Russian Revolution

Russian Revolution
Hope, Tragedy, Myths

Edited by
Ekaterina Rogatchevskaia

First published in 2017 by
The British Library
96 Euston Road
London NW1 2DB

On the occasion of the British Library exhibition
Russian Revolution: Hope, Tragedy, Myths

British Library Cataloguing-in-Publication Data
A catalogue record for this book is available from
the British Library

ISBN: 978 0 7123 5678 7 (paperback)
ISBN: 978 0 7123 5677 0 (hardback)

Half-title: Detail from *Velikaia voina v obrazakh i kartinakh*
(*The Great War in Images and Pictures*), 1917 (see page 76)
Frontispiece: Boys in Red Army uniform, c.1918–1920,
in Henri de Weidel, *Histoire des Soviets*, Paris 1922
Opposite acknowledgements: Socialist Revolutionary
election poster, 1917 (see page 151)

Designed by Andrew Shoolbred
Picture research by Sally Nicholls
Printed in Hong Kong by Great Wall Printing Co.

Contents

A Note on Conventions

In February 1918 Soviet Russia replaced the Julian calendar with the Gregorian calendar. Gregorian dates are usually referred to as 'new style' (N.S.); Julian are referred to as 'old style' (O.S.). In this volume, dates before February 1918 for Russian and world events are given as N.S. followed by O.S. in brackets

Russian and Slavonic names originally in Cyrillic characters are transliterated according to the Library of Congress transliteration scheme. The exception to this is where a different spelling is known in the English-language tradition (for example, Trotsky or Mayakovsky).

Most of the Russian terms are translated and transliterated. All translations in this volume for previously untranslated Russian sources are by Ekaterina Rogatchevskaia.

Some terms and abbreviations, such as duma, zemstvo, soviet or SR, are defined on their first use and then used throughout the book. Titles of images are given first in the original language (in transliteration if required) with a translation into English in brackets.

List of Contributors

Dr Sarah Badcock, Associate Professor, University of Nottingham. Publications include *Politics and the People in Revolutionary Russia: A Provincial History* (Cambridge University Press, 2007) and *A Prison Without Walls? Eastern Siberian Exile in the Last Years of Tsarism* (Oxford University Press, 2016). Sarah co-edited the volume *Russian Home Front In War And Revolution, 1914–22: Book 1. Russia's Revolution in Regional Perspective*, published by Slavica in 2015. Sarah contributed to the curation of the British Library's exhibition 'Russian Revolution: Hope, Tragedy, Myths'.

Dr Nick Baron, Associate Professor, University of Nottingham. Publications include *Soviet Karelia: Politics, Planning and Terror in Stalin's Russia, 1920–1939* (2007) and *The King of Karelia: Col. P. J. Woods and the British Intervention in North Russia, 1918–1919: A History and Memoir* (2007). Both books were also published in Russian. He was consultant to the British Library's 2016–2017 exhibition 'Maps and the 20th Century: Drawing the Line', and contributed to the curation of the exhibition 'Russian Revolution: Hope, Tragedy, Myths'. He is currently working on a cultural history of Soviet cartography.

Michael Carey, AHRC collaborative doctoral candidate, University of Nottingham and the British Library. Michael's research focuses on the impact of the Russian revolution on British socialism. He was involved in preparing and curating the exhibition 'Russian Revolution: Hope, Tragedy, Myths'.

Katie McElvanney, AHRC collaborative doctoral candidate at Queen Mary University of London and the British Library. Katie's research examines the work and role of women in the Bolshevik and anti-Bolshevik press during the October Revolution and civil wars. Katie was involved in preparing and curating the exhibition 'Russian Revolution: Hope, Tragedy, Myths'.

Dr Aaron McGaughey, Associate Lecturer in History, University of Kent. Aaron's research has focused mainly on the late Russian Empire in a transnational comparative context. Other work includes an AHRC CEKE-funded project with the Galleries of Justice Museum on the rehabilitation of young offenders in the early twentieth century. Currently he is attached to a project on the family of the last British ambassador to the Russian Empire, Sir George Buchanan, which includes interactive digital resources for schools and general outreach.

Dr Ekaterina Rogatchevskaia, Lead Curator of Central and East European collections, British Library. Before joining the British Library in 2003, Ekaterina taught various courses related to Russian literature, language and culture at the Russian State University for Humanities (Moscow), Glasgow and Edinburgh Universities, and she was research fellow at the Institute of World Literature (Moscow). She was review editor of *Solanus: International Journal for Russian and East European Bibliographic, Library and Publishing Studies*. She is lead curator of the exhibition 'Russian Revolution: Hope, Tragedy, Myths'.

Dr Jonathan Smele, Senior Lecturer in Modern European History, Queen Mary University of London. A long-standing member of the Study Group on the Russian Revolution, Jon edited its journal, *Revolutionary Russia* (2002–2012). Among his most recent publications are *The 'Russian' Civil Wars, 1916–1926: Ten Years that Shook the World* (London/New York: Hurst/Oxford University Press, 2016), and *Historical Dictionary of the 'Russian' Civil Wars, 1916–1926*, 2 vols (Lanham, MD: Rowman & Littlefield, 2015).

Acknowledgements

Curating an exhibition is an exciting project and hard but enjoyable teamwork. I am incredibly grateful to my former colleague and co-curator at the early stages of the exhibition planning, Roger Walshe, who enthusiastically supported the idea of a major exhibition at the British Library on the Russian Revolution to mark its centenary in 2017. However it is Susan Reed, co-curator of the exhibition *Russian Revolution: Hope Tragedy, Myths*, who deserves very special acknowledgement here. It is difficult to overestimate her role in curating the exhibition, but she was also very kind giving her time to reading this book and helping with its editing.

From the very beginning the project around the exhibition became part of the AHRC collaborative doctoral partnerships scheme between the British Library and the University of Nottingham and Queen Mary University of London. I was very lucky to have two wonderful PhD candidates, Michael Carey and Katie McElvanney, working with me on the project. Their creativity, dedication and passion for the project were of immense help. I am also indebted to their supervisors, especially Sarah Badcock and Nick Baron, who not only contributed to the book, but also helped with defining the scope of the exhibition and the book, read the drafts and provided helpful comments. My thanks also go to Richard Davies, Robert Henderson, Stephen Lovell and Tobie Mathew – external experts who gave me useful feedback and advice.

It was a great joy and pleasure working with colleagues in the exhibition production, interpretation, loans, conservation and publishing teams at the British Library. Susan Dymond, Oriana Calman, Robert Davies, Miranda Harrison, Alexandra Kavanagh, Mary Linkins, Sally Nicholls, Barbara O'Connor and Andrew Shoolbred were deeply interested in the subject, attentive to detail, accommodating and supporting.

Curators at the British Library were very generous with sharing their knowledge and ideas. I very much appreciate all assistance and support given to me in the process of preparing this book and the exhibition by Alison Bailey, Anna Chelidze, Michael Erdman, Irène Fabry-Tehranchi, John Falconer, Tom Harper, Barbara Hawes, Kristian Jensen, Olga Kerziouk, Elzbieta Kucharska-Beard, Marja Kingma, Chris Michaelides, Richard Morel, Matthew Neill, Yasuyo Ohtsuka, Paul Skinner, Magda Szkuta, Barry Taylor, Hamish Todd, Geoffrey West, Ildi Wollner and Janet Zmroczek.

The exhibition could not have happened without the fantastic work of British Library colleagues in marketing, media communications, content, design, events, learning, fundraising and commercial teams: Jonah Albert, Michele Burton, Silvia Dobrovich, Ian Douglas, Hanna Fayaz, Jon Fawcett, Hannah Gabrielle, Steven Gale, Elsie King, Stephanie Knox, Fiona McCarthy, Alex Michaels, Andrew Nelson, John Overeem, Chris Rawlings, Elliot Sinclair, Alex Stiles, Susannah Stevenson, Frances Taylor and Joanna Wells. I would also like to thank those colleagues in the business support, research development and international engagement teams who helped to sustain the project at its different stages: Edmund Connolly, Marcie-Jane Hopkins, Kate Marshall, James Perkins, Allan Sudlow and Jacqueline Wheeler.

I'm pleased to thank all organisations and individuals who kindly provided exhibition loans and expressed interest in collaboration in organising events at the British Library.

And last, but not least, special thanks go to the generous supporters of the exhibition: The Blavatnik Family Foundation, and the Friends of the British Library.

Timeline

Katie McElvanney

Note: The date column uses New Style (Gregorian calendar) dates.
Old Style dates are included in the event text, in brackets, where relevant.

1861–1899	
DATE *(Gregorian calendar)*	EVENT
1861	Tsar Alexander II passes the Emancipation Edict, ending serfdom in Russia (but keeps peasants tied to the land through continuing labour obligations).
1861	Louis Pasteur publishes his germ theory.
1861–1865	American Civil War.
1863	The Metropolitan Railway opens the world's first underground railway in London.
1865	Slavery is abolished in the United States.
1866	Publication of Fyodor Dostoevsky's *Crime and Punishment*.
1867	Swedish chemist Alfred Nobel invents dynamite. Within a decade, Russian revolutionaries are using dynamite to try to assassinate the tsar.
1867	The first volume of Karl Marx's *Das Kapital* is published.
1868	Nicholas II, the last tsar of Russia, is born.
1869	Dmitri Mendeleev publishes his periodic table.
1870	Vladimir Ilyich Lenin is born.
1877–1878	Russo–Turkish War.
1878	Vera Zasulich, a member of the secret revolutionary organisation Land and Freedom (*Zemlia i Volia*), is acquitted by the jury in her trial for the attempted murder of Dmitrii Trepov, Governor General of St Petersburg.

Events in (or relating to) Russia   World events   Statistics   Art, music and literature (including works by Lenin and Marx, and key fiction in Russian and English)   Science and technology

1880	Failed attempt (no. 5) to assassinate Tsar Alexander II by blowing up his palace dining room kills 11 and wounds 56. The tsar survives through being late to dinner.
1881	Tsar Alexander II is assassinated by a member of the radical group The People's Will (*Narodnaia Volia*) after five previously unsuccessful attempts on his life. He is succeeded by his son, Alexander III, who enacts anti-terrorism measures that curb civil rights and freedom of the press.
1882	Pogroms against Jews spread across the Russian Empire, leading to mass emigration of the Jewish population.
1883	The Emancipation of Labour group (*Osvobozhdenie truda*), the first Russian Marxist group, is founded in Switzerland.
1883	Karl Marx dies in London.
1884	The Representation of the People Act 1884 is passed in Great Britain, significantly extending male suffrage.
1887	Lenin's older brother, Alexander, is executed for his involvement in a plot to assassinate Tsar Alexander III.
1890	The Zemstvo Act restricts the authority of the *zemstvos*, rural government councils which were established in 1864.
1891–1892	Famine in Russia kills between 375,000 and 400,000 and affects millions more.
1891	Construction of the Trans-Siberian Railway begins.
1893	New Zealand becomes the first country to give women the vote in national elections.
1 November 1894	Tsar Alexander III dies after a sudden illness; his son Nicholas assumes the throne (20 October).
26 November 1894	Tsar Nicholas II marries Princess Alix (Russian Christian name – Alexandra Feodorovna), Queen Victoria's granddaughter (14 November).
20 December 1895	Lenin is arrested to be kept in solitary confinement for 13 months and then exiled to Siberia for three years (8 December).
26 May 1896	Coronation of Tsar Nicholas II (14 May).
30 May 1896	The Khodynka Tragedy – a stampede in Moscow occurs during festivities following Nicholas II's coronation, and results in the deaths of over 1,300 people. (18 May).
1897	Sergei Witte, Russian Minister of Finance, undertakes a major currency reform and puts the Russian rouble on the Gold Standard.
1897	According to census records, the overall literacy rate in the Russian Empire (excluding Finland) is 21.1 per cent (29.3 per cent for men and 13.1 per cent for women).
1898	The Russian Social Democratic Labour Party is founded in Minsk.
1898	Marie and Pierre Curie discover polonium and radium, and coin the term 'radioactivity'.
1899–1902	Second Boer War.

1900–1916

DATE (Gregorian calendar)	EVENT
1900	The average life expectancy at birth in Russia is 29.4 years for boys and 31.4 years for girls. By comparison, in 1901 life expectancy at birth in the UK is 45 years for boys and 49 years for girls.
1900	Boxer rebellion in China.
1901	Queen Victoria dies.
1901–1902	The Socialist Revolutionary Party (SR) is established.
1901–1905	Economic downturn in Russia creates discontent.
April 1902	Lenin enters the British Museum's round Reading Room for the first time under the pseudonym Jacob Richter.
1902	First publication of *Mrs Craddock*, one of the first novels by William Somerset Maugham, who in 1917 travelled to Russia as a British Secret Intelligence Service agent
1902	The Anglo–Japanese Alliance is signed.
1903	The Russian Social Democratic Labour Party meets for its Second Congress in London and splits into two factions: Mensheviks ('minority') and the more radical Bolsheviks ('majority').
1904	The first part of the Trans-Siberian Railway is completed between Moscow and Vladivostok. The entire railway was completed in 1916.
February 1904	The Russo–Japanese War starts. The Japanese fleet launches a surprise attack and siege on the Russian naval squadron at Port Arthur.
May–December 1904	The Russian army suffers defeats at the battles of Fu-hsien and Liao-yang.
12 August 1904	After having four daughters, Tsarina Alexandra gives birth to a son, Alexei (30 July).
January 1905	The Russian commander of Port Arthur surrenders the port to the Japanese without consulting his officers.
22 January 1905	Bloody Sunday. Troops and police open fire on a peaceful demonstration outside the Winter Palace and elsewhere in St Petersburg, killing between 200 and 1,000 people. The liberal press argued that Nicholas II was responsible for the bloodshed (9 January).
February–March 1905	The Russian army is defeated at the Battle of Mukden. Losses in the battle amount to approximately 89,000 Russian and 71,000 Japanese casualties.
April–May 1905	The Third Congress of the Russian Social Democratic Labour Party meets in London.
June 1905	Sailors mutiny on the battleship *Potemkin*, part of the Black Sea Fleet. The mutiny triggers riots in Odessa, which are quashed by troops on the tsar's orders.

| | Events in (or relating to) Russia | | World events | | Statistics | | Art, music and literature (including works by Lenin and Marx, and key fiction in Russian and English) | | Science and technology |

Summer 1905	Strikes, unrest and peasant uprisings continue, culminating in a general strike in October.
August–September 1905	Following Russia's defeat in the naval Battle of Tsushima in May 1905, Russia and Japan sign the Treaty of Portsmouth, ending the Russo–Japanese War.
October 1905	The St Petersburg Soviet of Workers' Deputies holds its first session.
October 1905	The Constitutional Democratic Party (Kadets) is formed.
30 October 1905	Tsar Nicholas II issues the October Manifesto, promising civil liberties and an elected parliament (Duma) (17 October).
December 1905	In response to the suppression of the St Petersburg Soviet, the Moscow Soviet launches a disastrous attempt to seize power. The government quashes the insurrection after five days.
1906	Finland, an autonomous part of the Russian Empire, becomes the first European country to give women the vote.
6 May 1906	Tsar Nicholas II issues the Fundamental Laws, a 124-point *de facto* constitution (23 April).
10 May 1906	The first Russian Duma meets (27 April).
November 1906	Prime Minister Petr Stolypin's Agrarian Reform Act, a series of measures aimed at ending the communal system of landholding, is implemented.
30 June 1908	The Tunguska event. A giant, mysterious explosion shakes Siberia, levelling an estimated 80 million trees over an area of 830 square miles (17 June).
1910	Leo Tolstoy dies.
1910	Artists and poets form a group that marks the start of the Russian futurist movement.
1911–1912	The Xinhai revolution overthrows China's last imperial dynasty and establishes the Republic of China.
6 March 1913	Nicholas II celebrates 300 years of Romanov rule in Russia (21 February).
1913	Andrei Bely's novel *Petersburg*, recognised as the most significant work of Russian symbolism and modernism, is published. The novel tells a story of a young revolutionary who is ordered to assassinate his father in autumn 1905, during the period of social and political unrest.
29 May 1913	Igor Stravinsky's ballet *The Rite of Spring* premieres in Paris, where it is met with outrage from the audience (17 May).
1913	Between 1908 and 1913 industrial production increases by almost 50 per cent in Russia, but working conditions remain almost the same.
1913	Natalia Goncharova, a prominent member of the Russian futurist movement, completes her futurist painting *The Cyclist*.
28 June 1914	Assassination of Archduke Franz Ferdinand, heir to the throne of Austria-Hungary (16 June).
28 July 1914	Austria-Hungary declares war on Serbia (16 July).

1 August 1914	Germany declares war on Russia and Russia enters the First World War (19 July). Three days later, on 4 August, Britain declares war on Germany (22 July).
1914	At the beginning of the First World War, the number of urban workers in Russia is estimated at between 12 and 22 million (approximately 10 per cent of the total population). Only 0.5 to 0.8 per cent of this industrial workforce were members of either the Bolshevik or Menshevik factions of the Social Democrats. The population of the Russian Empire in 1914 is approximately 170 million.
1914	Women comprise one-third of the industrial labour force in Russia, but receive significantly lower wages than their male counterparts.
1914	St Petersburg is renamed Petrograd to make it sound less German.
26–30 August 1914	Russia's 2nd Army suffers defeat at the Battle of Tannenberg, the first major battle on the eastern front. Over 30,000 Russian soldiers are killed or wounded, and more than 90,000 are taken prisoner by the Germans (14–18 August).
January 1915	The first use of gas warfare by the German forces.
April 1915 – January 1916	The Gallipoli campaign.
September 1915	Tsar Nicholas II becomes supreme commander of the Russian army.
1915	By the middle of 1915, the German army controls all of Russian Poland and Lithuania, and most of Latvia.
1915	Kazimir Malevich completes the first version of his *Black Square* painting.
July 1916	The Battle of the Somme begins.
30 December 1916	Grigorii Rasputin, the controversial 'holy man' and close friend of Tsar Nicholas II's family, is murdered (17 December) after several failed attempts.
1916	By 1916 Russia's war casualties total 1.7 million military dead and 5 million wounded.

1917

DATE (*Gregorian calendar*)	EVENT
1917	The overall literacy rate in Russia is approximately 43 per cent.
January 1917	A Russian pound (or *funt*) of sugar in Moscow costs 28 kopecks, compared to 15 kopecks before the war. (The Russian pound is an obsolete unit of measurement equal to 409.5 grams.)
8 March 1917	On International Women's Day, demonstrators and striking workers – many of whom are women – take to the streets to protest against food shortages and the war (23 February).
10 March 1917	Strikes spread across Petrograd (25 February).

Events in (or relating to) Russia   World events   Statistics   Art, music and literature (including works by Lenin and Marx, and key fiction in Russian and English)   Science and technology

12 March 1917	The Duma meets against the Tsar's wishes. The Petrograd Soviet of Workers' and Soldiers' Deputies forms and holds its first meeting. The death penalty is abolished (27 February).
14 March 1917	Order Number 1, the first official decree of the Petrograd Soviet of Workers' and Soldiers' Deputies, is issued (1 March). Tsar Nicholas II abdicates and also removes his son from the succession. The following day Nicholas's brother Mikhail announces his refusal to accept the throne.
15 March 1917	The Provisional Committee (Government) of the State Duma is formed and replaces the tsarist government (2 March). Prince Lvov becomes leader of the Provisional Government.
6 April 1917	The US declares war on Germany and enters the First World War.
April 1917	Lenin returns from exile, travelling to Petrograd in a sealed train from Switzerland via Germany and Finland.
1 May 1917	The 'Miliukov note'. A telegram sent to the Allied Powers by Foreign Minister (and member of the Kadet Party) Pavel Miliukov states the Provisional Government's intention to continue the war. The note is leaked, resulting in protests and increased support for the Bolsheviks (18 April).
May 1917	Miliukov resigns and members of the Socialist Revolutionaries and Mensheviks join the government.
June 1917	The first All-Russia Congress of Workers' and Soldiers' Deputies opens.
July 1917	Russia launches an offensive against Austria-Hungary.
July 1917	The death penalty is re-introduced at the front.
16–20 July 1917	The July Days begin in Petrograd (3–7 July). A new Provisional Government is set up with Alexander Kerensky at its head. Lenin goes into hiding.
July 1917	The Provisional Government grants women the right to vote and hold office.
24 July 1917	Alexander Kerensky becomes Prime Minister of the Provisional Government (11 July).
August 1917	A Russian pound (funt) of sugar costs 2.25 roubles in Moscow and is being sold on the black market.
August 1917	Trotsky joins the Bolshevik Party. He had previously been a member of the Menshevik faction and later was head of the Mezhraiontsy – a small independent faction of the Russian Social Democratic Labour Party.
4–9 September 1917	The Kornilov affair, a failed coup by General Kornilov, commander of the Russian army, takes place (22–27 August).
September 1917	Russia is officially declared a republic, several months after the de facto end of the monarchy.
7 November 1917	The October revolution; the Bolsheviks seize control of Petrograd (25 October).
8 November 1917	The Bolsheviks take control of the Winter Palace, the last remaining holdout of the Provisional Government (26 October).
8 November 1917	The decrees on land and peace are issued by the new government. Subsequent workers' decrees outline measures for an eight-hour working day, minimum wage and the running of factories. The death penalty is abolished once again (26 October).

9 November 1917	The Decree on the Press, the first Bolshevik censorship decree, abolishes the 'bourgeois' press (27 October).
15 November 1917	The Bolsheviks gain control of Moscow after a week of bitter street fighting (2 November).
November 1917	The Central Rada (parliament) takes power in Kyiv.
25 November 1917	Elections to the Constituent Assembly take place (12 November). The Socialist Revolutionaries win the largest number of seats, while the Bolsheviks win less than one-quarter of the vote.
6 December 1917	Finland declares its independence from Russia (23 November).
December 1917	A Russian pound (funt) of sugar costs 6 roubles in Moscow. Each person receives ¼ pound of bread per day. Bread and flour are still being sold openly, but for extortionate prices.
December 1917	Lenin appoints Felix Dzerzhinsky as Commissar for Internal Affairs and head of the All-Russian Extraordinary Commission for Combating Counter-Revolution and Sabotage (Cheka).
15 December 1917	An armistice between Russia and the Central Powers is signed, and fighting stops (2 December).
22 December 1917	Russian–German peace negotiations begin at Brest-Litovsk (9 December).
23 December 1917	Orthographic reform is introduced by the People's Commissariat for Education (10 December). However, the reform does not take effect until 10 October 1918.

1918–1924

DATE (Gregorian calendar)	EVENT
18–19 January 1918	The Constituent Assembly meets but is dissolved by the Bolsheviks (5–6 January).
January 1918	Alexander Blok completes his poem *The Twelve*.
January 1918	The Russian delegation, led by Leon Trotsky, denounces the German Peace Terms as unacceptable and walks out of the peace negotiations at Brest-Litovsk.
28 January 1918	The Council of People's Commissars (*Sovnarkom*) issues a decree forming the Workers' and Peasants' Red Army (15 January).
February 1918	A Russian pound (funt) of sugar in Moscow costs 10 roubles.
14 February 1918	Russia adopts the Western (Gregorian) calendar.
3 March 1918	The Brest-Litovsk Treaty ends Russia's participation in the First World War. Russia accepts territorial losses.

Events in (or relating to) Russia World events Statistics Art, music and literature (including works by Lenin and Marx, and key fiction in Russian and English) Science and technology

6–8 March 1918	At the 7th Congress of the Russian Social Democratic Labour Party, the Bolsheviks change the name of their party to the Russian Communist Party.
1918	Spanish flu pandemic kills 50 to 100 million people worldwide.
March 1918	British troops land in Murmansk.
March 1918	The Russian capital is moved from Petrograd to Moscow.
April 1918	For an eight-hour day, skilled male workers receive 18 roubles and women workers of the same category receive 15 roubles 30 kopecks. Unskilled workers receive 10.65 roubles and 9.35 roubles, respectively.
May 1918	Czechoslovak legionaires storm Chelyabinsk railway station and occupy the city.
6 July 1918	Wilhelm von Mirbach, the German ambassador to Soviet Russia, is assassinated in Moscow by members of the Left Socialist Revolutionary Party.
10 July 1918	The first constitution of the Russian Socialist Federated Soviet Republic grants equal rights to men and women.
16 July 1918	Gorky's *Novaia zhizn'* (*New Life*), the last opposition newspaper, is banned.
16–17 July 1918	Tsar Nicholas II and his family are executed by the Bolsheviks in Yekaterinburg.
July 1918	US President Woodrow Wilson approves a 5,000-strong American force to support the White Army in northern Russia.
11 August 1918	Lenin sends a telegram to communists in Penza, Central Russia, complaining about uprisings in the area and calling for the public execution of 100 *kulaks*.
30 August 1918	Moisei Uritskii, head of the Bolshevik secret police (Cheka) in Petrograd, is assassinated.
30 August 1918	An assassination attempt on Lenin by the Socialist Revolutionary Fanny Kaplan leaves him seriously wounded. The attempt, together with the murder of Uritskii, sparks a period of mass arrests and executions known as the 'Red Terror'.
October 1918	A Russian pound (*funt*) of sugar in Moscow costs 35 roubles.
October 1918	The Bolshevik Family Law clarifies and expands earlier reforms on the legal status of marriage, divorce and parenthood.
7–8 November 1918	Revolution breaks out in a number of German cities, including the capital, Berlin. Uprisings continue over the following months until the final suppression of the Munich Soviet in May 1919.
11 November 1918	First World War ends.
11 November 1918	Poland declares its independence.
19 November 1918	The first All-Russian Congress of Women meets. The congress results in the foundation of the *Zhenotdel*, the world's first government department exclusively concerned with the affairs of women, in 1919.
December 1918	Perm (in central Siberia) falls to the White Army, led by Admiral Kolchak.
15 January 1919	German communist leaders Rosa Luxemburg and Karl Liebknecht are murdered in Berlin.

18 January 1919	Paris Peace Conference convenes, resulting in the Treaty of Versailles.
January 1919	The *Sovnarkom* formally announces the beginning of *Prodrazverstka* (compulsory grain requisitioning), which leads to peasant revolts.
1919–1921	Polish–Soviet War.
March 1919	American journalist and socialist John Reed's *Ten Days that Shook the World* is published in New York.
March 1919	The Hungarian Soviet Republic, led by Béla Kun is established; it lasts until August before being dispersed.
March 1919	The Comintern (or Third International) is formed in Moscow, with the aim of spreading revolution all over the world.
July 1919	Finland becomes a republic.
1920	Communist parties form across the world.
10 January 1920	The League of Nations is established.
August 1920	Peasant insurrection in Tambov (300 miles south-east of Moscow) begins.
November 1920	The Red Army invades and occupies Crimea and the White Army is forced to withdraw.
November 1920	Abortion is legalised.
1920	Evgenii Zamyatin completes his dystopian novel *We*. It is the first work to be banned by the Goskomizdat (State Committee for Publishing) and is first published in English in New York in 1924.
1921	The population of Petrograd has fallen from 2.5 million in 1917 to 600,000 in 1920.
1921	By the beginning of 1921 the rouble has lost 96 per cent of its pre-war value; industrial production has fallen to 10 per cent of its 1913 level.
March 1921	The Kronstadt mutiny, an unsuccessful uprising against the Bolsheviks, takes place.
March 1921	End of 'War Communism' and the introduction of the 'New Economic Policy' (NEP).
18 March 1921	The Peace of Riga ends the Polish–Soviet War.
1921	Extreme inflation in Germany.
1921–1922	Between 6 and 7 million children are living on the streets, with a further 540,000 living in orphanages.
3 April 1922	Stalin is appointed General Secretary of the Communist Party.
16 April 1922	Soviet Russia and Germany sign the Treaty of Rapallo, renouncing all territorial and financial claims against each other following the Brest-Litovsk Treaty and the First World War.

Events in (or relating to) Russia	World events	Statistics	Art, music and literature (including works by Lenin and Marx, and key fiction in Russian and English)	Science and technology

October 1922	Mussolini marches on Rome.
December 1922	Creation of the Soviet Union.
1922	Five million people have died as a result of two years of famine.
1923	The Soviet nationalities policy *Korenizatsiia* (indigenisation) is introduced.
23–25 October 1923	The Hamburg uprising, an attempted communist coup, is crushed within 24 hours.
21 January 1924	Lenin dies, leading to a power struggle within the party. Stalin emerges as party leader. His rival Leon Trotsky is dismissed, then exiled and finally murdered in 1940.
31 January 1924	Constitution of the USSR that legitimises its creation is ratified.
1 February 1924	Britain, led by its first Labour government, recognises the Soviet Union. Several other countries, including Italy and China, quickly follow.
1924	The majority of Western countries close their borders to immigrants from Eastern Europe following almost 40 years of mass migration.

1925–1991

DATE (*Gregorian calendar*)	EVENT
1928–32	The first five-year plan.
1 December 1934	Sergei Kirov, a member of the ruling Politburo, is murdered. Over the next four and a half years, millions of party members and others are arrested, many of whom are executed.
1937–1938	More than 1 million people are estimated to have been killed during Stalin's Great Purge.
1 September 1939–2 September 1945	The Second World War.
1 October 1949	Chinese Communist leader Mao Zedong declares the creation of the People's Republic of China (PRC).
5 March 1953	Death of Joseph Stalin.
25 February 1956	Stalin's successor Nikita Khrushchev denounces him in his 'Secret Speech'.
14–28 October 1962	Cuban missile crisis.
1985	Soviet leader Mikhail Gorbachev introduces a programme known as *Perestroika*, designed to restructure Soviet political and economic policy.
26 April 1986	Chernobyl nuclear disaster.
December 1991	The Belavezha Accords – the agreement that declares the Soviet Union effectively dissolved – is signed.

Явился новый человек!
Да здравствует коммуны век.

Яя

Яя

Introduction

Ekaterina Rogatchevskaia

One hundred years after the revolution took Russia by storm, it might be the right time to re-examine why it happened, how it developed and why its lessons can still shape our vision and understanding of the world we live in now. Finding new facts about the revolution and new angles for their re-examination and re-interpretation is creating a new discourse, in which the phenomenon of the Russian Revolution can be used as a reference point for debates around current political situations in the world. Such fundamental questions as relations between the masses and the elites, the vulnerability of democratic procedures faced with organised violence, or of humanitarian values confronted by a large-scale refugee crisis, as well as contradictions between the principle of fairness in society and the practical impossibility of achieving it, are still among those being discussed with the experience of the Russian Revolution in mind.

By no means do the exhibition *Russian Revolution: Hope, Tragedy, Myths* (The British Library, 28 April–29 August 2017) and the book that accompanies it attempt to present a detailed sequence of all the revolutionary events, nor do they give definite final answers to such questions as 'Why did the revolution happen?', 'Which roles did the social classes and groups play?', 'Were there any alternative ways of resolving the crisis?', and, perhaps most critical of all, 'What was the point of no return?' Covering the chronological period from the late nineteenth century until the mid-1920s, with landmarks being the formation of the Soviet Union in 1922 and Lenin's death in 1924, this book is neither another 'popular history' nor a collection of academic papers. Original essays, written in an accessible style by the contributors to this volume and based on their knowledge of the topic, illustrate the complexity of the Russian Revolution, leaving space for readers to draw their own conclusions. In addition to giving a general overview of events and explaining the motives and causes of decisions and actions, the authors do not avoid discussions of complicated issues that help to reveal tensions, ambiguities and controversies, and show events as a palette of mixed colours with numerous shades rather than a black-and-white chessboard.

For over 70 years since the Bolsheviks took power in Russia, interpretations of the events of the revolution and its consequences were determined by the political views of the interpreters. From the first days in power the Bolsheviks tried to control the revolutionary narrative, creating a canonical view of selected events and their analysis, propagating it and eliminating the chances of breaking or even adjusting the canon. Locking away and destroying primary sources, documents and archives was part of this endeavour. It is not surprising that most of the counter-arguments and views outside the Bolsheviks' control were also formed within the framework set up by the Bolsheviks. The collapse of the USSR in 1991 created opportunities to examine a large body of various textual, visual and material sources, which helped to formulate new research questions and compensate for big gaps in our knowledge by writing micro-histories and bringing small social or political groups, separate regions and limited time periods into focus. The exhibition and the book also present, alongside iconic images and documents such as Soviet propaganda posters, some rarely seen materials, for example White Army propaganda and original photographs made in Russian refugee camps. One of the aims of the book is to take readers on a visual journey through the events in Russia 100 years ago and to explore history through objects. At the same time the authors do not approach the book as an exhibition guide or as a catalogue. Their focus on interpretations of the objects makes it possible to weave them into the general historical narrative and to present this in a multi-dimensional and memorable form.

Access to new sources also stimulates a development of new approaches, interpretations and frameworks. It would probably be fair to say that historians nowadays have largely turned from studying crucial events and major figures to the grassroots activities and various actions that influenced and informed 'big' decisions. The new research brings a human dimension into the story of global political and economic changes. This human dimension was also pivotal for the story that the exhibition and the book tell. Among the book's goals is to bring together an overview of the revolution as one of multiple personal experiences. Throughout the book its contributors bring together the narratives, views and feelings of people of different social backgrounds, political opinions, professional qualifications and nationalities, possessing various degrees of knowledge of the Russian language, culture and politics – including foreign observers who witnessed the Russian revolutionary scene or constructed their opinions based on the information available to them. Various perspectives on the Russian Revolution are presented in the book through documents, newspapers articles,

diaries, memoirs, letters, and literary and artistic works. At the same time, many extracts describe everyday events, such as going to the theatre, conversations with colleagues and children's school routines. People's lives were determined not only by large-scale political actions or fighting, but also by love, envy, passion, devotion to their work and millions of other emotions and episodes, for which the revolution was a set backdrop. We know now that this backdrop expanded to take over the entire stage, sweeping some actors from it and giving new roles to the rest. What we are trying to do is to encapsulate a moment in history that has not yet been calibrated in relation to time past. By representing a wide diversity of voices – excited and thoughtful, confused and resolute, scared and hopeful, sad and happy, alarmed and astonished – the contributors endeavoured to focus not necessarily on the revolution witnessed by people, but on the people just living their lives through the revolution.

Introducing the reader to the global context in which the revolution took place, the Timeline at the beginning of the book,

Kommunisticheskii rai (The Communist Heaven), anti-Bolshevik propaganda poster, c.1919–20.

Initially, artists who worked on the propaganda campaigns of both sides referenced religious symbols and concepts, as they thought that the people would have more empathy with these images. However, White propaganda made it one of its explicit features. This poster mocks Lenin, Trotsky and other Bolshevik leaders who, at a sumptuous feast, toast those whom they 'liberated from violence and hunger' and to whom they 'gave an opportunity to glimpse the Communist heaven'. In the lower image people are dying in the street in front of a shop with a large sign saying 'No bread'.

1856.g.8.(8).

compiled by Katie McElvanney, presents a selection of events, facts and statistical data related to Russia and the outside world. By switching the perspective through which one can look at or learn about the events, the Timeline aims to give the reader a resonant experience of history.

In the first chapter, 'Tsar and His People', Aaron McGaughey sets up the scene by examining the Russian social structure and introducing 'a burgeoning but fragmented civil society'. He presents the sequence of events from 1905 to 1916 through the discussion of 'politics of change' and explores the reasons for the failure of this 'politics of change' in Russia. Among the 'heroes' of this chapter, such figures as the revolutionary Prince Petr Kropotkin, Prime Minister Petr Stolypin and Nicholas II share the author's attention with a doctor, Ekaterina Slanskaia, 'one of the only one hundred doctors who qualified from the Women's Medical Courses in St Petersburg', and an ordinary Bolshevik, Semen Kanatchikov.

Sarah Badcock's analysis of the year 1917 in chapter 2, '1917: The Weeks When Decades Happened', includes such interesting perspectives as popular expectations at the time of economic collapse and the role and activities of soldiers' wives. The discussion of the grain crisis and the focus on rural communities and their practices during 1917 give the reader a chance to appreciate the extent and importance of local governance and grassroots movements. In the spotlight in this chapter are Maria Botchkareva, a peasant and a female soldier; Viktor Shklovsky, a recent graduate of St Petersburg University and a Provisional Government commissar in 1917, who became a well-known scholar and writer in Soviet Russia and lost all his siblings to the revolution or its aftermath; and 'the saviour of the revolution' Alexander Kerensky. The chapter leaves the reader with an open question on what freedom meant for various social groups and what it brought to the country.

In chapter 3, 'Cursed Days', Jonathan Smele argues that between 1916 and 1926 Russia went through a series of civil wars and presents a picture of the diverse forces that took part in military conflicts. The author examines the roots of the 'White movement' – the term that is applied to describe opponents of Bolshevik rule from all sides of the political spectrum – from far-right monarchists to socialists who, just months before, had worked with the Bolsheviks. The chapter also discusses the role played by non-Russian regions that saw the revolution as an opportunity to establish independent governments and therefore supported the Bolsheviks or their enemies depending on the immediate benefit, while Russia's war allies backed the forces that would keep Russia in the world war. The story of the creation of the regular Red Army is told in conjunction with analysis of the main reasons for its ultimate victory.

Meeting of invalids in Petrograd on 29 (16) April, 1917. Photograph from *Voina i revoliutsiia*, Petrograd, *c*.1918.

This shows a patriotic meeting of wounded soldiers who were getting treatment in Petrograd hospitals. The slogans demanded 'War until victory' and 'Down with Lenin and co'. The soldiers agreed to organise the defence of Petrograd. All males of conscription age were to be mobilised and sent to the front from Petrograd.

X.802/4756.

Written by the exhibition curator Ekaterina Rogatchevskaia, chapter 4, 'The New World is Born', is a survey of the initial steps taken by the Bolsheviks in building communism. The Bolsheviks' responses to various internal and external challenges to their power was taking Russia further and further away from what idealists might have dreamt of. Organised famine, the rising cult of Lenin and the increasing influence of the internal police – the infamous Cheka – became part of everyday life, together with establishing new forms of propaganda and a very distinct artistic language to celebrate the victorious revolution.

Chapter 5, 'Russia and the World on Fire' by Mike Carey and Nick Baron, gives the reader an overview of the international scene at the time of the Russian Revolution. The chapter suggests that it was not 'the Russian Revolution that set the world on fire', but rather the new Bolshevik state that in a seemingly unstoppable process of radicalisation under the banner of worldwide revolution 'became the brightest and hottest of flames'. Such topics as the personal experience of foreigners in Russia (including military personnel, spies, journalists, left-wing activists and many others), revolutions in other countries, and the exploration of tension between the national peripheries and the Russian centre in the period between the collapse of the Russian Empire and formation of the Soviet Union, are presented by a selection of rarely seen material and unexpected juxtapositions.

The Epilogue, 'Putting History into Words: Russian Novelists Write the Revolution' by Ekaterina Rogatchevskaia, shows how the theme of the Russian Revolution has been dealt with in Russian literature and how writers responded to the events and consequences of the Revolution. Focusing on works by four Nobel laureates (Ivan Bunin, Mikhail Sholokhov, Boris Pasternak and Alexander Solzhenitsyn), it explores the ways in which Russian and Soviet writers have engaged with both their own society and the world at large.

1 Tsar and His People: The Russian Empire on the Brink of the Twentieth Century

Aaron McGaughey

The Russian Empire stretched continuously across one-sixth of the world's landmass, from Poland to the Pacific and from the Arctic Circle to the deserts of Central Asia. Second largest among the contemporary empires after the British empire, it was home to some 150 million people divided into around 170 ethno-cultural groups. Their lifestyles ranged from nomadic steppe herdsmen and tribute-paying fur trappers to communal agriculturalists, industrial workers and wealthy nobles. In some areas of Siberia the population density hardly reached 10 people per square mile, while in the country's western parts, including Poland and Finland, it was over 100 people per square mile.

Full maps of the empire were usually published in two sections: European and Asian. The kaleidoscopic diversity of geography, agriculture, industry, culture, ethnicity, religion, history and social structures sustained enduring notions of a land of paradox and unknowable mystery. The population of the Russian Empire was formally arranged in a system of estates (*sosloviia*), each with different duties and privileges. The four principal estates were nobility, clergy, merchants and peasants. There were many sub-divisions within these estates, such as hereditary or service nobility, merchants, monks and craftsmen. The non-Russian and non-Orthodox population of Siberia and Central Asia was designated as *inorodtsy*, meaning 'those of other birth'. By the mid-nineteenth century this term was widely used to refer to all non-Russians. The empire's Jewish population were also legally assigned to this estate, much to the annoyance of their representatives.

The changes wrought by succeeding bouts of social and economic reform from the 1850s onwards eroded the economic, social and cultural status quo that underpinned the estates system and facilitated the ascent of the 'other ranks' (*raznochintsy*) that did not fit within the existing structure. Movement between estates was ill-defined, but possible in some instances. Although portrayed by reactionary and Slavophile elements as sacred,

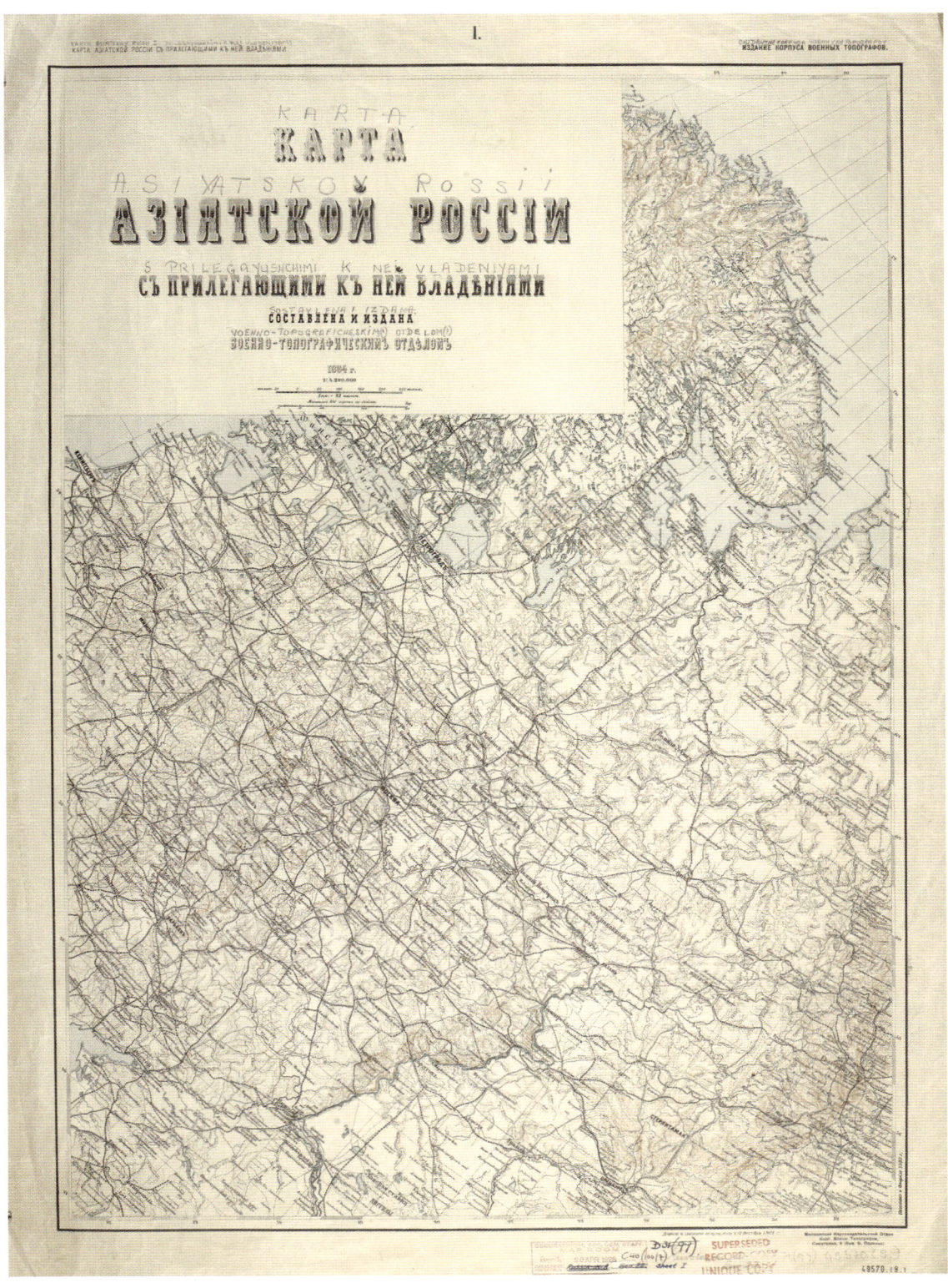

Karta zheleznykh, vodnykh I shosseinykh putei soobshcheniia Evropeiskoi Rossii (Map of the European part of Russia, showing the development of transport routes), St Petersburg, Ministry of Transport, 1914.

Maps. 35872.(16).

Karta Aziatskoi Rossii s prilegaiushchimi k nei vladeniiami (Map of the Asian part of Russia). St Petersburg, Ministry of Transport, 1914.

Maps. 49570.(9).

МОРДОВКА. ЧЕРЕМИСКА. ЧУВАШКА. ФИННЪ.

ЕВРЕИ: КАРАИМЫ И ТАЛМУДИСТЪ.

Page from *Zhivopisnyi al'bom Narody Rossii (The Picturesque Album: The Peoples of Russia)*, St Petersburg, 1880.

Representatives of four indigenous peoples of Russia (on the left) and religious Jews (right) are shown. From the 18th century onwards, 'visualising' the empire was an important part of creating state identity. Albums presenting various ethnic groups in national costumes alongside descriptions of their 'life and customs' were very popular.

1783.b.3.

timeless and unchanging, in reality the estates system was only formalised in the 1820s on the basis of seventeenth- and eighteenth-century laws. What had begun as a means to facilitate the extraction of resources from a large, diverse and relatively poor population became an ideological justification of social and political ossification.

Official propaganda projected Tsar Nicholas II, Europe's last autocrat, as the sacrosanct 'Little Father', whose innate connection to his subjects ensured that he acted in their best interests. In this mythology, the 300-year-old Romanov dynasty acted as a divinely ordained centripetal force rooted in the candlelit grandeur of old Muscovy, standing apart from temporal politics and above reproach. Just four years after leading his dynasty's tercentenary celebrations in 1913, a popular revolt swept away Nicholas and the Russian monarchy.

Rival historicising voices have laid sweeping narratives of twilight, decline, missed opportunities and inevitable revolution over the final decades of the Russian Empire. However, claims of historical certainty, like Nicholas's Muscovite pageantry, mask a destabilising conflict between modernisation and reaction. Far from being a divine artefact, the tsarist state was an imperialist Great Power, a member of the Triple Entente and a vital component of the European balance of power. The Romanov family tree was deeply entwined with other European royal houses: Nicholas numbered both Kaiser Wilhelm II of Germany and George V of Great Britain among his cousins.

Centuries of chronic under-government had created such acute deficiencies in administration, taxation and data collection that Nicholas knew barely anything about his people, let alone what was best for them. Nor could the autocratic tsars claim to stand above politics. In 1861 Nicholas's grandfather, Alexander II, initiated what became known as the Great Reforms. The social disruption they fomented culminated in his assassination in 1881. His son, Alexander III, embarked on reactionary counter-reforms as the tsarist security state fought a running battle against a burgeoning but fragmented civil society. A growing number of men and women – politicians, bureaucrats, academics, professionals, philanthropists, entrepreneurs and revolutionaries – sought to shape Russia as they saw fit by acquiring the knowledge and means decisively to answer the 'peasant question', the 'resettlement question', the 'women question', the 'Jewish question' and myriad others. Intellectual

(below left) From left to right: Tsarina Alexandra Feodorovna (Alix of Hesse and by Rhine before marriage), with nine-month-old daughter Olga, Tsar Nicholas II, Queen Victoria and Edward, Prince of Wales, at Balmoral, 1896.

(below) King George V and Tsar Nicholas II in Berlin, 1913.
This picture was taken during the wedding of the Kaiser's daughter, Princess Victoria Louise of Prussia. The cousins are in the uniforms of their respective German regiments – Nicholas II is in the uniform of the Westphalian Hussars and George V is in the uniform of the Rhenish Cuirassiers.

and political debates on the nature of 'Russia', its past, future and its place in the world had rumbled interminably for decades, but these seemingly esoteric disputes had important practical implications. From the 1890s state-driven industrialisation spurred unprecedented urbanisation and social change. The following quarter of a century provided a stark illustration of the fact that the autocracy and the entire social system of prescribed estates on which it rested were an anachronism, woefully insufficient to handle change and the expanded role required of it.

Nicholas tried to demonstrate the vitality of the autocracy through foreign adventures. He hurled Russia into a short, calamitous war against Japan in 1904. This was followed in short order by a street revolution that forced him grudgingly to concede a measure of political and social liberalisation in October 1905. The regime was already teetering on the brink of catastrophe when Nicholas repeated his Japanese mistake and staggered into a general European war in the summer of 1914. The brief flurry of patriotism that greeted the outbreak of hostilities was soon crushed by familiar, pervasive incompetence on the front line and at home.

The Russian Peasantry

On his deathbed in 1855, Nicholas's great-grandfather and namesake, Tsar Nicholas I, lamented to his son and heir Alexander that his inheritance was a ramshackle army, an empty treasury and an ineffective, corrupt state. The ongoing debacle of the Crimean War (1853–1856) against Britain and France showed just how far the Russian Empire had fallen behind its European rivals since Alexander I's troops had marched triumphantly through the streets of Paris in 1814. The soon-to-be Alexander II was a pragmatic but committed autocrat. He understood the symbiosis between an efficient state, military victories and autocratic prestige, and that defeat gave him political space to implement his Great Reforms. Alexander was influenced by Russia's tradition of sweeping autocratic reform, but the fate of his forebears – Nicholas I faced the Decembrist revolt upon his accession to the throne in 1825, and both Paul I (1801) and Peter III (1762) had been murdered in palace coups – gave him an appreciation of the limits of divinely ordained authority. This led him to adopt a gradual, at times indecisive, approach. Nevertheless the Great Reforms fundamentally reshaped the Russian Empire. They covered disparate areas, but shared a common goal of addressing endemic administrative, economic and military weaknesses to secure both the autocracy and Russia's position as a great power.

The cornerstone was the emancipation of serfs, who constituted 37 per cent of the population. In a speech to the Marshals of the Moscow Nobility in 1856, Alexander II reflected that as such a change seemed inevitable: 'it is much better

(opposite) *My tsarstvuem nad vami...* (*We Reign Over You*), designed by Nikolai Lokhov for the Union of Russian Social Democrats, 1901.

In this clandestine poster, the idea of an unjust hierarchy is visually presented by a pyramid. The message is clear: the people at the bottom, who work for and feed those on the upper levels, will soon overthrow the those who 'eat for them', 'shoot them', 'lie to them' and 'reign over them'.

that this business be carried out from above, rather than from below'. By the tsar's will, more than 20 million people were freed from personal bondage and given the right to buy the land they worked. State-owned serfs – who were personally free but restricted on movement – were emancipated several years later. To replace seigneurial rule in the countryside and address provincial under-government, local councils (*zemstvo*) were created. Equivalent municipal councils were established in large cities such as Moscow and St Petersburg. Education reforms in 1864 granted autonomy to Russian universities and censorship was relaxed. The same year Alexander decreed the opening, but not the provision, of primary education to all estates. In 1874 fundamental military reforms were undertaken in an attempt to create a modern army that could defend Russia's Great Power status and imperial interests.

Emancipation was so important because the 'peasant question' lay at the centre of the debate on the future of the Russian Empire. More than 80 per cent of the imperial population was registered to the peasant estate; peasant conscripts filled the rank and file of the imperial army, and Russia's exports and tax base were overwhelmingly agrarian. Emancipation was a complex and titanic task, with extensive surveys, tentative trials and half-measures having begun as early as 1803 during the reign of Alexander I. Emancipated peasants were to be allotted land commensurate to their needs, mortgaged for 49 years. Both land and debt were to be held collectively by the village commune (*mir*). However, questionable prices and numerous delays to fiscal reforms meant that many peasants quickly fell behind on their redemption payments. These were reduced in 1881, before being cancelled altogether in 1907.

Popular understanding of landholding was linked to need and work; peasants did not understand why they had to pay for land that they saw as already theirs. Moreover, plots were generally smaller than had been allotted under serfdom, and many landlords denied access to pastures and meadows. Given the restrictions on formal education, most of the peace arbiters who oversaw the division of land between freed peasants and their former masters were nobles themselves. Worst of all, during the two-year lead-in period, peasants were obliged to continue paying their seigneurial dues, either in cash (*obrok*) or in services rendered (*barshchina*). Widespread rumours claimed that the nobility had spread a 'false edict' and that the tsar would soon deliver full and free land redistribution, the so-called 'Black Repartition'. For their part, many nobles resented the compulsory sell-off and payment in state bonds that left little capital available to invest in modernising their farms.

Five decades of freedom saw a mixture of continuity and change in rural Russia. Taking into account regional and chronological variation, and the scarcity of reliable statistics,

BLESSING THE GROUND BEFORE SOWING: LITTLE RUSSIA

'Blessing the Ground before Sowing: Little Russia.' Plate in Hugh Stewart and Frederic de Haenen, *Provincial Russia*, 1913.

Blessing the ground before sowing took place was an important Orthodox ritual performed by village priests. Special service books – the so-called *Trebniks* (*Books of Needs*) – contained a variety of prayers specifically linked to the agricultural cycle.

10292.h.36.

there was a concomitant small, slow growth in both the rural economy and living standards. However, agriculture remained so close to subsistence levels that few peasants could run a surplus, and rapid population growth reinforced the widespread notion of 'land hunger' in the empire's European provinces. Communalism remained the only protection against potentially catastrophic events such as bad harvests or the sudden loss of family members or livestock. Poor harvests in 1891 and 1892, for example, led to the deaths of around half a million people from famine and disease. The state perpetuated the crisis with a half-hearted relief effort and aggressive fiscal policies.

Alexander's reforms had also attempted to redress the isolation of the peasantry from wider society. The success or otherwise of incorporating isolated settlements into a national community of 'Russians' informs many of the questions about the nature of popular unrest and the Russian Revolution. Peasants were not passive recipients of 'modernisation'; rural communities adapted to outside forces in various ways in an effort to improve their lives. Through the land arbitration

Idealised image of a Russian peasant. Plate in Hugh Stewart and Frederic de Haenen, *Provincial Russia*, 1913.

10292.h.36.

process, *zemstvo* councils and the newly created court system, peasants engaged with a variety of bodies far beyond the village. However, their already small allotment of *zemstvo* seats was reduced in 1889, and the creation of the office of land captain the next year restored a measure of noble authority. Rural communities recognised the value of literacy and numeracy in their more frequent dealings with the bureaucratic state and market economy, but only 30 per cent of the empire's literate population lived outside its few cities by the turn of the century. Continued poverty, conscription and social discrimination did little to diminish revolutionary sentiment or to facilitate capitalist reform. Failure to solve the land question led to increasingly frequent outbursts of rural unrest, which played a significant role in undermining the autocracy in 1905 and 1917. Millions of peasants voted in the first national elections to the Duma in 1906, and continued to do so even when the already disadvantageous franchise was changed to neutralise their radicalism.

Urban Workers

In an attempt to compete with its Great Power rivals, the Russian state embarked on a rapid, state-directed industrialisation drive from the mid-1880s. The results were uneven but undoubtedly impressive, with massive increases in the production of coal, iron, oil and textiles, connected by an expanding rail network. However, while Russia's industrial growth outstripped many of its rivals, overall production, productivity and per capita income still lagged well behind. Moreover, industrialisation spurred intense social change. Between 1890 and 1912, the empire's urban workforce more than doubled to 2.9 million, concentrated mainly in St Petersburg, Moscow, Ukraine and Poland. However, it still constituted only 15 per cent of the imperial population. This was mostly due to the migration of peasants to the cities, as opposed to a natural increase in population. Migrants were disproportionately young males, drawn by the prospect of finite working hours and wages, disposable income and opportunities to live beyond the strictures of the patriarchal commune.

The exchange of people, goods, attitudes and customs had a transformative effect on urban and rural areas, but neither wholly assimilated the other. Migrants remained tied to the peasant estate with the duties and constraints associated with it, and were inescapably attached to their home commune. Most returned home seasonally to contribute their share of labour and redemption payments to the commune that retained control over internal passports. Moreover, workers commonly had wives and children in the village, and worked only a few years in cities before returning home permanently. Returning migrants brought disruptive ideas and attitudes, and often showed less deference to patriarchal authority. Their experiences also personalised the plight of urban workers for many peasants and drew town and countryside closer together.

The changes taking place in the countryside were captured by the ethnographer and painter Olga Semenova-Tian-Shanskaia. From the famed Semenov Tian-Shanskii family of explorers, she spent four years observing peasants in Ryazan province. She

Pair of men's shoes. Birch-bark, 19th century.

This type of traditional footwear was worn mainly in the northern areas of Europe. It became a symbolic stereotype of Russia, along with the samovar, Fabergé eggs and Orthodox icons. In Russia itself, the word for these shoes (*lapti*) acquired a derogative meaning of cheap shoes that belonged to uneducated and 'simple' villagers. This would be one of the first things city newcomers would want to change in their appearance.

British Museum, Eu.4222.a-b.

recorded the following conversation with a peasant named Pyotr on the attraction, beyond alcohol, of moving to Moscow:

> Pyotr, giving the question some thought, replies: 'It seems to me that many of them go there for clothes, too. Here you can go around in the same old rags winter and summer, but in town you can get decent clothes and shoes. Why, the way they look when they come back from town, we can't even stand next to them.' Indeed, it is a matter of honour for a young man to return from town to his village looking like 'a Moscow dandy', sporting a vest, a jacket, galoshes and even slacks.
>
> I: 'Did you really want to go to Moscow, then? Are you sorry you weren't able to get there?'
>
> Pyotr (smiling quietly): 'I wanted to, of course. Even now I sometimes want to go there, especially when one of the fellows comes back with a lot of good stories. I get envious. But when I don't hear anything about living in Moscow, I all but forget that the place exists. I just go on living and don't give it a thought.'
>
> I: 'So, what do they tell you about Moscow?'
>
> Pyotr: 'They say that pay is good there, and people dress better, and there is plenty of everything – tea, liquor, food – not like here in the village. The pay is high, and lots of everything, they say.'[1]

More often than not, a collective (*zemliachestvo* or *artel'*) of peasants from the same area helped new arrivals acclimatise to city life and find work and board. These networks were vital as the rapid influx of people sharply increased demand for a host of basic amenities – sanitation, housing, roads, water, electricity, transport, communications, policing, medicine and so on, that were well beyond the needs, and often the aspirations, of metropolitan and national governments. As workers had no electoral influence with municipal dumas, these services were usually concentrated in wealthy districts. As in Western Europe, a mixture of public bodies and private philanthropy tried to fill the breach, but succeeded only intermittently. People lived and worked in appalling conditions. The chronic shortage of adequate housing led to severe overcrowding, where a single squalid room in a sub-divided flat could be shared by 20 people or more. Many lived in lodgings provided by factory owners or slept on workshop floors, with food and entertainment deducted from their meagre wages. Shifts of 12 hours or more, highly unsafe working conditions and arbitrary labour discipline were standard practice. As the majority of workers were unskilled, they

Two photographs from Eric Baschet, *Russland 1904–1924: eine historische Foto-Reportage*, Kehl am Rhein, 1978.

Top: 'In diesem Keller von Petersburg bringt ein Transportunternehmer fünfzig seiner Fahrer fürdie Nacht unter' ('In this Petersburg cellar the owner of a haulage company shelters fifty of his drivers for the night').

Bottom: 'Sie verschlinger den ‚Kasscha'-Brei (Buchweizen), die Kohlsuppe und den Fisch' ('They wolf down "kasha" (porridge), cabbage soup and fish').

X:805/475.

were engaged as day labourers with no job security. In these circumstances malnutrition, chronic health problems and epidemic disease were rife. Alcohol was a readily available means of coping with this often brutal existence.

This unprecedented population movement had a destabilising effect on the empire's frayed social fabric. To wealthy urbanites, the presence of so many impoverished migrants, encroaching on public spaces and displaying a lack of social deference, led to widespread fears of an uncontrollable tide of 'hooliganism' swamping Russian cities. However, these workers were not a homogenous mass. Although Russian industry had a disproportionate number of large factories containing thousands of workers, the majority worked in smaller concerns. There were hierarchies of occupation, gender and skill within individual industries. Men monopolised jobs in heavy industry and the scarce skilled or semi-skilled jobs that commanded higher wages, while women worked predominantly in domestic service and textile production. As workers began to take permanent residence in cities, communal ties and a prescribed social station were replaced by a strong shop-floor camaraderie, infused with hatred of foremen and wealthy industrialists. While some migrant workers retained their traditional habits due to poverty or personal choice, wealthier workers in industries such as steelmaking determinedly expressed their separation from village life by adopting new styles of dress and behaviour. These established, self-consciously urban workers often mocked the newly arrived peasants for their coarse manners and rustic dress. In his autobiography, Semen Kanatchikov describes his early days in the city:

> Awkward, sluggish, with long hair that had been cut under a round bowl, wearing heavy boots with horseshoes, I was a typical village youth. The skilled workers looked down on me with scorn, pinched me by the ear, called me a 'green country bumpkin' and other insulting names ... The pattern shop was considered to be the 'aristocratic' workshop. Most of the patternmakers were urban types – they dressed neatly, wore their trousers over their boots, wore their shirts 'fantasia' style, tucked into their trousers, fastened their collars with a lace instead of a necktie, and on holidays some of them wore bowler hats. They cut their hair 'in the Polish style' or brush-cut. Their bearing was firm, conveying their consciousness of their own worth. They used foul language only when they lost their tempers and in extreme situations, or on paydays, when they got drunk, and even then not all of them at that.[4]

Workers joined educational societies and temperance movements, and became increasingly politicised as the state

showed time and again that it prioritised cheap labour and GDP over their welfare. The factory inspectorate established by the Ministry of the Interior was scuppered by its political rivalry with the Ministry of Finance. Trade unions were illegal, activists were arrested and troops were used to enforce the outright ban on industrial action. Clandestine socialist agitators cultivated links with these 'conscious workers' to foment strikes and promote revolution as the only means of redressing their grievances. This symbiosis of political and worker socialism played a key role in the downfall of the autocratic regime.

Privileged Society

In 1894 Tsar Alexander III died aged 49, to be succeeded by his son Nicholas. Accepting his inheritance with a reluctant sense of duty rather than any great enthusiasm, the now Nicholas II hastened his marriage to Princess Alexandra of Hesse. The unfortunate coincidence of the two events made for an awkward spectacle, but Nicholas was loath to face such a task without the woman upon whom he became increasingly reliant.

The official coronation happened 18 months later, in May 1896. Russian imperial coronations were imbued with much religious symbolism and a strong emphasis on the sacred nature of autocratic power. Traditionally, coronations took place in the Moscow Kremlin, with festivities continuing throughout the old capital. Common people also partook in celebrations in the city's large open spaces. However, the coronation of the last

Poklon s Krasnogo kryl'tsa narodu (*Bowing to the People from the Red Porch*), chromolithograph of the original watercolour by Andrei Riabushkin, from *Les Solennités du saint couronnement. Ouvrage publié avec l'autorisation de Sa Majesté l'Empereur par le Ministère de la Maison Impériale sous la direction de M. V. S. Krivenko,* French translation by M. G. Korsow, St Petersburg, 1899.

The crowning service was held at the Dormition Cathedral in Cathedral Square in the Kremlin. So-called 'Coronation Albums' documented the ceremony. The most lavishly produced editions were presented as gifts to foreign courts; cheaper and less detailed editions were also in circulation. The 1896 ceremony was also filmed by the French journalist Camille Cerf.

L.R.25.c.20.

Narodnyi prazdnik 18 maia 1896
(*People's celebration on 30 (18) May
1896*), chromolithograph of the original
watercolour by Vladimir Makovskii, from
*Les Solennités du saint couronnement.
Ouvrage publié avec l'autorisation de
Sa Majesté l'Empereur par le Ministère
de la Maison Impériale sous la direction
de M. V. S. Krivenko,* French translation
by M. G. Korsow, St Petersburg, 1899.

L.R.25.c.20.

Souvenir enamel mug to commemorate
the coronation in 1896.

This formed part of a free gift, which
included cake, sausage, a gingerbread
with a coat-of-arms and a small bag of
sweets. Because of the tragic stampede
for souvenir gifts on coronation day, it was
later referred to as the 'mug of sorrow'.

Private collection.

tsar and tsarina was overshadowed by events at one such mass gathering. At Khodynka Field, to the north-west of the city, over 500, 000 people rushed to get free souvenirs. In the stampede, 1,389 people were killed and another 1,300 injured. Despite the carnage, the scheduled celebrations continued. The new tsar described events in his diary:

> 18th [30] of May. Saturday. Until now, everything was going, thank God, like clockwork, but today a great disaster happened. The crowd staying overnight at Khodynka, awaiting the start of the distribution of lunch and mugs, pushed against buildings and there was a terrible crush, and awful to say trampled around 1300 people!! I learned about this at 10½ … At 12½ we had lunch and then [Empress] Alix and I went to Khodynka to be present at this sad 'national holiday'. Actually there was nothing going on: we looked from the pavilion at the huge crowd that surrounded the stage from which the orchestra played all the time the anthem and 'Glory'. Went to Petrovsky [Palace], where at the gate I received several delegations and then entered the yard. Here dinner was served under four tents for all township heads. I had to make a speech, and then another for the assembled marshals of the nobility. After going around the table, we left for the Kremlin. Dinner at Mama's at 8. Went to the ball at [French ambassador] Montebello's. It was very nicely arranged, but the heat was unbearable. After dinner, left at 2.[5]

Nicholas has been cast as both a helpless victim and a villain of the Russian Revolution. He was polite, attentive and reasonably intelligent, and worked with a strong sense of duty. Most of all, Nicholas was a dedicated family man. He shunned the glamour of St Petersburg society for the life of a country squire at Tsarskoe Selo, some 13 miles outside the capital. However, such parochialism made Nicholas wholly unsuited to his task. He lacked the dominating personality and political nous to be an effective autocrat, but disdained bureaucratic formalism and had an unthinking suspicion of anything he felt undermined his son's 'sacred inheritance'. Nor could he be shaken from his romantic belief in the unswerving loyalty of the peasantry. As the increasing complexity of state business overwhelmed him, Nicholas shunned policymaking and obstinately sought refuge in his faith, family and trivial administrative tasks. This made him unwilling or unable to recognise the need for a fundamental renovation of the state machinery, and left the tsarist government sluggish and directionless in the face of unprecedented challenges. Meanwhile, Alexandra's shy and reserved nature meant that she was ill-equipped for the empress's traditional role in the notoriously acerbic St Petersburg society. However, as Nicholas's most trusted confidante, she played a key role in

Nicholas and Alexandra at a fancy-dress ball. Photographs from *Album du bal costumé au Palais d'hiver: Février 1903 (Album of Winter Palace Fancy-Dress Ball Costumes, February 1903)*, St Petersburg, 1904.

On 24 (11) February 1903, Nicholas and Alexandra made a rare social appearance at the annual Winter Palace fancy-dress ball, where all the guests appeared in costumes of Russian 17th-century nobility (the time before Peter the Great 'westernised' Russian lifestyle). It was uncommon for a tsar to appear in costume, but the choice of theme was very much in keeping with Nicholas's perception of the Russian Empire and his place in it.

K.T.C.11.b.2.

the reactionary clique that sought to banish his pious fatalism. Four daughters – Olga, Tatiana, Maria and Anastasia – were born before the long-awaited son and heir, Alexei, arrived in August 1904. Alexandra's greatest fears were realised when it became clear that the young crown prince (*tsesarevich*) had inherited the haemophilia passed down from her grandmother, Queen Victoria. It was this grief that spurred her damaging association with the dissolute peasant mystic Grigorii Rasputin. The British Ambassador Sir George Buchanan, who first met the royal couple in 1893, described the tsar as 'a lovable man, possessed of many good qualities, a true and loyal ally, having, in spite of all appearances to the contrary, his country's true interests at heart'. Similarly, he believed that 'though a good woman, actuated by the best of motives, [Alexandra] was instrumental in bringing about the final catastrophe', and that her 'natural sadness of heart manifested itself in many ways'.[6]

Russian Nobility

The 1897 census recorded that 1.5 per cent of the imperial population was assigned to the noble estate. Of these, 1.2 million were hereditary nobility or gentry and another 630,000 were non-hereditary, lifetime nobility. The empire had traditionally secured territories into which it had expanded through intermarriage with local elites, which meant that in the late imperial period half of the nobility were non-Russian. A particularly large number were Polish and German gentry. From the eighteenth century the nobility enjoyed significant corporate rights, including trial by their peers, a monopoly of high civil and military office and exclusive ownership of serfs and other private property, which gave them significant advantages over the other estates.

The Great Reforms unintentionally accelerated the decline and fragmentation of the Russian nobility. Even before emancipation, noble rank did not necessarily entail affluence and many estates were so small or inefficient that they were not economically viable. With the state providing little cash to improve estates after emancipation, many owners sold up and moved to cities. Nor could Alexander III's Gentry Land Bank, with more capital and more favourable terms than those offered by the Peasant Land Bank, reverse the trend: noble landholding shrank about 1 per cent per year after 1861, and over half had no land at all by 1905. The more enterprising nobles took a leading role in Russia's emerging industries such as metallurgy, petrochemicals and railways, reinventing themselves as the empire's pre-eminent capitalists.

The endemic problems facing the Russian Empire in the late nineteenth century would have tested any leader or system of government. However, they were exacerbated by the anachronistic tsarist state, as its effectiveness depended on the competence of those in charge and their chosen officials. Nicholas faced the same insoluble problem as his predecessors: how to create an efficient administration, promote economic growth and educate the population in the ever-growing range of skills necessary to sustain Russia as a great power, but at the same time limit social agency and maintain the archaic system of autocratic government. In the face of rapid socio-economic change, the nobility retained their grip on high civil and military office.

Nicholas lacked a circle of astute advisors who could have helped him face his many challenges. As such, he inherited many officials who had been influential figures in his father Alexander III's 'counter reforms' in the 1880s. The continued absence of cabinet government meant that individual minsters had sweeping powers and vast, ever-increasing remits far beyond the capabilities of any single individual. The result was overlapping jurisdictions and contradictory policies.

The Contested Middle

Indeed, noble dissatisfaction with the autocracy went much deeper. Supporters of the autocracy shared personal experience, and often personal acquaintance, with proponents of reform and even revolutionaries. Alexander II's Great Reforms and industrialisation were designed to refurbish the autocracy, and noble birth unquestionably remained an advantage, but the increased availability of education gave access to information and opportunities for a broader range of people. Increased social mobility disrupted existing social patterns and did much to foster a civil society of groups and individuals pursuing their aims through economic, social, political or violent means.

The *zemstvo* were a key motor of change. Before the Great Reforms, Russia had about one-quarter of the officials per capita of its Great Power rivals. This historic paucity of qualified personnel bred venality and arbitrariness. The 1864 statute devolved powers over education, healthcare, veterinary services, infrastructure and 'caring for local economic needs and wants' which allowed enterprising local councils to undertake wide-ranging programmes. However, secondary and higher education institutions struggled to meet the demand for tens of thousands of new professional workers such as doctors, lawyers and veterinarians. Many – but by no means all – came from the gentry, particularly in established fields such as law and in the upper echelons of the *zemstvos*. However, the vast *zemstvo* support staff of semi-professional workers, for example nurses and administrators, came from lower estates. This demand was also somewhat self-perpetuating, in that the more *zemstvos* became capable of doing, the more they saw the need to do.

Economic change also played a key role. Industrialisation and urbanisation demanded thousands of engineers, technicians, accountants and managers who were often of low birth. Greater wealth, free time and demographic concentration for professionals of all levels allowed them to participate in civic life. As old estate allegiances receded, they were replaced by nascent sectoral identities. This led to a boom of professional associations, cultural groups and philanthropic societies. They built theatres and museums, founded temperance and educational societies and promoted actions for the public good rather than private gain.

Many people gravitated to ideologies of liberalism and constitutionalism that were prevalent in Western Europe. Concepts such as the protection of private property, civil rights, legal equality and a legislative assembly appealed to those who had benefitted from access to education and industrialisation, or who had experienced a modicum of power through the *zemstvos*. The first liberal political organisation was the Union of Liberation (*Soiuz Osvobozhdeniia*), founded in 1903. It did not advocate insurrection, but its activities were semi-clandestine due to their political content. The liberal movement played a vital role in the 1905 and February 1917 revolutions. The liberal Constitutional Democratic Party, popularly known as the Kadets, was formed in October 1905. Situating itself within European liberal tradition, the Kadet manifesto proclaimed that its founding was 'so natural, so uncontrived, indeed, so necessary and inevitable in view of the present political situation, that life has already anticipated our formal resolution, and the Constitutional Democratic Party is regarded as an entity that has been in existence for a long time, which even possesses its own traditions and its own definite political physiognomy'.[7] However, the diversity of Russia's civil society – professional, generational, ethnic, regional – meant that it was not able to present a united front, and was overtaken by representatives of Russia's longstanding tradition of revolutionary socialism.

Revolutionary Movement vs Police State

There was no legal means of expressing political dissent in the Russian Empire before 1905. The social and economic dislocation created by the Great Reforms and industrialisation, allied to the growing disillusionment of many educated people with the intransigent autocratic government, was a fertile breeding ground for political dissent. As the empire remained overwhelmingly agrarian, it is unsurprising that Russia's first significant revolutionary movement had a strong agrarian focus. The Populists (*Narodniks*), as they later became known, were radical students driven by various romantic, liberal and Slavophile readings of the concept of *narodnichestvo* – the idea that personal and national salvation lay in uncovering an unspoilt, primordial 'Russianness' among the Russian people (*narod*). In 1874 they sought to foment revolution by 'going to the people'; they moved to isolated villages, established workshops, schools

Nobles in revolution

A noble background was not unusual for revolutionaries. One of the most colourful examples was the famed explorer, geographer and revolutionary anarchist Prince Petr Kropotkin (1842–1921). The Kropotkin family was from the highest echelons of nobility. Kropotkin graduated from the prestigious Corps of Pages, and personally served Tsar Alexander II. However, he was repulsed by serfdom and the autocracy it sustained. He was imprisoned in 1874, but escaped to Europe two years later. In exile, Kropotkin became a famed proponent of 'scientific anarchism'. He returned to Russia after the February revolution, but abhorred the Bolshevik seizure of power in October.

There was also a strong tradition of revolutionary noblewomen. For instance, in 1878 Sofiia Subbotina was sentenced to eight months in exile for her role in the Populist revolutionary movement. Vera Figner, scion of a hereditary noble family from Kazan, was a member of the People's Will organisation assembled from the ashes of the Populists. Her death sentence for involvement in the assassination of Alexander II in 1881 was commuted to Siberian exile. Vera Zasulich, tried in 1877 for the attempted murder of the Governor of St Petersburg, was from a minor noble family in Smolensk.

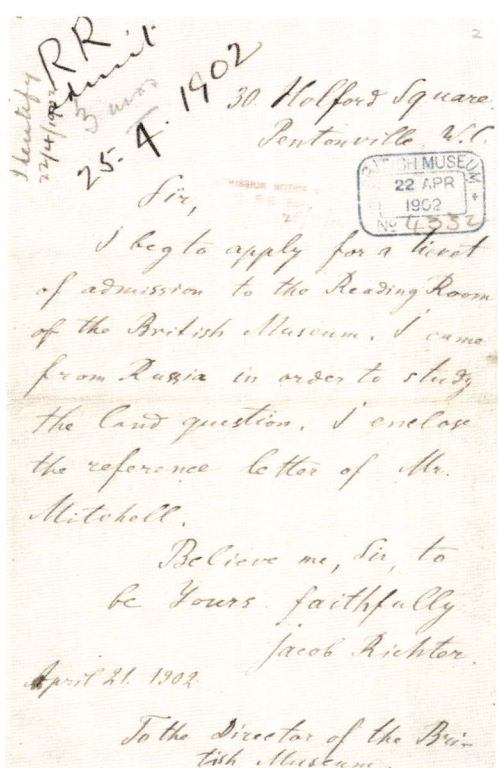

Vladimir Lenin's application for a reader's ticket at the British Museum, using the false name of Jacob Richter, April 1902.

Add MS 54579.

Book of Prince Petr Kropotkin's own press-cuttings on the question of the emancipation of women, presented to the Library of the British Museum in 1917.

1884.a.11.

and libraries, and sought to raise both living standards and socialist consciousness.

The movement was quickly crushed and hundreds of activists were arrested, but not due to peasant denunciations as was widely claimed at the time. Educated urbanites were conspicuous in the countryside, their propaganda and revolutionary songs providing ready evidence for local authorities. The Populists' failure led some to switch their focus from the people to the state. In 1876 the populist Land and Freedom (Zemlia i Volia) group split into the non-violent Black Repartition (Chernyi Peredel) and the revolutionary terror organisation People's Will (Narodnaia Volia). The People's Will hoped to destabilise the state by killing regime officials. The group made several attempts to assassinate Tsar Alexander II and finally succeeded on 13 (1) March 1881. The group's Executive Committee then issued a lengthy open letter demanding widespread reform, but did not attract widespread support.

Vladimir Lenin's elder brother Alexander was a member of the People's Will, and was executed in 1887 for plotting the assassination of Alexander III. Shortly after, Vladimir, then a law student, also got involved with the Populists and was expelled from university. He migrated towards Marxism over the next several years. He was arrested in 1897, aged twenty-seven. On his way to Siberian exile he wrote to his mother:

> I still have two more days' journey ahead of me. I drove across the Ob in a horse-sleigh and bought tickets to Krasnoyarsk. Since traffic here is still 'temporary', I had to pay the old rates, which meant handing over 10 roubles for a ticket and 5 roubles for luggage for something like 700 versts![8] The way the trains run here is beyond all bounds. To do that 700 versts we shall crawl for forty-eight hours. Beyond Krasnoyarsk, the railway goes only as far as Kansk, i.e., for 220 versts – and altogether to Irkutsk it is about 1,000 versts. And so I shall have to go on by road – *if I have to go at all*. Another 24 hours is taken up by those 220 versts on the railway; the further you go, the slower the trains crawl along.[9]

The regicide of Alexander II had repulsed many moderates and was to lead to the rehabilitation of the Populists. Their legacy was a key influence on the Socialist Revolutionary (SR) Party, formed in 1901. The SR's focus remained on the peasantry, particularly the issue of land redistribution, but they advocated an alliance of 'toilers' – peasants, workers and intellectuals – against 'exploiters' such as landlords, capitalists and the state. However, direct action retained many devotees and extreme SRs killed more than 10,000 officials between 1901 and 1914. The SR's great rival was the Russian Social Democratic Labour Party, commonly

31-го октября 1898 г. № 300

Памяти Е. П. Карцовой.

27-го октября на кладбищѣ Новодѣвичьяго монастыря совершилось погребеніе замѣчительной русской женщины, настоятельницы общины сестеръ милосердія св. Георгія, Елизаветы Петровны Карцовой, скончавшейся 24-го октября, на 76 году.

Е. П. была одной изъ первыхъ русскихъ сестеръ милосердія и проработала на этомъ тяжеломъ поприщѣ 43 года, до самой смерти. Покойная, дочь помѣщика Новгородской губ., родилась въ 1823 году. Во время севастопольской обороны, когда, по иниціативѣ великой княгини Елены Павловны, была сдѣлана первая попытка организаціи женской помощи раненымъ на театрѣ военныхъ дѣйствій, Е. П. обратилась къ великой княгинѣ съ просьбой включить ее въ число сестеръ, направляемыхъ въ Севастополь. Худенькая, слабенькая, она казалась совсѣмъ не созданной для такой тяжкой работы, и великая княгиня рѣшилась послать ее, только уступая горячимъ просьбамъ покойной. На театрѣ военныхъ дѣйствій Е. П. сдѣлалась ближайшей сотрудницей Н. И. Пирогова, оцѣнившаго высокій даръ ея и самоотверженное отношеніе къ своему долгу. Тяжко было работать среди ужасовъ войны при полномъ отсутствіи самой элементарной организаціи медицинской помощи. Не разъ покойная приходила въ отчаяніе отъ чувства безсилія облегчить участь несчастныхъ страдальцевъ и только громадная воля и горячая любовь къ ближнему помогали ей пережить эти трудныя минуты. Какъ работали на войнѣ первыя русскія сестры, уже достаточно извѣстно: встрѣченныя сначала съ недоброжелательствомъ и скептицизмомъ, онѣ своимъ самоотверженіемъ заслужили общее уваженіе и обезпечили будущее этому новому дѣлу.

Поступивъ въ сестры милосердія сначала на одинъ годъ, Е. П. такъ привязалась къ служенію больнымъ и раненымъ, что осталась сестрой на всю жизнь. По скончаніи войны, покойная работала до 1867 года старшей сестрой Крестовоздвиженской общины, а съ 1867 г. по 1871 г. въ частной больницѣ Миловидова въ Москвѣ.

Въ 1871 году, при основаніи общины сестеръ милосердія св. Георгія, Ея Высочество Принцесса Евгенія Максимиліановна Ольденбургская и графиня Е. Н. Гейденъ съ согласія Ея Величества Государыни, въ то время Цесаревны, Маріи Ѳеодоровны пригласили покойную Е. П. взять на себя организацію новой общины и занять мѣсто ея настоятельницы. Съ этого времени покойная отдалась всецѣло новому учрежденію, которое обязано ей всѣмъ своимъ образцовымъ устройствомъ. Но главная заслуга передъ общиною Е. П.—это духъ полнаго самоотверженія и безкорыстной преданности дѣлу, который она умѣла внушить своимъ ученицамъ.

Во время войны Черногоріи съ Турціей въ 1875 году Е. П., во главѣ отряда общины, работала на театрѣ военныхъ дѣйствій и завоевала общее уваженіе и любовь между черногорцами; когда отрядъ покидалъ Черногорію, эти люди, закаленные въ постоянной борьбѣ съ врагами, плакали и цѣловали руки старушки, а князь черногорскій, въ письмѣ къ Государынѣ Маріи Александровнѣ, въ трогательныхъ словахъ выразилъ благодарность своего народа Е. П. и русскимъ сестрамъ милосердія.

Во время русско-турецкой войны покойная работала съ отрядомъ Георгіевской общины въ Болгаріи, всюду раздѣляя трудъ сестеръ и служа имъ образцомъ.

Позднѣйшіе годы жизни покойной были посвящены дальнѣйшему развитію руководимаго ею учрежденія. За это время она воспитала цѣлый рядъ поколѣній сестеръ. Нравственное вліяніе ея на ученицъ было громадно, потому что онѣ видѣли въ ней живой образецъ, видѣли человѣка, у котораго слово никогда не расходится съ дѣломъ, идеально чистаго и безъ завѣта отдавшагося облегченію людскихъ страданій. Отъ своихъ ученицъ Е. П. требовала полнаго безкорыстія. Для сестры не должно быть иной награды, кромѣ сознанія исполненнаго долга—такъ смотрѣла она на дѣло сестры и такъ поступала всегда сама. Кончина ея была подвигомъ, достойнымъ всей ея жизни; до послѣднихъ минутъ она переносила страданія съ кротостью и терпѣніемъ и продолжала постоянно заботиться о дорогой ей общинѣ, старалась и немногіе, оставшіеся ей часы употребить на добро. Ея нравственное вліяніе отражалось не только на сестрахъ, но и на всѣхъ, работавшихъ съ нею, и каждый, соприкасавшійся съ этой благородной личностью, навсегда сохранитъ о ней самое теплое, благодарное воспоминаніе.   Н. Чистовичъ.

ПЕТЕРБУРГСКАЯ ЖИЗНЬ.

А. И. АБАРИНОВА.

(Къ 25-ти-лѣтнему юбилею ея сценической дѣятельности).

ПЕТЕРБУРГСКАЯ ЖИЗНЬ.

Е. Н. ВОДОВОЗОВА.

(По случаю 35-лѣтія ея литературно-педагогической дѣятельности).

known as the Social Democrats (SDs). They were inspired by Emancipation of Labour (*Osvobozhdenie Truda*), a circle of Russian exiles in Switzerland who translated Marx into Russian. Marxism had little cachet in Russia until the 1880s and 1890s, when the effects of industrialisation and urbanisation seemed to give credence to this imported 'scientific', worker-oriented socialism.

The Russian Social Democratic Labour Party was founded in 1898, but split at the Second RSDLP Congress in London in 1903. After winning a policy vote, the faction led by Lenin seized the opportunity to claim the name *Bolsheviks* (the majority) and label their defeated opponents *Mensheviks* (the minority), even though neither side was dominant. Although the split had been over a seemingly semantic issue on party membership (as well as personal animosity), it spoke to deep divisions on revolutionary theory. In his 1902 book *What Is To Be Done?* Lenin argued that to overcome Russia's lack of industrial development, the party had to create socialist consciousness in the workers and lead the revolution. To do this and evade the intrusive security state, membership should be limited to a disciplined 'revolutionary vanguard' with strong central leadership. This led to the party, and Lenin in particular, assuming increasing importance in Bolshevik thinking. Their Menshevik opponents argued for a slightly broader membership and a less rigid hierarchy. This made Menshevism more ideologically diverse, fostering cooperation with other anti-regime elements.

Upon his accession to the throne in 1881, Alexander III had taken steps to reorganise the security apparatus that failed to protect his father. He dismissed the 'criminal and hasty' plans that Alexander II had made for consultative committees and embarked on a period known as the 'counter reforms'.

The Security Law introduced in 1881 granted two tiers of extraordinary police powers to governors-general, Reinforced

Safeguard and Extraordinary Safeguard. The former was immediately implemented in ten provinces, including the capitals. These safeguards allowed for the internment of 'suspicious' persons, bans on assembly, the dismissal of *zemstvo* officials and all but the most senior bureaucrats, the closure of publications and the suspension of universities. The autocracy's dreaded secret police, commonly known as the *Okhrana*, operated outside the law and answered directly to the Minister of the Interior rather than the judiciary. Where evidence for a prosecution was lacking, a committee within the ministry used its powers of 'administrative exile' to send undesirables to Siberia for several years. They also had a Corps of Gendarmes at their disposal. However, the Russian security state was not unique in Europe at the time, and the 1881 statute represented the bureaucratisation and systematisation of police powers in an under-governed state rather than pervasive repression.

The *Okhrana* was actually a loose affiliation of agencies employing a couple of thousand agents, and its per capita was dwarfed by its Great Power rivals. There were only 100,000 police officers for the entire empire, and they were especially scarce in rural areas. Rather than weight of numbers, the *Okhrana* achieved success by operating at the cutting edge of policing technology, deploying innovative methods such as fingerprinting, photo-fits and phone taps to collect vast amounts of information on activists and intellectuals of all political persuasions. Torture was not widely used and death sentences were rare, even for those found guilty of sedition. Moreover, such 'politicals' represented a very small fraction of the prison population. Many were not punished at all, and the *Okhrana*'s success in 'turning' arrestees allowed them to shut down or take over workers' groups, political parties and clandestine organisations such as the People's Will and the SR Combat Organisation. There was also a bureau in Paris to track exiles. However, public perception was of an omnipotent, highly invasive security apparatus engaged in morally dubious activities, with tens of thousands of spies embedded across the country and perlustration cabinets interfering with postal services in every city. The lines between agents and revolutionaries were increasingly blurred. The most extreme case was the double agent Evno Azef, who was involved in many murders as head of the SR Combat Organisation. Although Nicholas sought to continue his father's policies, he was soon overtaken by events. The policies and practices of the *Okhrana* alienated many moderates, and proved unsuitable to the increased movement of people and ideas in the late nineteenth century.

Nationalities and Foreign Policy

National identity became an increasingly powerful political

Leg irons brought from Siberia by a British artist and journalist of the *Illustrated News*.
Science Museum, A40051.

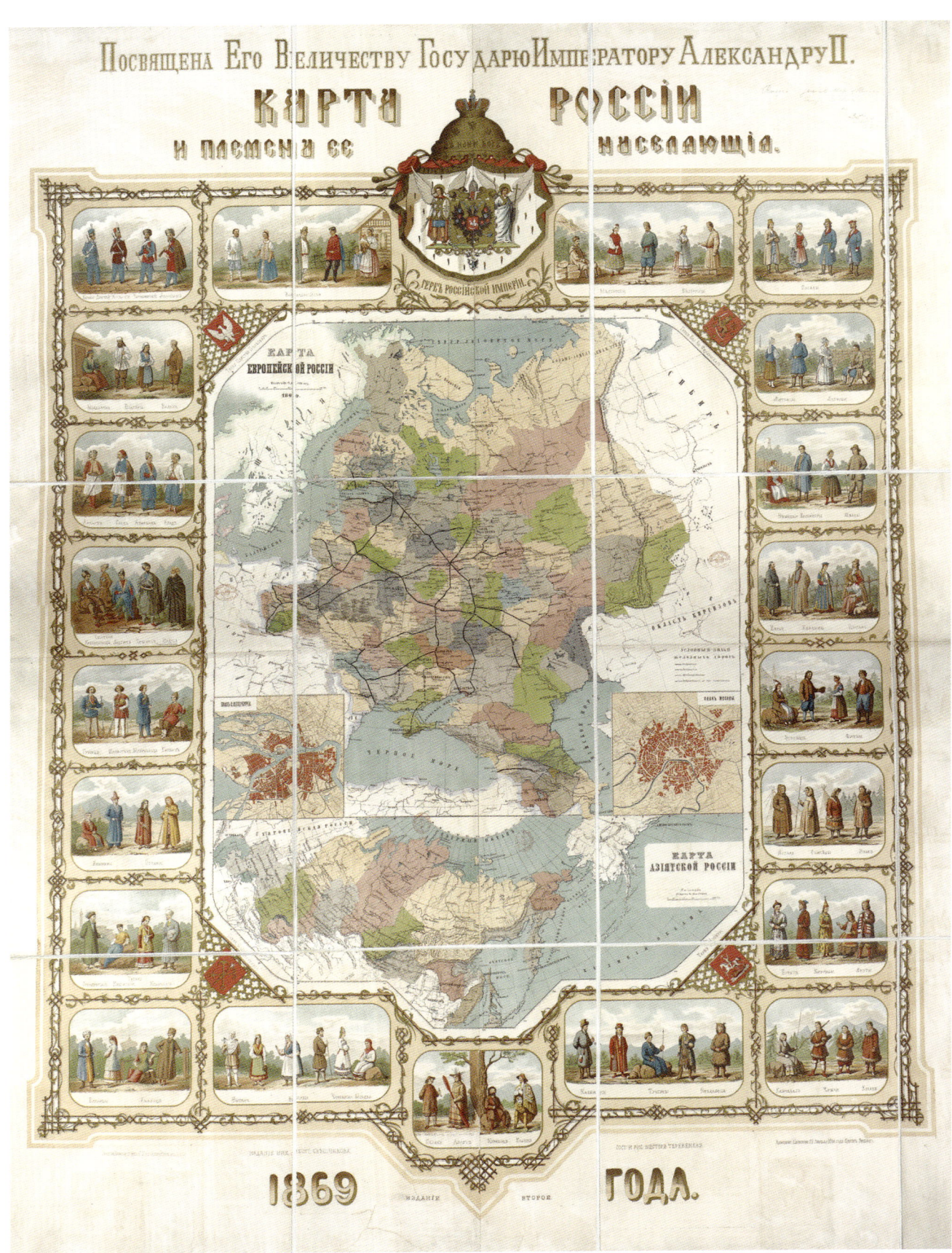

force across Europe in the nineteenth century. However, it was an uneasy fit for the rulers of a multi-ethnic empire who claimed to rule by divine right and were vehemently opposed to the notion of popular sovereignty. Two competing but overlapping concepts of the Russian 'nation' emerged. 'Russian' (*rossiiskii*) was a statist identification based on dynastic legitimacy and pertaining to all imperial subjects, regardless of origin. It was challenged by the concept of 'Russian' (*russkii*) denoting all who were perceived as ethnically 'Russian'. An innate Russian Orthodox faith was an enduring element in depictions of ethnically Russian people until the fall of the Romanovs. The Russian word for peasant derived from the word 'Christian' and, for the non-Orthodox, baptism was the closest equivalent to Russian citizenship. The autocracy pursued Russification policies in both the western and eastern halves of the empire at various times. However, prior to the First World War, Russification remained limited and initiatives were often abandoned on pragmatic grounds. The Pan-Slavist offshoot of Russian nationalism that styled the autocracy as the protector

(opposite) *Karta Rossii i plemena ee naseliaiushchiie* (*Map of Russia and its Peoples*), designed by Nestor Terebenev, St Petersburg, 1869.

Maps 35795.(38).

(left) Icon of the Virgin Hodegetria. Tempera on panel, 19th century, Russia.

The Virgin Hodegetria means the Virgin 'who shows the way.' Until the fall of the Romanovs, baptism was the closest thing there was to acquiring Russian citizenship for subject peoples.

Victoria and Albert Museum. E.69:1-2-1997.

of the Balkan Slavs was an often unwanted entanglement that helped to draw Russia into war in 1914.

Although the empire had been expanding eastwards for centuries, Russian settlement was sparse due to heavy legal restrictions on peasant movement. As the late imperial period wore on, anxiety mounted in both official and private circles regarding the 'land hunger' engendered by the supposed overpopulation of the empire's European core. Eastward peasant migration grew steadily following the emancipation of the serfs in 1861, but the most significant increase came in the last two decades of the nineteenth century, when resettlement restrictions were gradually eased and the Trans-Siberian Railway became operational. By 1906, the 'great resettlement movement' and natural increase had brought the Siberian population to 9.4 million.

In the 1890s, 'peaceful penetration' of the Far East by extracting railroad concessions in Manchuria and Korea brought Russia into contact with Japan, an emerging power on the world stage. In response to increasing provocation, the Imperial Japanese Navy attacked the Russian base Port Arthur on 9 February (26 January) 1904. Neither the Russian army nor navy were remotely ready for such a conflict and the Trans-Siberian Railway proved slow in carrying troops and supplies over the vast distance to the front. The Russians suffered a series of humiliating defeats, most notably at Port Arthur and at the Battle of Mukden. Tens of thousands of troops were killed or captured, and the Russians were forced to sign a humiliating peace at Portsmouth, New Hampshire in September.

The Politics of Change

Defeat in the war was damaging for the autocracy in several ways. Calling up combat troops had weakened European Russian garrisons and continued defeats further strained resources and officer–soldier relations. More than a hundred small mutinies occurred between October and December 1904 alone. The loss of face diminished popular faith in the autocrat and emboldened the burgeoning liberal movement. In February 1905 Sergei

Territorial growth
Perhaps above all else, the Russian Empire was successful in the formal annexation of territory. The Partitions of Poland in the late eighteenth century added a vast swathe of Eastern Europe, but further expansion towards the Balkans and Central Asia was made complicated by the post-1815 balance of power in Europe. A section of the Pacific coast was tenuously grasped as early as 1647, and the empire reached its greatest extent with the annexation of Alaska in 1733. There were also small, short-lived outposts at Fort Ross in California and Fort Elizabeth on the Hawaiian island of Kauai in the early nineteenth century. However, fearing it would be indefensible in the event of a British attack, Alaska was sold to the United States in 1867 for $7.2 million. At the same time, Russia redoubled its efforts in the Far East as the European Great Powers, the USA and the emerging empire of Japan jostled to carve up the struggling Qing Empire.

КАРТА
РАЗВИТИЯ РУССКОЙ ЖЕЛЕЗНО-ДОРОЖНОЙ
СЕТИ с 1838 по 1913 год

УСЛОВНЫЕ ОБОЗНАЧЕНИЯ:
ЖЕЛЕЗНЫЕ ДОРОГИ, ПОСТРОЕННЫЕ

- в 1838—1857 г.
- в 1858—1867 г.
- в 1868—1877 г.
- в 1878—1892 г.
- в 1893—1902 г.
- в 1903—1913 г.

АЗИАТСКАЯ РОССИЯ

Karta razvitiia russkoi zheleno-dorozhnoi seti s 1838 no 1913 god (Map of the Russian Railway Network, 1838–1913).

Maps 35797.(8.).

Two posters from the series *K voine Rossii s Iaponiei* (*Russian War with Japan*), 1904.

The above image symbolically represents Russia as a warrior beauty and Japan as a dragon-type monster. In the image on the left, a pitiful Japanese character is effortlessly beaten by a strong and cheerful Russian sailor. Russian *lubok* (popular lithographic prints) played the role of illustrated news stories. They had a wide range in tone, from humorous to instructive to sharp political and social commentary. They could be reproduced inexpensively, and were thus a way for the masses to display art at home. They were published in large quantities by leading publishing houses who specialised in popular cheap literature.

N.Tab.2005.12
N.Tab.2005.13.

Witte, Minister of Finance (1892–1903) and the man behind the Trans-Siberian Railway project, wrote to the Minister of War and military commander Alexei Kuropatkin:

> If the war had ended in a few months, it would have strengthened Russia's spirit, her international prestige. Even if she had not achieved real benefits from it, she might perhaps have taken heart and her prestige been revived. But the war has grown sour … and Russia's social fabric has gone to pieces.[11]

In January 1905, 'Bloody Sunday' was to be a catalyst for simmering unrest in St Petersburg. The unrest began when four members of the Assembly of Russian Factory Workers were fired from the Putilov Steelworks in St Petersburg's Vyborg district. The Assembly was part of the autocracy's short-lived policy of 'police socialism', whereby state-run workers' groups aimed to ward off socialist agitators. It was run by Father Georgii Gapon, a controversial figure accused of being an agent of both the *Okhrana* and the Socialist Revolutionaries. His brief was to provide recreational activities in a wholesome, apolitical environment, but political elements within the Assembly fostered increasing radicalisation.

The dismissals at the Putilov plant triggered a wave of strikes. Gapon reluctantly agreed to lead an unauthorised protest march on 22 (9) January. Up to 150,000 workers and their families converged on the Winter Palace to present a petition asking Nicholas II for improved conditions and political reform. Troops ordered the crowd to disperse, but events accelerated when warning shots and cavalry charges turned into deadly volleys of fire. The official count was 96 dead and 333 wounded, but press estimates put the death toll at over 4,000. The symbolism of this act – imperial troops murdering unarmed people carrying icons and singing hymns, appealing to their benevolent 'Little Father' – provoked outrage and did lasting damage to popular perceptions of the autocracy.

Months of unrest followed as strikes spread to every sector of the workforce: railwaymen, telegraph operators, professionals, salesmen, bank clerks and even theatre companies joined in, and some factory owners continued to pay their workers. Cooperation between workers, professionals and intellectuals led to the formation of the Union of Unions in May. This added respectability to the strike movement and made some regime figures reluctant to implement a crackdown. Unrest spread across the empire. In 50 cities workers formed councils of their representatives (soviets), autonomously from the trade unions. In the countryside, peasant communities seized land, burned manor houses and targeted the symbols and wielders of state power. By October the autocracy was

Deviatyi val (The Ninth Wave), no.2, 1906, cover.

The Ninth Wave is a reference to a well-known painting of a stormy sea by the marine artist Ivan Aivazovskii. On the cover of this issue, marking the first anniversary of Bloody Sunday, one reads 'Freedom' and 'You fell victim to the fatal fight', which are quotes from a popular revolutionary song of the period. Such publications flourished in the short period between 1905 and 1907 when preliminary censorship was temporarily abolished.

LB.31.c.10733.

backed into a corner. Strikes and urban unrest gripped the empire, tentative plans for a consultative assembly had been rejected by the public and the humiliation of the war with Japan hung over the army. Only when Nicholas could find no one willing to carry out a bloody crackdown in his name did he reluctantly follow the advice of 'almost everybody [he] had an opportunity of consulting' and agree to make concessions.

Tatiana Naidenova, 18-year-old daughter of a textile factory owner, astutely observed in her diary:

> The General Strike is still on, but in my view it can be called 'revolution'. There are rumours that constitution will be announced shortly. If they think that they could pacify the people, they are very wrong. It's too much out of order, and nobody knows what he wants. It is very sad to hear such things as 'there were lots of killed and injured there', or 'well done, the Cossacks!' said with excitement. This is all terrible. The unrest was bound to happen, and of course, our government is to blame.[12]

Plate from Henri de Weidel, *Histoire des Soviets,* Paris, 1922.

Left *Sviashchennik Georgii Gapopn and gradonachal'nik I.A.Fullon nad otkrytii Kolomenskogo ordeal 'Sobraniia Russkikh fabrichno-zavodskikh rabochikh g. Sankt-Peterburga')* (*Priest Georgii Gapon and mayor Ivan Fullon at the opening ceremony of the Kolomenskii department of Assembly of Russian Factory Workers, St Petersburg, autumn 1904).* Photograph by Karl Bulla, 1904.
Right: Artist's impression of the events of Bloody Sunday, near the Narva gates in St Petersburg.

1854.g.15.

LE POPE GAPONE ET LE CHEF DE LA POLICE DE SAINT-PÉTERSBOURG
Photographie prise à l'inauguration de la 3e section du Club ouvrier.

AVANT LA FUSILLADE DU 22 JANVIER 1905, A LA PORTE DE NARVA
Le pope Gapone à la tête des ouvriers, face à la troupe prête à tirer.

Svobodnyi smekh (Free Laughter), no.8, 1906, cover.

Russian political chaos was mocked in the press. On the cover of this satirical magazine, the Duma is presented as a headless Russian beauty. She is surrounded by laughable bustling politicians, offering her a head as they think fit.

LB.31.c.10759.

The October Manifesto was promulgated on 30 (17) October 1905. Nicholas insisted on issuing an imperial proclamation, rather than accepting the ambitious Witte's offer of presenting it as a bureaucratic programme. The manifesto was short and made three promises: the granting of inviolable civil freedoms of association, speech, religion and assembly, underpinned by 'the principles of true inviolability of person; the establishment of the State Duma, elected by all estates; and the 'unshakable principle' that no law could pass without Duma consent. Although the manifesto was deliberately vague, it received widespread acclaim and achieved the government's goal of dividing the opposition movement. The Constitutional Democratic Party (the Kadets) and the Union of 17th October, known as the Octobrists, emerged. While the Kadets did not feel the manifesto went far enough, the Octobrists sought conciliation with the state in the belief that it provided a sound basis for the development of 'the principle of constitutional monarchy'. Nicholas was aided by the increasingly strident demands and potency of the radical workers' movement, which led many liberals to turn back to the seemingly reformist autocracy as a force for order. At the same time, many workers and peasants began to return to work, seemingly satisfied with their gains. The state seized the chance to suppress the workers' soviets in Russian cities and sent punitive expeditions of soldiers to quell rural unrest.

Although it seemed that Russia might be embarking on the path to constitutional monarchy, Nicholas could not reconcile himself to what he referred to privately as a 'terrible decision'. Although he refused to revoke a decree issued in his name, the tsar and the reactionary clique surrounding him sought to thwart Russian constitutionalism at every turn. The revised Fundamental Laws of the Russian Empire, which belatedly appeared in spring 1906, signified Nicholas's intentions. The Duma could not enact legislation, only approve bills brought before it. The tsar retained an absolute veto and appointed half the members of the State Council, which acted as an upper house. Ministerial appointments remained a royal prerogative, which meant that they did not have to carry the confidence of the Duma. Moreover, the tsar could dismiss the Duma at any time and allow ministers to pass laws using Article 87 of the Fundamental Laws. Nicholas also retained control over the security services. The 1881 Security Law remained in effect, and was used to suspend the civil liberties granted in October.

First Duma

The electoral law of December 1905 combined a relatively broad franchise with a convoluted system of electoral colleges for separate estates and property qualifications. There was minimal representation for urban workers, but a large peasant voting body, due to the mistaken belief that they would unquestioningly support the tsar. The Socialist Revolutionaries and the Social Democrats refused to contest the elections for the First Duma, which resulted in the Kadets becoming the largest party for the only time. Many peasant votes went to a loose faction of socialists known as the Labourists or Toilers (*Trudoviks*). Along with 60 seats won by minorities, there was a clear majority in favour of immediate, radical reform.

The First Duma was opened with great solemnity by Nicholas II on 10 May (27 April) 1906. Following the German model, all deputies were invited to the throne room of the Winter Palace to receive the 'Address from the Throne'. The mutual hostility was evident from the start. Nicholas's speech was lacklustre and his demeanour uninterested; the military band struck up as soon as he finished to pre-empt any heckling. The Duma's official reply was a direct challenge to the autocracy. It demanded vast increase in its powers, the repeal of the 1881 Security Law, pardons for all political prisoners, full legal equality and the compulsory requisitioning of private land for distribution to the peasants. After 70 days of unproductive recriminations and weeks of dithering from Nicholas, the Duma was prorogued in July by royal decree. The Kadets and some *Trudoviks* fled to the Finnish provincial town of Vyborg and issued a call for non-

The hostility of the majority of the First Duma toward the throne was clearly shown on the first day of its sessions. All the Duma members attended the Imperial reception in the throne room of the Winter Palace dressed in a deliberately careless fashion. Be it said, however, that there was a certain lack of tact on both sides. The court had decided that this reception was to be particularly solemn and brilliant ... On one side of the corridor were members of the State Duma and on the other members of the State Council, senators, and the other higher civil and military officials. The contrast was striking. The court and the government, flourishing gold-laced uniforms and numerous decorations, was set opposite the grey, almost rustic group representing the people of Russia ... This Oriental method of impressing upon spectators a reverence for the bearers of supreme power was quite unsuited to the occasion. What it did achieve was to set in juxtaposition the boundless Imperial luxury and the poverty of the people.
Vladimir Gurko, Assistant Minister of the Interior, on the opening of the First Duma, 10 May (27 April) 1906.[13]

Pamiatnaia knizhka pervoi Gosudarstvennoi dumy (Commemorative Book of the First Duma), no.1, St Petersburg, 1906, cover.

Presenting portraits of all Duma delegates, the commemorative book was published in installments. By the time a luxury edition, in one thick volume, was printed, the Duma was about to be dissolved.

RB.31.c.577.

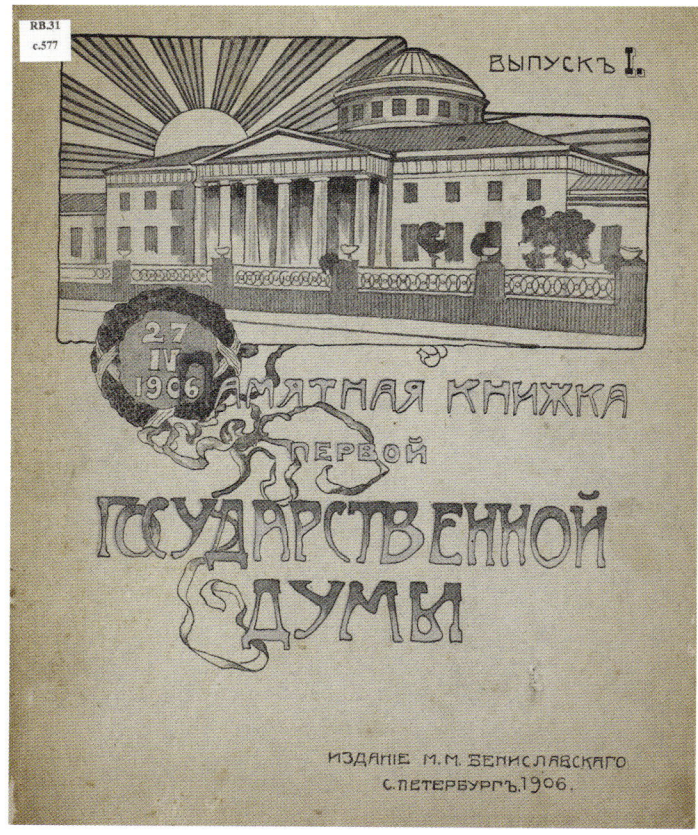

Ilya Repin, *17 October 1905*, 1907.
In this painting the artist's aim was to portray 'the atmosphere of overwhelming excitement' when a crowd of liberal intelligentsia is carrying an amnestied revolutionary. Some of the people in the picture resembled those whom Repin and his audience knew and would recognise. In 1911 it was shown at the Fine Arts exhibition in Rome. Due to censorship restrictions, it was not displayed in Russia until a year later.

violent civil disobedience. However, they had badly misjudged the popular appetite for more unrest and soon backed away from it. The fallout from this split did tremendous damage to the Kadets, and the participation of the socialist parties returned an even more radical Duma in the election of March 1907. The presence of hundreds of socialist deputies and the continued lack of a strong conservative bloc made the relationship between state and assembly even more fraught. The Second Duma achieved very little before it was predictably disbanded on trumped-up charges of political conspiracy based on SD agitation among the army.

At the height of the crisis, in the spring of 1906, Petr Stolypin was appointed as both Minister of the Interior and Chairman of the Council of Ministers. That Nicholas allowed such a concentration of power was unusual and spoke to his desperation. Stolypin was something of an outsider in elite circles, but his success in crushing unrest as Governor of Saratov Province saw him cast as the empire's latest strongman

Ceremonial opening of the State Duma, St George Hall in the Winter Palace, 27 April 1906. Photographer: K. von Gann.

saviour. The radical wing of the SRs (Maximalists) had killed 4,500 officials since January. The socialist parties continued their agitation among workers and soldiers, and the Kadets felt unable to condemn any of it lest they be accused of plotting with the state. Almost every province in the empire was under Reinforced Safeguard. In response, Stolypin established a system of military courts, which executed 3,000 political activists within nine months. Stolypin also devastated the nascent trade union movement, with 1,000 shut down or pre-emptively barred. Using Article 87 of the Fundamental Laws (only employable with the sovereign's backing), in June 1907 Stolypin altered the electoral law to favour the wealthy and diminish worker and peasant representation. One per cent of the population now elected the majority of the deputies.

The revolution was now definitively over. Russia passed into the era of Stolypin's political domination, which lasted until he died at the hands of an *Okhrana* double agent at the Kiev Opera House in 1911. Stolypin also sought to modernise the Russian Empire. He introduced free, universal primary education, social insurance schemes and full civil equality. His most significant act was an attempt to solve the interminable 'peasant question' by the most radical reform seen since Emancipation.

Peasants were given the chance to consolidate an enclosed plot of land and remove it from the commune, which had its legal protections stripped away. Through this, Stolypin hoped to encourage agricultural modernisation, boost production and replace impoverished communes with a class of industrious, prosperous smallholders to serve as the bedrock of autocratic support they were always believed to be. The reform was a modest success. Some 10 per cent of households had withdrawn from their communes by 1914, but at the cost of a vast increase in the number of landless peasants so feared by the state. Stolypin's biggest success was perhaps related to migration. A law on the freedom of movement, together with increased state subsidies and planning, helped 4 million people move to Siberia. After Stolypin's death, his reforms lost impetus. Rural disorders became increasingly frequent in the years leading up to the war, with some 17,000 outbreaks in the period 1910–1914.

While rural reform measures met with modest results, there was little attempt to improve the lives of the empire's growing urban workforce. An increased focus on military production led to another economic 'spurt' after 1908, but there was little benefit to workers and wages remained low. The state remained unable or unwilling to improve pay and conditions, or to make workers' lives tolerable by investing in adequate public utilities. Strikes were increasingly frequent. Although demands were still largely economic and trade unions remained weak, the continued agitation of clandestine socialist activists sharpened working-class consciousness in cities such as St Petersburg and Moscow.

However, as shown in 1905, labourism could be a destabilising, revolutionary force. The deaths of some 200 striking gold miners in the Lena region of north-east Siberia in April 1912 led to rolling strikes across the empire. The wave of unrest crested with the St Petersburg general strike in July 1914 that brought tens of thousands of workers on to the streets. To head off rising labour radicalism and peasant frustration required concessions that the regime was incapable of making. Its heavy-handed repression and undermining of the October Manifesto alienated liberals and moderates, who increasingly came to see that the autocracy was incompatible with the wholesale liberal reforms they sought. It seemed to be a question of when, not if, another direct confrontation between state and society would occur. However, international events would intervene as Europe tumbled into war in the summer of 1914. Under Stolypin, Russia had tried to avoid foreign entanglements. Having repeatedly eschewed confrontation, Nicholas, amenable to pan-Slavic sentiment, felt that to stand aside as Austria subjugated the Kingdom of Serbia would be to abrogate Russia's Great Power status.

The First World War

The outbreak of war afforded the regime a temporary respite. Significant investment in the armed forces had given Russia a standing army of 1.4 million, with the potential to call up more than three times as many, and a misplaced sense of strength. Patriotic demonstrations broke out in major Russian cities, with all parties except the Bolsheviks voting to support the conflict. It soon became evident that the autocracy was incapable of prosecuting a successful war. On 1–2 August (20–21 July) Meriel Buchanan, daughter of the British Ambassador Sir George Buchanan, described in her diary the swell of patriotism and how quickly it evaporated:

> Today the order for general mobilisation has gone out. The streets are full of crying women walking about with their husbands, the shops are crammed with officers and soldiers buying stockings, boots and all kinds of different provisions... Last night there was again a big manifestation. A whole crowd of people joined hands around the statue of [the famed General] Suvorov and stood with their hats off while a gentleman in a cab made a speech. Then they elevated a picture of the Emperor and all went down on their knees...The Germans mobilise today at twelve and there seems nothing more to do. The streets now are full of soldiers marching out the reservists, with a few poor crying women still clinging onto them here and there. Some of them have babies in their arms, some of them stumble along blindly, sometimes they go hand in hand with the men keeping step with them as well as they can. And then

The Royal Decree on mobilisation ... mobilisation, war – everything is so unexpected! Of course, Russia has always been protecting Slavs and she could not indifferently watch how dangerous the situation was becoming in the Orthodox Serbia. But I felt, and I think that many felt likewise, that not only Serbia, but the entire Slavic world was challenged. War is not an inevitable result of developments in European history. It could have been avoided. But Germany's intention to write history with a bayonet, ignoring the natural rights of other people, led to the events, the seriousness of which goes without saying.

Anatolii Ditrikh, 29, photographer and journalist, diary entry, 30 (18) July 1914.[14]

Война Россіи съ нѣмцами День объявленія войны.

Площадь передъ Зимнимъ Дворцомъ въ Петроградѣ 20 Іюля 1914 г., въ день обнародованія Манифеста о войнѣ объявленной намъ нѣмцами, когда Государь выйдя на балконъ, восторженно привѣтствуемый наро-

домъ обратился къ нему съ призывомъ постоять съ Нимъ за Россію, защитить своей грудью ея честь и достоинство и дать могучій отпоръ дерзкимъ врагамъ.

Voina Rossii s nemtsami. Den' ob"iavleniia voiny (The War with Germany. On the Day of the Announcement of War), Moscow, 1914.

This poster depicts an outbreak of patriotic fervour at a meeting in Winter Palace Square in St Petersburg on the day the war was announced.

Private collection.

afterwards one sees them coming back alone, crying bitterly as with hard, miserable eyes that see nothing around them.[15]

Despite success against the similarly dilapidated Austro-Hungarian army, the war on the Eastern Front proved disastrous. Chronic shortages of rifles, machine guns and artillery soon became apparent, as did a dearth of capable commanders. The Russian railway network buckled under the large, complex demands of wartime logistics and bureaucratic ossification prevented the shifting of adequate resources from the civilian economy. The numerically superior Russian army was consistently bested by its German adversary, which by the end of 1915 had seized all of Poland and parts of Ukraine, Belarus and the Baltic. These areas had contained much of the empire's industrial and agricultural output, which exacerbated shortages. So too did the High Command's decision to implement a scorched-earth policy in retreat, which resulted in millions of refugees fleeing eastward into the already overstretched interior. Losses were heavy even by the unprecedented standards of the

Геройская борьба казака Козьмы Крючкова съ 11 нѣмцами.

First World War, and renewed offensives in 1916 only increased the death toll. On the eve of the revolution the imperial army had lost 3.6 million dead and wounded, with another 2.1 million being held as prisoners of war. The High Command's fecklessness with human life sapped morale, and desertion and mutiny became ever more frequent. An increasing number of proletarian conscripts brought a sharper political edge, as did the work of clandestine socialist agitators. All of this served to connect the suffering of the soldiers to that of their families on the home front, as did the necessity of placing local recruits in city garrisons.

Even though the war shut off exports and food production increased in 1914 and 1915, agriculture and consumer manufacturing declined markedly in 1916; labour shortages set in, and peasants preferred to eat any surplus rather than sell at the low prices demanded by the government. In any event, the loss of manufacturing capacity and labour led to an acute shortage of essential consumer goods, which left both peasants and workers with little to buy. The regime failed to

Pervyi Georgievskii kavaler Kuz'ma Kriuchkov (The First St George 'Cavalier', Kozma Kriuchkov), Moscow, 1915.

Born in 1890, Kozma Kriuchkov died in 1919 in the Russian Civil War. He was the first hero of the First World War to be awarded the Cross of St George, a reward for 'undaunted courage' by the lower ranks of the military. He received the Cross for a battle in which he fought single-handedly against the Germans, killing 11 of them. He later became a popular figure in mass literature and culture. His portrait even appeared on sweet wrappers branded as 'St George' sweets. Here he appears in a *Lubok* (popular print) – these prints played an important role in official propaganda.

HS.74/273.

establish a functioning system of price-setting, requisitioning and distribution, and disturbances linked to food shortages in towns broke out as early as 1915. By 1916 fuel shortages had become acute. The long queues of cold, hungry and frequently disappointed people that snaked along city streets provided a public space for the frank expression of grievances where public meetings or demonstrations would have been prohibited. Women took a leading role in anti-regime protests. That many were the wives of soldiers (*soldatki*) serving on the front line made suppressing dissent problematic both politically and in practice, as the shared experiences and personal interaction between protesters and troops outweighed abstract notions of patriotism or loyalty to a supposedly semi-divine ruler.

The war, rather than party affiliation, was the defining political issue in the final years of tsardom. Flush with patriotism, a deeply frustrated civil society eagerly stepped in to remedy the shortcomings of the tsarist war effort in 1914. A flurry of organisations drew together politicians, professionals, industrialists and officials from across the political spectrum under the banner of prosecuting the war more effectively. Their existence helped to broaden anti-regime sentiment and seemed finally to answer the question of who was best placed to run the empire. The reformed Union of *Zemstvos* (*Zemgor*) and the Union of Towns representing municipal dumas set up hospitals, collected food and provided aid to hundreds of thousands of refugees. The Special Commission for State Defence, formed in May 1915 by concerned industrialists, sought ways to improve production and provision to the army and home front. This was followed in August by committees dedicated to food, fuel and transport, overseen by a Central War Industries Committee. As the crisis became more acute, the regime even consented to the creation of the Central Workers Group of the War Industries Committee by a 'revolutionary defensist' alliance of Mensheviks and liberals.

On a lower level, hundreds of civil and professional associations strove to help the war effort. These bodies contained men such as the Oktobrist leader Alexander Guchkov, the Kadet Chairman of *Zemgor* Prince Georgy Lvov and the moderate socialist Alexander Kerensky who would later play vital roles in the Provisional Government. When the Duma was recalled in July 1915, they broadened their struggle for control with the state. The Progressive Bloc was formed in August 1915 by the same combination of moderate conservatives and liberals who had sought to aid the war effort.

It soon became apparent that the regime remained suspicious of groups outside its control, even as they became ever more indispensable to the war effort. Their members were placed under heavy police surveillance and any attempt to expand their operations was rebuffed. Nicholas bristled at such upstart

Novyi Satirikon (New Satiricon), April 1917, cover.

The negative image of the 'trusted friend' of Nicholas's family – Grigorii Rasputin, a peasant and healer who had influence on the tsarina – was widely used in revolutionary propaganda. This caricature of Rasputin was published several months after he was murdered by a group of plotters.

LB.31.c.900.

politics. He dismissed ministers who had been sympathetic to the Duma and turned to a dwindling circle of ageing arch-conservatives, whom the Empress described as 'the good old sort'. At the start of the war, Nicholas had promulgated the Statute on the Field Administration of the Army in Wartime, which empowered military commanders at the expense of the civil administration. The dynamics of power shifted even further when Nicholas, ignoring the pleading of his ministers, chose to oversee the conduct of the war personally. He left the imperial capital for the High Command (*Stavka*), which was based in Mogilev, in modern-day Belarus. Even though he did not take strategic decisions, Nicholas was thenceforth explicitly associated with the continued military defeats and attendant hardships.

In Nicholas's absence, Alexandra effectively took over the day-to-day running of the government. She was quixotically opposed to any conciliation with civil society or political parties, and held a personal resentment against their representatives. She continued the tsar's strategy of increasingly reactionary and short-lived appointments, which exacerbated the broad sense of crisis enveloping society, the economy and the war effort. From Nicholas's departure for the front until February 1917, the period of so-called 'ministerial leapfrog' saw the appointment of four Prime Ministers, five Ministers of the Interior, four Ministers of Agriculture and three apiece to the Ministries of Foreign Affairs, War and Transport. Alexandra's unpopularity was intensified by baseless but widespread rumours about the nature of her

Nicholas II with his first cousin Grand Duke Nicholas, whom he replaced as commander-in-chief of the Russian armed forces after the great retreat in autumn 1915.

Photograph from *Ego Imperatorskoe Velichestvo Gosudar' Imperator Nikolai Aleksandrovich v deistvuiushchei armii* (*His Imperial Majesty Nicholas II in the Army in the Field*), four volumes. Petrograd, 1914–16.

9082.h.21.

Kit of field dressings issued from a first aid depot in Moscow named after Empress Alexandra Feodorovna. The kit is part of the Miss Florence Farnborough collection of relics from the First World War on the Russian Front.

Imperial War Museum, SUR 833.

relationship with Rasputin, which presented the tsar as a hapless cuckold while the German-born tsarina and the degenerate Siberian wanderer luxuriated at the head of a foreign conspiracy. Even her and her daughters' involvement in the treatment of injured soldiers served only further to demystify the sainted image of the imperial family in a wartime cultural climate that produced bawdy images of nurses.

The rapid deterioration of the Russian war effort and the home front pushed the Progressive Bloc to take a stronger anti-government line. On 14 (2) November the Kadet leader Pavel Miliukov made strident criticisms of the government in a speech in the Duma, renewing calls for a responsible ministry:

> Gentlemen, if our own Government wanted deliberately to set itself a task, or if the Germans wanted to employ their own means for the same purpose – the means of influencing and of bribing – they could not do better than to act as the Russian Government has acted ... And, does it matter, gentlemen, as a practical question, whether we are, in the present case, dealing with stupidity or treason? When the Duma keeps everlastingly insisting that the rear must be organised for a successful struggle, the Government persists in claiming that organising the country means organising a revolution, and deliberately prefers chaos and disorganisation. What is it, stupidity or treason?[16]

The speech was not intended to provoke unrest nor to be widely circulated, but it was distributed illegally and had an incendiary effect on a population that had been fed a diet of nationalist rhetoric by the state and anti-state propaganda by political agitators.

By the turn of the year, the tsarist government was on the brink. The economy had collapsed, the countryside was increasingly restless and the state was unable to acquire or distribute foodstuffs and essential consumer goods. The loyalty of both front-line troops and rear garrisons was undermined by their officers' inept prosecution of a vainglorious war that sent their comrades to die unshod, unarmed and unknown. Liberals abandoned lingering hopes of the state cooperating in good faith. The patriotism of the army high command was increasingly linked to prosecuting the war successfully, and many conservatives lamented the risible diarchy of Nicholas and Alexandra. In the capital strikes became larger, more frequent and increasingly political and anti-war in character. Although the leaders of the socialist parties were not present, their seconds and shop-floor activists were emboldened by the rolling discontent and became increasingly active. On 22 (9) January 1917, the anniversary of Bloody Sunday, a massive strike brought almost 200,000 workers out on to the streets. Despite all of this,

Nicholas had refused to return to St Petersburg. On 8 March (24 February) 1917, while his empire crumbled, the last Emperor wrote to his wife from *Stavka*:

> My brain is resting here – no ministers, no troublesome questions demanding thought. I consider that this is good for me, but only for my brain. My heart is suffering from separation. I hate this separation, especially at such a time! I shall not be away long – direct things as best I can here, and then my duty will be fulfilled.[17]

NOTES

1. David L. Ransel (ed.), *Village Life in Late Tsarist Russia: An Ethnography by Olga Semenova Tian-Shanskaia*, trans by David L. Ransel with Michael Levine. Indiana: Indiana University Press, c.1993.
2. S. I. Kanatchikov, *A Radical Worker in Tsarist Russia: The Autobiography of Semën Ivanovich Kanatchikov*, trans and ed by Reginald E. Zelnik. California: Stanford University Press, 1986.
3. Toby W. Clyman and Judith Vowles (eds), *Russia Through Women's Eyes: Autobiographies from Tsarist Russia*. New Haven and London: Yale University Press, 1996.
4. S. I. Kanatchikov, *A Radical Worker in Tsarist Russia: The Autobiography of Semën Ivanovich Kanatchikov*, trans and ed by Reginald E. Zelnik. California: Stanford University Press, 1986.
5. S. V. Mironenko (ed.), *Dnevniki imperatora Nikolaia II, 1894–1918*. Moscow: Rosspen, 2011. Vol. 1 (1894–1904).
6. G. Buchanan, *My Mission to Russia, and Other Diplomatic Memories*. London: 1923.
7. O. V. Volobuev et al (ed.), *S"ezdy i konferentsii konstitutsionno-demokraticheskoi partii: 1905–1920 gg.: v 3 tomakh*. Moscow: Rosspen, 1997–2000. Vol.1 (1905–1907).
8. 1 versta = 1.07 km = 0.66 miles.
9. V. I. Lenin, *Collective Works. Vol. 37: Letters to Relatives, 1893–1922*. Progress Publishers: 1967.
10. F. I. Shikuts, *Dnevnik soldata v Russko-iaponskuiu voinu: v dvukh chastiakh*, ed by V. I. Przhevalinskii. Moscow: GPIB, 2003 (reproduction of 1909 edition). Part 2. (cited: http://prozhito.org/person/200). Access date: 12 November 2016.
11. 'Perepiska S. Iu. Witte i Kuropatkina' in *Krasnyi arkhiv*, no.19, 1927.
12. Aleksandr Aleksandrovih Naidenov, *Al'bom fotografii 1889–1915. Semeinaia khronika. Dnevnik Tani Naidenovoi 1904–1907*, ed by T. Barkhina. Bliznetsy: 2001 (cited: http://prozhito.org/person/330). Access date: 12 November 2016.
13. V. I. Gurko, *Cherty i siluty proshlogo: pravitel'stvo i obshchestvennost' v tsarstvovanie Nikolaia II v izobrazhenii sovremennika*. Moscow: Novoe literaturnoe obozrenie, 2000.
14. E. Matveeva and A.Azemshi (eds), 'Ditrikh A.P. Iiul' chetyrnadtsatogo: Otryvki iz dnevnika', in *Nashe nasledie*, 2006. (cited: http://prozhito.org/person/471). Access date: 12 November 2016.
15. Meriel Buchanan, *Petrograd, the City of Trouble, 1914–1918*. W. Collins, Sons & Co: c.1918.
16. P. Miliukov, 'Rech' na zasedanii Gosudarstvennoi Dumy', in *Rech'*, no.330, 13 December 1916. Cited by Frank Alfred Golder, ed., *Documents of Russian History, 1914–1917*, trans by Emanuel Aronsberg. The Century Co: 1927.
17. A. L. Hynes (trans), *The Letters of the Tsar to the Tsaritsa, 1914–1917*. Translated from the official edition of the Romanov correspondence, edited by M. N. Pokrovsky. London: John Lane / New York: Dodd, Mead & Co: 1929.

2 1917: The Weeks When Decades Happened

Sarah Badcock

The miracle had happened! Tsarism, which enslaved us and thrived on the blood and marrow of the toiler, had fallen.
Maria Botchkareva, Russian soldier, recalling news of the February revolution at the front, 1917.[1]

There were two seismic political revolutions in Russia during 1917. The first was in February, when the 300-year-old Romanov dynasty was toppled by an unlikely alliance between lower-class residents and soldiers in Petrograd (as the city was renamed in 1914), and the country's political and military elites. The second revolution was in October, when the Bolshevik party, led by Vladimir Lenin, seized political power in the capital. Both these revolutions marked the beginnings of social and political contestation and transformation, but neither revolution defined the social and political changes that they initiated.

The elite political narrative played out in the streets of Petrograd. Yet the story of 1917 is as much about the dissolution of a great empire as it is about political transformation within one state. Ordinary men and women played an integral role in unfolding political events, and all parts of the Russian Empire's vast and complex web were connected to one another. Ordinary people made the revolution their own, and dictated the terms of what the revolution was to the political elites. The latter were not

Russia's key political parties in 1917
The Socialist Revolutionary Party (SR) was a socialist party with a distinctive blend of populist (Russian socialist) and Marxist ideas. The SR party was the most popular political party in 1917, with a strong support base from the rural population and urban workers. Its chief theoretician and leading figure was Viktor Chernov. The Russian Social Democratic Workers' Party was a Marxist group. In 1902 it split into two factions: the Bolsheviks, led by Vladimir Lenin, and the Mensheviks, led by Georgii Plekhanov, Irakli Tsereteli, Iulii Martov and Fedor Dan. The Democrat Party (Kadets) was Russia's main liberal party, and was led by Pavel Miliukov. Their ideas were based around the rule of law, and they favoured a constitutional monarchy.

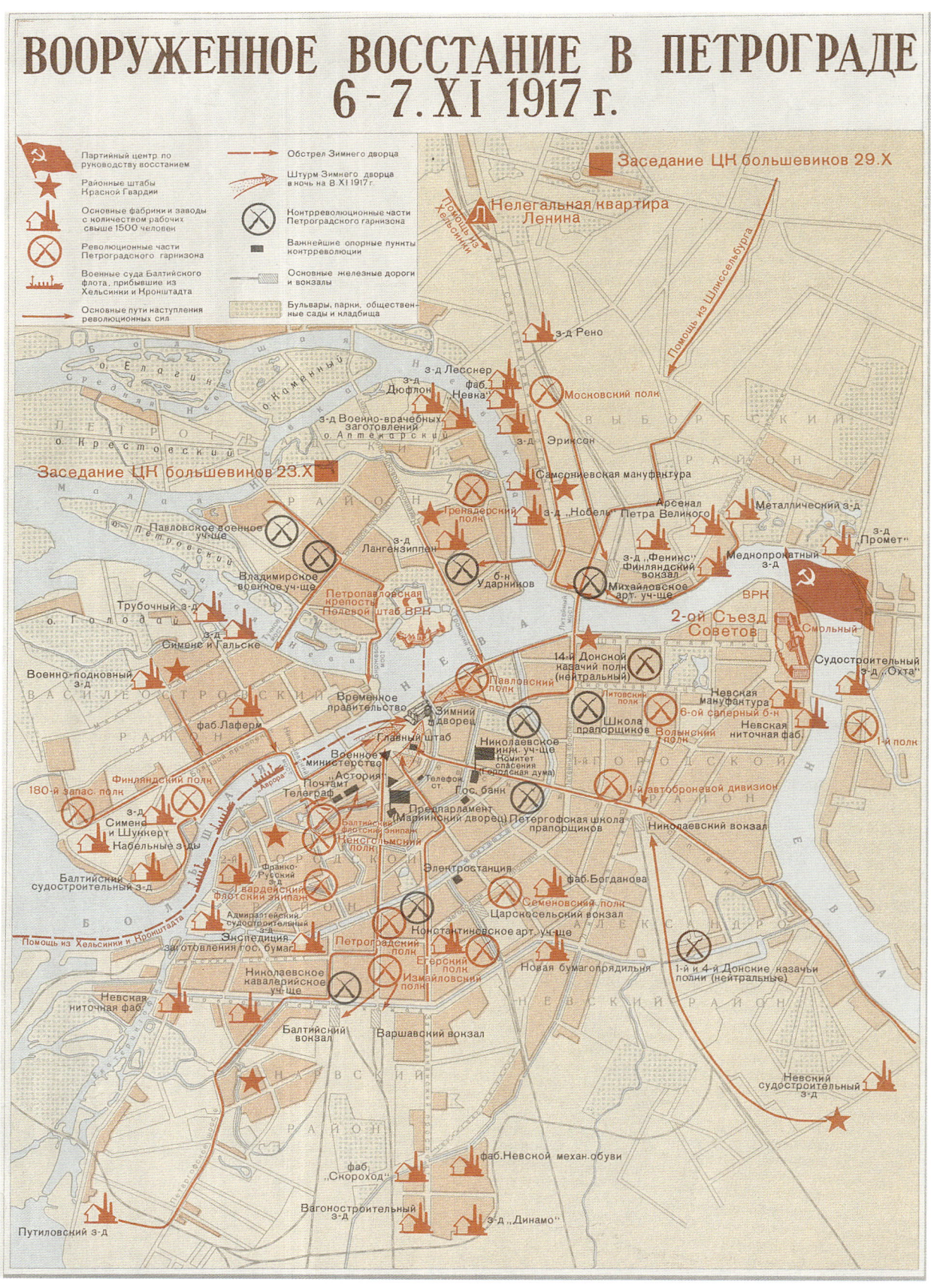

(opposite) *Vooruzhennoe vosstanie v Petrograde 6-7.IX, 1917 g. (Military insurrection in Petrograd 6-7.IX, 1917).*

Soviet maps typically depict only military insurrections in Petrograd and Moscow, ignoring events elsewhere. The red banner indicates the Smolny Institute for Noble Maidens – the Bolsheviks' headquarters before moving to Moscow in 1918. The large triangle at the top points to 'Lenin's clandestine apartment', where he hid to avoid arrest. Red factories, stars and crossed bayonets are included to demonstrate overwhelming support for the Bolsheviks from workers, Red Guards and military units. Two black banners in the centre indicate strongholds of the Provisional government. Its last residence – the Winter Palace – is barely visible.

Maps X.1709.

.

(above) Meeting in Kazan cathedral square, Petrograd, 1917.

Photograph from *Voina i revoliutsiia*, Petrograd, c.1918.

X.802/4756.

puppet masters in the centre of power, defining the revolutionary dance across the empire. Rather they were themselves dictated to by the events that took place across the collapsing empire.

We can demarcate central political developments during 1917 into four key phases, each of which was marked by a re-configuration of the Provisional Government: (i) from the February revolution to the April crisis, (ii) from the April crisis to the July Days, (iii) from the July Days to the Kornilov affair, (iv) from the Kornilov affair to the October revolution.

The first period was characterised by popular hope for a better future. The Mensheviks, the Socialist Revolutionaries and the liberal Kadets dominated the political landscape in this

The political centre – 1917 in a nutshell

The political framework of 1917 is characterised by a swing to the political left across the year in Petrograd from February to October. The moderate socialists and liberals who assumed responsibility for governing the country after the February revolution oversaw Russia's progressively collapsing economy. The government was unable to improve living conditions or resolve the food supply crisis. Russia's active army disintegrated in the course of 1917, despite the Provisional Government's enduring commitment to participation in the First World War. The government lacked any means to enforce its power and authority across the empire, enabling the development of separatist and nationalist movements in Russia's peripheries and autonomous political action in Russia's rural areas. The Bolshevik Party capitalised on economic collapse, societal polarisation and discontent with the war among the active army to build a numerically small but significant base of support among soldiers, sailors and industrial workers. With the Bolshevik seizure of power in the name of the soviets in October, Russia's civil war was initiated, as contestation began across the fracturing empire over the shape of the future.

period. The February revolution, when striking workers and the mutinying Petrograd garrison precipitated the abdication of the tsar, was met with broad optimism. The Provisional Government was formed to govern the empire until full and fair elections could take place, which would enable Russia's whole population to select democratically the country's future government.

Prince Georgy Lvov, a non-partisan public activist, headed the first Provisional Government. Its members included other non-party activists, liberal Kadets and one socialist – the renowned lawyer and Duma deputy Alexander Kerensky. The new Minister of Foreign Affairs, Pavel Miliukov, believed that Russia's participation in the First World War should continue to be defined by the imperial war aims laid out by the autocratic government; these focused on securing the Straits of Dardanelles for the Russian Empire. The publication of Miliukov's so-called 'secret note' to the Allies, which assured them of Russia's continued commitment to imperial war aims, precipitated public outcry. It forced Miliukov's resignation and the collapse of the first Provisional Government.

(right and opposite)
Velikaia voina v obrazakh i kartinakh (The Great War in Images and Pictures), April 1917.

Art academicians, professors, prominent journalists and public figures contributed to this popular and colourful publication, which included symbolic artistic representations of revolution such as those shown here.

Cup.1264.hh.22.

The second phase was heralded by formal coalition in the Provisional Government between the liberals and non-party activists on the one hand, and the moderate socialists in the Petrograd Soviet on the other. Viktor Chernov, leader of the Socialist Revolutionary Party, and Irakli Tsereteli, one of the Mensheviks' leaders, took ministerial office. In so doing, they committed themselves and their parties to the coalition, and to the government's attempts to continue the war effort and to govern Russia.

The Provisional Government's war aims were modelled on proposals made by the Petrograd Soviet that there should be peace without annexations or indemnities and with the right to national self-determination. The newspaper of the Petrograd Soviet, *Izvestiia*, published the 'Soviet's appeal to all the peoples of all the world' on 28 (15) March 1917:

> Comrade-proletarians and toilers of all countries:
> We, Russian workers and soldiers, united in the Petrograd
> Soviet of Workers' and Soldiers' Deputies, send you warmest

greetings and announce the great event. The Russian democracy has shattered in the dust the age-long despotism of the Tsar and enters your family of nations as an equal, and as a mighty force in the struggle for our common liberation. Our victory is a great victory for the freedom and democracy of the world. The chief pillar of reaction in the world, the 'Gendarme of Europe', is no more. May the earth turn to heavy granite on his grave! Long live freedom! Long live the international solidarity of the proletariat, and its struggle for final victory!

Our work is not yet finished: the shades of the old order have not yet been dispersed, and not a few enemies are gathering their forces against the Russian revolution. Nevertheless our achievement so far is tremendous. The people of Russia will express their will in the Constituent Assembly, which will be called as soon as possible on the basis of universal, equal, direct and secret suffrage. And it may already be said without a doubt that a democratic republic will triumph in Russia. The Russian people now possess full political liberty. They can now assert their mighty power in the internal government of the country and in its foreign policy. And, appealing to all people who are being destroyed and ruined in the monstrous war, we announce that the time has come to start a decisive struggle against the grasping ambitions of the governments of all countries; the time has come for the people to take into their own hands the decision of the question of war and peace.

Conscious of its revolutionary power, the Russian democracy announces that it will, by every means, resist the policy of conquest of its ruling classes, and it calls upon the peoples of Europe for concerted, decisive action in favour of peace.

We are appealing to our brother-proletarians of the Austro–German coalition, and, first of all, to the German proletariat. From the first days of the war, you were assured that by raising arms against autocratic Russia, you were defending the culture of Europe from Asiatic despotism. Many of you saw in this a justification of that support which you were giving to the war. Now even this justification is gone: democratic Russia cannot be a threat to liberty and civilization.

We will firmly defend our own liberty from all reactionary attempts from within, as well as from without. The Russian revolution will not retreat before the bayonets of conquerors, and will not allow itself to be crushed by foreign military force. But we are calling to you: Throw off the yoke of your semi-autocratic rule, as the Russian people have shaken off the Tsar's autocracy; refuse to serve as an instrument of conquest and violence in the hands of kings, landowners, and bankers – and then by our united efforts we will stop the horrible butchery, which is disgracing humanity and is beclouding the great days of the birth of Russian freedom.

Toilers of all countries: We hold out to you the hand of brotherhood across the mountains of our brothers' corpses, across rivers of innocent blood and tears, over the smoking ruins of cities and villages, over the wreckage of the treasuries of civilization; – we appeal to you for the reestablishment and strengthening of international unity. In it is the pledge of our future victories and the complete liberation of humanity.

Proletarians of all countries, unite!
Petrograd Soviet of Workers' and Soldiers' Deputies.[2]

Viktor Shklovsky was a Provisional Government commissar during 1917, and had been an officer in the tsarist army before the revolution. His recollections of the revolutionary period offered a vivid evocation of the importance of war aims within the military:

Novyi Satirikon (New Satiricon), no.11, March 1917.

The unity of the revolutionary forces was stressed in liberal periodicals, as in this 'revolutionary' issue of a popular satirical magazine.

L.B.31.c.900.

Three photographs from *Voina i revoliutsiia*, Petrograd, c.1918.

Left: A meeting at the Moscow city Duma, July 1917. Unknown photographer.

Right: View of Winter Palace Square, where the disarmed military units that sided with the Bolsheviks were assembled, 1917. Photograph by Iakov Shteinberg.

Opposite: Shooting at a street demonstration on Nevsky Prospekt, 4 July 1917. Photograph by Viktor Bulla.

Iakov Shteinberg and Alexander and Viktor Bulla – sons of German-born Karl Bulla (the 'father' of Russian photography) – were responsible for the most well-known photographs of the events of 1917. Viktor Bulla also took part in shooting *Chronicle of the Revolution in Petrograd,* a documentary film on the February revolution of 1917, and he also documented the October uprising, sending his photographs to the Petrograd Soviet. The third image shown here was widely reproduced in Soviet history textbooks – although the name of the photographer was erased from history, as both Bulla brothers died in the Stalin purges.

X.802/4756.

The Allies, damn them, would not give their consent to our definition of a peace 'without annexations and reparations'; and these words, bandied about in the newspapers – I know how sacred they were to every soldier, whose feet were rotting in the water of the trenches, whose neck was gnawed by lice. These words were truly sacred to the barefoot soldiers. Those who repudiated them are guilty of blood, filth and callousness. Oh, if we could have unfurled before the June regiments the holy banner of a just war. I wouldn't want to cry over your graves now, my poor comrades.[3]

As Shklovsky so eloquently pointed out, the Allies' refusal to accept and adopt Russia's definition of war aims was very damaging to the Provisional Government. A truly revolutionary government could only prosecute a war with revolutionised war aims. Lenin's Bolsheviks were the only mainstream party to condemn the Provisional Government, and to call openly for immediate peace.

There was a steady rise in popular hostility towards coalition with liberals in government, particularly among soldiers, sailors and urban workers. These tensions culminated in a series of demonstrations in Petrograd on 16–18 (3–5) July. When Viktor

Chernov, the Minister of Agriculture, tried to remonstrate with the crowd, someone shouted to him, 'Take power when it's offered to you, you son of a bitch!'

The Bolshevik Party had supported the July demonstrations, and faced concerted hostility and suppression after the events. Rumours abounded of Bolshevik links with the Germans, and treacherous behaviour. Eduard Dune was a skilled worker who had joined the Bolshevik party in 1916, when he was just 17 years old. He was in Moscow during 1917, and played an active role in the revolution there. He recalled a small Bolshevik demonstration in central Moscow in July 1917:

> The demonstration turned out to be most unimpressive. Afterwards propagandists remained on the square, surrounded by groups of glaring, inquisitive onlookers, obviously inclined to be hostile. Similar knots of unfriendly citizens had gathered around the numerous orators along Tverskaia boulevard and were heckling them fiercely: 'German agent', 'Where's your German money?', 'Adventurers', 'Did you happen to come to Moscow via Germany?' Toward the back of the crowd that surrounded me was a slightly rotund young beauty, beside herself with

КОШМАРЫ НЕДАВНЯГО ПРОШЛАГО

184

4-го Іюля 1917 г. на Невскомъ (у публичной библіотеки) проспектѣ въ 2 часа дня
Съ чрезвычайно рѣдкаго снимка, сдѣланнаго въ моментъ стрѣльбы по проходящимъ войскамъ.

rage, who tried to stab me with her umbrella. I felt that at any minute she and I would exchange punches.[4]

The Provisional Government was reformed on 6 August (24 July), with Alexander Kerensky as its new Prime Minister. The sense of crisis intensified in Petrograd from August onwards. The backdrop was of progressive disintegration of the army, rising disaffection towards moderate socialists in the garrisons and factories across the country, and deepening fears of a counter-revolution – both from the Bolsheviks on the left and the conservatives on the right.

Rising fear of counter-revolution culminated in the Kornilov affair of 7 September (25 August), when General Kornilov moved troops towards Petrograd. Kornilov argued that he had been authorised to do this by Kerensky in order to suppress the Bolsheviks in the capital, and to restore order. Kerensky denied this, and presented Kornilov's actions as an attempted right-wing coup. This shrill response enabled a mobilisation of the left, as Bolsheviks in the capital, who had lost political traction after the events of July, were key figures in arming and mobilising workers, and in rallying soldiers to resist Kornilov. The affair itself was short-lived, with Kornilov quickly ousted and forced into hiding, but its implications were profound. The event secured enhanced power and credibility for the Bolsheviks among Petrograd's workers and soldiers, and it crushed the credibility of coalition government as Kadets, and even Kerensky himself, were implicated in the affair.

Kerensky ignored calls for a socialist-only administration and formed the third coalition government on 8 October (25 September). Rising disaffection among the capital's factory workers, soldiers and sailors gave the Bolsheviks the power to overthrow the Provisional Government in the name of the soviets.

J. Butler Wright, the counsellor of the American Embassy in Petrograd, reported the Bolshevik seizure of power in his diary entry on 7 November (25 October) 1917:

> Last night at 1:30 very heavy firing (machine guns, rifles, and artillery) was heard – and this morning it appears that the Peter and Paul fortress and the warship Aurora opened fire on the Winter Palace to dislodge the ministers who were concentrated there, protected only by a regiment or two of cadets and by the women's regiment. The palace is literally pockmarked with bullet holes and two shells apparently took effect. Armed civilians of a villainous type patrol the city. A squad of sailors and soldiers shot down in cold blood a young cadet in front of the National City Bank and never paused! The Bolsheviks are in complete power and no cables have come in today. Our cables are accepted, but we have no assurance as to whether they are dispatched. Kerensky

(opposite) E. Barnard Lintott, *The Attack on the Winter Palace, Petrograd 1917*, watercolour, 1917.

(below) Sergei Eisenstein, *October*, 1927, film still.

Lintott was Secretary at the British Embassy in Moscow during the Russian Revolution. The view through the gateway to the Winter Palace was made iconic by the films *October* by Sergei Eisenstein (1927) and *Lenin in October* by Mikhail Romm (1937) – both made for revolution anniversaries. Stills from these films were later reproduced in Soviet history books as if they were original photographs. The opening of the gates is one of the most expressive moments in *October's* storm scene (although in actual fact the gates were not shut, as shown in Lintott's watercolour).

Imperial War Museum, ART 992.

The Bolsheviks in the soviets
'All power to the soviets!' was one of the Bolsheviks' rallying cries in 1917. There was strong grassroots support for soviet power, as the soviets were seen as the natural defenders of lower-class Russians and were exclusively socialist. The Bolsheviks were quick to marginalise the other socialist parties within the soviets. In reality, many supporters of soviet power were simultaneously opposed to the notion of Bolshevik dictatorship.

is rumoured to have reached Pskov and to be arrested there; and the reports state that troops are on their way to relieve the city. The quiet is very ominous and committees for protecting private property are being founded.[5]

The Bolshevik takeover of power in Petrograd started a wave of attempts to re-form and consolidate centres of power. In many provincial centres, the Bolsheviks' advance signalled the final collapse of central authority and increased a drive for regional and local autonomy. Along the perimeters of the empire numerous national governments emerged, and the larger, anti-Bolshevik movement gained momentum in response to Bolshevik central policies. In January 1918 the Bolsheviks forcefully disbanded the All-Russian Constituent Assembly, a democratically elected representative organ, and in March the Soviet government signed the Brest-Litovsk Treaty with Germany.

Russia's exit from the war and the premature demise of the Constituent Assembly galvanised anti-Bolshevik forces. These regrouped on the imperial periphery, where Bolshevik control was not particularly strong and where they could expect to get external help from Russia's First World War Allies. The forces that arrayed against the Bolsheviks in 1918 were extremely diverse, both in their backgrounds and in their visions for Russia's future. They included not only conservatives and former tsarist elites, but also a wide array of socialists and liberals who were appalled by Bolshevik attacks on democratic institutions and by the 'treacherous' peace made with Germany.

The February Revolution and the Shape of Power

February 1917 saw a convergence of factors that were to overwhelm the regime. Women, including a strong component of soldiers' wives, inspired a series of demonstrations and strikes from Petrograd's factory workers. Mutinies among the Petrograd garrison turned these revolts into a revolution. The 'great unwashed' of the city, swaths of factory workers and shopkeepers and soldiers, women and children, armed and unarmed, filled the streets of the capital. Russia's political elite struggled to come to terms with the power of the streets, and many expressed barely veiled fear and disgust for the politics that unfolded there.

Confusion and uncertainty came from men who had not anticipated a revolution in their lifetime and who had no contingency plans. Viktor Shklovsky described the scenes in the Tauride Palace on 12–13 March (27–28 February): 'Chaos reigned in the Tauride Palace. Weapons were being brought; people were trailing in; provisions were being hauled around; bags were being stacked in a room near the entrance. Prisoners were already being brought in.'[8]

The situation is serious. The Capital is in a state of anarchy. The Government is paralysed; the transport service is broken down; the food and fuel supplies are completely disorganised. Discontent is general and on the increase. There is wild shooting on the streets; troops are firing at each other. It is urgent that someone enjoying the confidence of the country be entrusted with the formation of a new Government. There must be no delay. Hesitation is fatal. I pray God that at this hour the responsibility may not fall upon the monarch.

Excerpt from telegram to Tsar Nicholas sent by Chairman of the State Duma Mikhail Rodzianko, 12 and 13 March (27 and 28 February) 1917.[6]

Home of the State Duma, the Tauride Palace presented an obvious alternative centre of power in revolutionary Petrograd. The State Duma's members lacked the courage and revolutionary conviction required by the moment. The tsar prorogued the State Duma on 11 March (26 February), and its members were unwilling to meet in contravention of Nicholas's orders. A handful of its bolder members gathered in a side room of the Tauride Palace on 12 March (27 February) as the 'Temporary Committee of the State Duma'. They were unlikely revolutionaries, with Alexander Kerensky the only socialist among a group of liberals, industrialists and a committed monarchist.

The 'Temporary Committee' commissioned Pavel Miliukov (leader of the Kadet Party) and Vasilii Shul'gin to meet Nicholas II on his train bound towards Petrograd, in order to request his abdication. On 15 (2) March Nicholas wrote in his diary:

> For several days we had been living on a volcano. The eruption had begun. The street began to speak.
>
> *Memoirs of Vasilii Shul'gin, a conservative deputy of the State Duma.*[7]

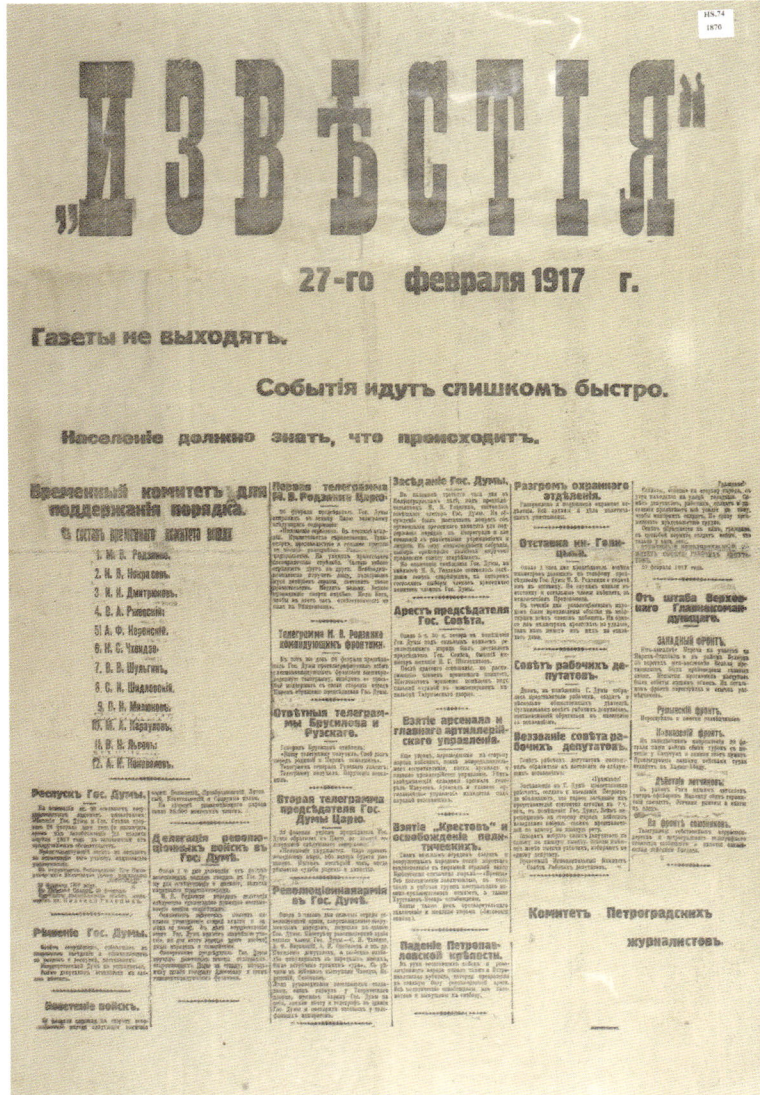

Izvestiia (*News*). Billboard issued on 12 March (27 February) 1917.

The text includes the headline news and the names of the 'Temporary Committee of the State Duma'. Below the title is written: 'Newspapers are not being published. Events are happening too fast. The population should know what is going on.'

HS.74.1870.

Ruzski came in the morning and read me the text of an extremely lengthy conversation with Rodzianko over the telegraph apparatus. The situation in Petrograd is such that a Ministry of the Duma would now be powerless to do anything, for it has to contend with the Social-Democratic Party, represented by the workers' committee. My abdication is needed. Ruzski transmitted this talk to Headquarters, and Alexeev sent it on to all the commanders-in-chief. At 2.30 answers came. The essence is that in the name of saving Russia and maintaining calm in the army at the front, it is necessary to take this step. I have agreed. From Headquarters has been sent a draft of a manifesto. In the evening Guchkov and Shulgin arrived from Petrograd, with whom I discussed the matter, and I handed them the signed and altered manifesto. At 1 o'clock in the morning I left Pskov, with a heart heavy from suffering over this. All around me there is treachery, cowardice, and deceit.

A day later he wrote:

Slept long and soundly. Woke up far past Dvinsk. The day was sunny and frosty. Talked to people close to me about yesterday's events. Read a lot about Julius Caesar. At 8:20 arrived in Mogilyov. All the ranking officers from Headquarters were on the platform. Received Alekseev in the railcar. At 9:30 made it into the house. Alekseev came with the latest news from Rodzianko. It turns out that Misha renounced the throne. His manifesto ends with a flourish about elections to the Constituent Assembly within six months. Lord knows who gave him the idea to sign such a disgusting thing! The disorders have ceased in Petrograd – if only this can keep up.[9]

Group photograph taken in the Ministry of Transport the day after the tsar's abdication, 1917.

Sitting behind the table, second from the left, is Yurii Lomonosov, transport engineer. On his left is Alexander Bublikov, railway engineer, member of the last Duma, and later a commissar in the Provisional Government. Both men played an important part in the abdication. Taking control of the railways, they prevented the tsar's train from reaching Petrograd; it was re-directed to Pskov, where Nicholas was compelled to abdicate.

Special Collections, Leeds University Library, LRA MS 716.

A small group of State Duma members masterminded the Provisional Government. It sought to provide interim governance for Russia until the convocation of an elected assembly that would have the power and the authority to decide on Russia's future. Its claim to legitimacy lay in its rather tenuous link to the State Duma.

In an adjacent meeting room of the Winter Palace, another group of committed public activists met on 12 March (27 February) to form what was to become an alternative site of political power for 1917. The Petrograd Soviet of workers' deputies was formed at the initiative of members of the workers' group from the War Industries Committee, who had just been released from prison, and several socialist Duma members, including the Menshevik Nikolai Chkheidze. Factories all over Petrograd elected delegates to the Soviet by shows of hands and open votes. Many of these delegates were lower-class Petrograd workers. The Soviet's Executive Committee, however, which shaped and directed Soviet policy, was dominated by intellectuals and party activists.

The soldiers whose mutiny had enabled the capital's revolution were not to be ignored. General Kutepov was sent by the district commander to restore Petrograd to order. Kutepov started the day with a group of disciplined men, and when he saw large groups of soldiers milling about, clearly undecided about the course of action, he successfully enjoined them to accompany him. As the day progressed, however, his new recruits melted away into the swirling mass of humanity, and he had to return to barracks at once before his own men, thought to be loyal, succumbed to the temptations of joining the milling crowds. Nikolai Sukhanov, a Menshevik political activist and one of the revolution's great chroniclers, described the 'Dreadful rifles, hateful greatcoats, strange words!' of the crowds of mutinying soldiers.[11]

Soldiers gathered at the Petrograd Soviet of workers' deputies to pledge their support for the revolution. They quickly transformed the workers' soviet into a soviet of workers and soldiers' deputies. The Petrograd garrison was not to be denied its share of political influence.

The Petrograd Soviet provided an alternative seat of power and authority in the capital, a situation that came to be known as dual power. While the Petrograd Soviet recognised the Provisional Government as Russia's legitimate ruling power, its support was conditional on the Provisional Government's rejection of imperialist war aims. In practice, the Soviet's Executive Committee supported the Provisional Government until the Bolsheviks gained ascendancy in the Soviet's worker section in September and decided to seize power through a military coup.

Dual power in 1917 was often more about the shape of power than about its practice. In regional centres across Russia, local

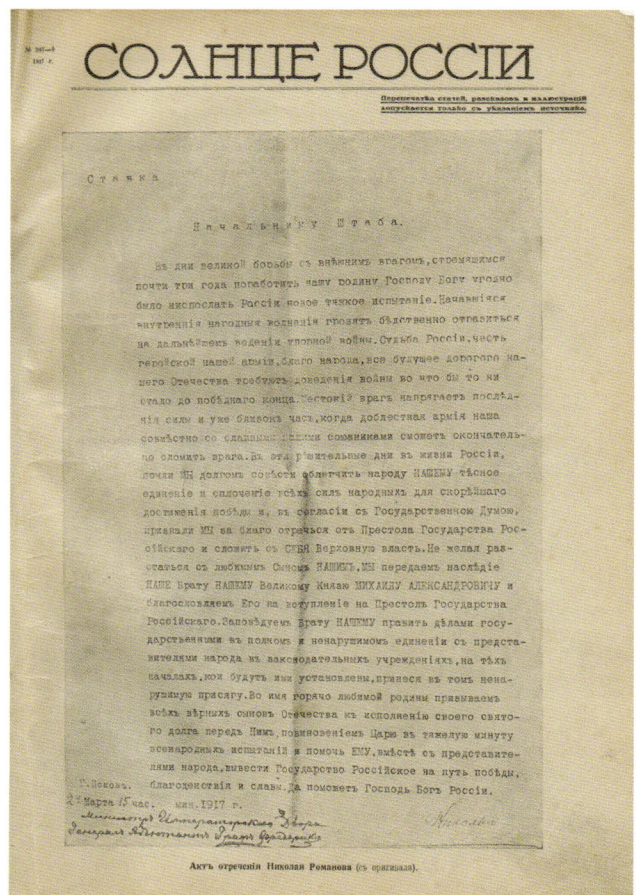

government incorporated Soviet and Provisional Government affiliated institutions, but divisions between these organisations remained blurred, or even non-existent, throughout the year.

The Guardians of the Revolution and Order Number 1

The Petrograd garrison was in many respects 1917's kingmaker. There were around 180,000 soldiers garrisoned in Petrograd, of which 65 per cent were either new recruits or veterans of the front recuperating from wounds or illness in the capital. A significant number of the new recruits were workers who had been punished with military draft because of strike action. Another important group within the garrison were men over the age of 40, who had been called up in 1916 and 1917 and who tended to be reluctant to submit to military discipline.

The autocracy was brought down in February 1917 by this incendiary mix of front-line veterans, reluctant older recruits and labour activists, as widespread mutinies enabled workers' protests to become a revolution.

Viktor Shklovksy described the make-up of the Petrograd garrison:

(opposite). *Solntse Rossii* (*The Sun of Russia*), no.365, April 1917.

A facsimile of the abdication act was published in this issue of this popular illustrated magazine

(right) Group of soldiers reading the same issue of *Solntse Rossii* that is pictured opposite. Photograph from *Voina i revoliutsiia*: c.1918.

X.802/4756.

At this time, a regular soldier – in fact, any soldier from the ages of twenty-two to twenty-five – was a rarity. They had been savagely and senselessly slaughtered in the war … The Petersburg soldier of those days was either a dissatisfied peasant or a dissatisfied city-dweller. The men were not even dressed in their new grey greatcoats, but just hastily wrapped in them, then lumped into crowds, bands and gangs called reserve batallions. In essence, the barracks became simply brick pens to which more and more red and green draft notices drove ever-increasing herds of raw humanity.[12]

The first official decree of the Petrograd Soviet of Workers' and Solders' Deputies, issued on 14 (1) March 1917, was Order number 1. This transformed the fundaments of military discipline in Russia's army, and is testament to the power and authority of the Petrograd garrison. It was issued without the consent of the Provisional Government. The garrison was promised that its soldiers would not be sent to the front, but would remain in Petrograd as guardians of the revolution. Order number 1 initiated a new era of soldier–officer relations. Soldiers no longer had to salute or use formal address, and were to be treated respectfully by their superiors. Soldiers were authorised to form committees, and when they were off duty they enjoyed the same rights as civilians. Shklovsky remembered the order's reception in the Petrograd garrison:

Poster of Order no.1, 14 (1) March 1917.
The poster would have been glued to walls or advertising columns.
HS.74/1870.

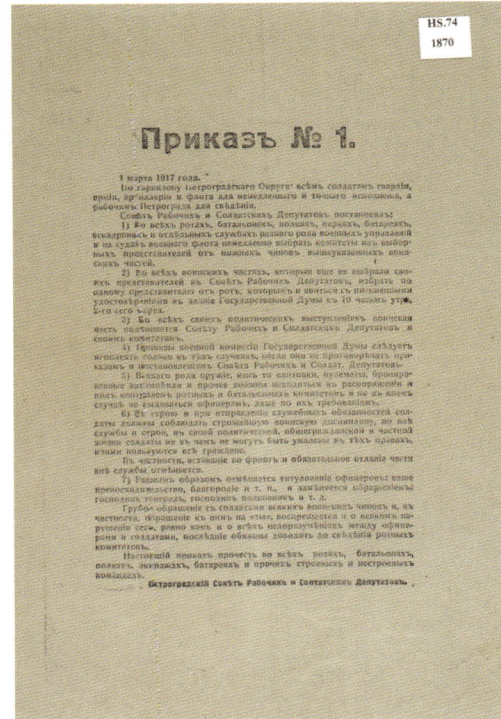

Order number 1 was brought to the riding school and distributed in the ranks during a review. The soldiers started replying 'Hello, mister colonel!' and they brought it off very well, very amiably. I think that order number 1 – though apparently it anticipated events, since there were as yet no committees in the units – was timely and indispensible. It was impossible to hold the units together only with officers just back from a long absence. Although committees are completely impossible in an army – even less possible than elected officers – still they were the only thing that somehow or other held the army together.[13]

Order number 1 was widely condemned by those who sought to maintain Russia's war effort as irreparably corroding military discipline. In this excerpt, though, Shklovsky presents things rather differently, suggesting that the introduction of committee rule was in fact the only thing that could have allowed the army to function at all in spring 1917.

The order was only intended to apply to the Petrograd garrison. Despite this restriction, it was printed in large numbers and sent through the whole army, which legitimised these revolutionary changes across the military, and contributed to an unravelling of military discipline through 1917.

Economic Collapse and Popular Expectations

The banknotes printed in 1917 came to epitomise the period's economic collapse, as the value of currency crumbled and costs of living spiralled. The revolution had a profoundly negative effect on Russia's economy, already in tatters after three years of war spending. The government covered four-fifths of its expenses with deficit spending by 1915–1916, and this proportion actually worsened in 1917. As the revolutionary government printed more and more money to cover the deficit, inflation surged out of control. A basket of household goods in the second half of 1917 cost about five times what it had in 1913. People in the towns and countryside found it increasingly difficult or even impossible to obtain life's daily necessities. Material realities contrasted sharply with popular expectations of the revolution. Long-held political dreams and wartime mobilisation had politicised ordinary Russians, and the February revolution empowered and filled them with hope to build a new, just regime. They participated in mass political festivals that sacralised the new political freedoms and got involved in multiple grassroots committees and soviets that sprang up across the country. The deteriorating economic climate together with rising popular expectations made it increasingly difficult for the Provisional Government to consolidate its power. The country's continuing participation in the First World War aggravated the situation dramatically.

For Russia's urban workers the revolution's promises were particularly heady, and its disappointments sharply felt. Labour activism, in the form of mass strikes, had been instrumental in ending the autocracy, and workers were the key constituents in the soviets that sprang up in Petrograd and in Russia's other towns and cities. Workers were usually cited as the most important group in 'organising' the new revolutionary order. Urban groups were disproportionately represented in provincial

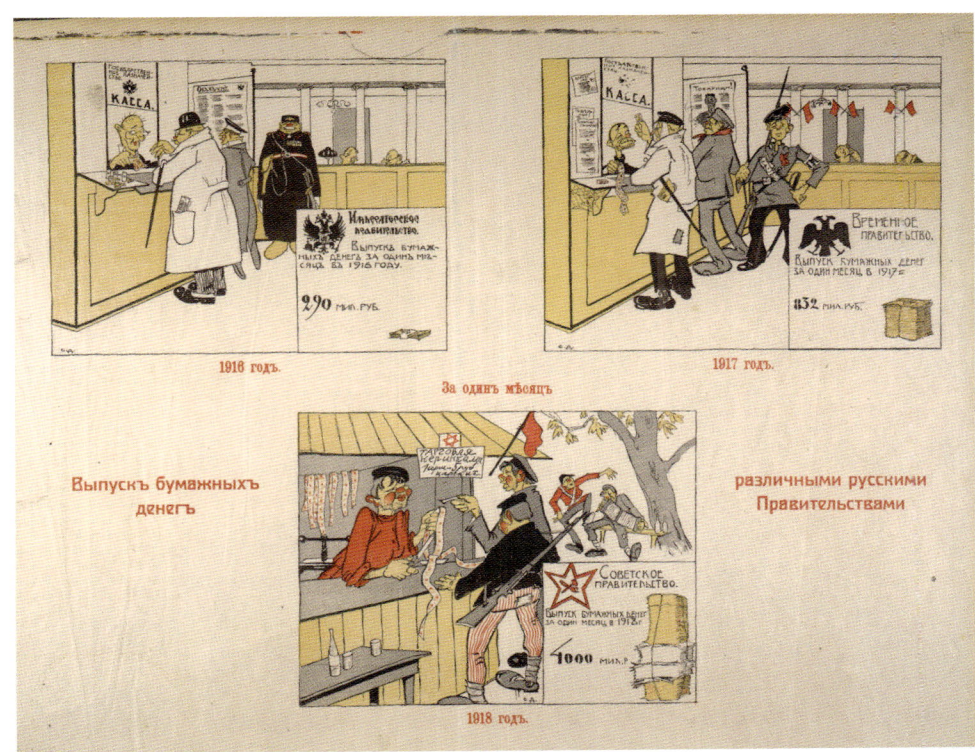

(left) Anti-Soviet satirical poster: *Vypusk deneg raznymi russkimi pravitel'stvami* (*Issuing banknotes by various Russian governments*), 1918.

1856.g.8.

(below) Banknotes issued by the Provisional Government.

Private collection.

One of the first acts of the Provisional Government was to order a new issue of banknotes. In spring 1917, 5-rouble and 10-rouble notes were issued in the design of 1909, with simplified series numbers. These banknotes were in circulation until 1922. New designs were also created. Printed in the United States, some notes only reached Russia in 1918, and were in circulation in Siberia and the Far East under various temporary governments. In August 1917, 20-rouble and 40-rouble notes were issued. Most of these were printed by the Soviet government, and were also in circulation until 1922. The banknotes were known as 'kerenki' after the prime minister of the Provisional Government. As hyperinflation continued, the banknotes stopped being cut, leading to people exchanging long ribbons of money (as shown in the poster).

level power structures, and workers were disproportionately represented among urban groups. Workers' key demands, for an eight-hour working day, paid overtime and the establishment of factory committees to represent and defend workers in negotiation with factory management and the state, were all agreed in the first days of the revolution. Disputes between factory management and workers could be resolved in newly established chambers of conciliation, which enabled workers' demands to be met as never before.

The Provisional Government and the soviets regarded striking as a legitimate tool for the conscious labour movement. Despite the relative success of many strikes in achieving their demands, workers' real pay continued to deteriorate, and job security looked increasingly uncertain as a result of shortages and imminent demobilisation. Workers were increasingly alienated from the Provisional Government by the failure of strikes to improve real conditions, despite their apparent victories. Strikes were legitimised as a means of struggle with factory management, and they were called repeatedly in 1917. Urban workers in Russia's industrial centres turned away from the moderate socialists in the course of 1917, and increasingly supported Bolshevism, which offered a clear alternative to the coalition government that seemed to be failing workers.

Meanwhile the labour movement itself contributed to Russia's economic collapse, as costs rose and production fell in factories. In Sormovo, a major metal-working factory complex near Nizhnii Novgorod, the director of the factories resigned in July 1917, unable to cope with the new revolutionary world:

> In view of violence upon technical personnel, mass refusal of personnel employees to carry out their duties, constant meetings in working time of sections of the craftsmen's profession, it follows that there is total disorganisation of work. Reconciliation chambers are practically ignored. I demand that the most energetic measures be rapidly taken in order that the guilty do not get away with their unlawfulness. I give a week's notice to the Minister of Labour and from 1 August I consider myself free from occupied duties, since I do not wish to participate in chaos. Four months of workers' power together with regional workers' organisations does not guarantee positive results.[15]

Alexander Kerensky – Saviour of the Revolution?

In his article published in the 25 (12) July 1917 issue of *Russkoe Slovo*, Prince Georgy Lvov emphasised the unique qualities of his successor as Prime Minister of Russia, Alexander Kerensky: 'At such times a strong government is needed. And to bring it about, a combination of elements of authority is needed such as are embodied in the person of Kerensky.'[16]

Photograph of Alexander Kerensky, *Illustrated London News*, 18 August 1917.

Having moved the cabinet and his personal residence into the Winter Palace in summer 1917, Kerensky sat in Nicholas II's office for two artists – the famous portraitist Ilya Repin, and his former student Isaak Brodskii. All the portraits (Repin made two) were finished in the artists' studios in 1918. Kerensky's image in this photograph echoes his posture in the portraits.

The leading political figure in the first months after the February revolution, Alexander Kerensky became the subject of the revolution's first cult of personality. He was renowned for his stirring and emotional oratory, as well as for his commitment to coalition government and to Russia's continued prosecution of the war. His intuitive knowledge of the appropriate action for the moment in the early days of the revolution was unmatched by the other leading political figures of the time. On 12 March (27 February) former tsarist ministers were seized in the street and roughly escorted to the Winter Palace. Kerensky stepped forward and declared the captives 'prisoners of the revolution'. In so doing he may well have averted lynchings. While his colleagues lacked the impetuosity and courage simply to arrest men such as Vladimir Sukhomlinov, the disgraced Minster of War – for so long symbolic of power and corruption in the old regime – Kerensky could see that only by legitimising their capture with arrest could they be protected from the angry mobs in Petrograd.

George Buchanan, the British Ambassador in Petrograd, recalled Kerensky's qualities as a public figure: 'Kerensky was the only minister whose personality, if not altogether sympathetic, had something arresting about it that did not fail to impress one. As an orator he possessed the magnetic touch which holds an audience spellbound, and in the earlier days of the revolution he unceasingly strove to instil into the workmen and soldiers some of his own patriotic fervour.'[18]

The ability to deliver speeches that would connect with their audiences was an important skill for any public figure in 1917. Kerensky's experience as an advocate served him well in this respect. Over and over in his rather cliché-ridden but very

Photograph of the trial of General Sukhomlinov and his wife, *Illustrated London News*, 6 October, 1917.

In his memoirs, the general recalled his arrest: 'A gang of armed men came to arrest me in the apartment and to take me to the Tauride Palace, where the new government was already being organised. On our way there in a truck a bloke in glasses held a pistol against my temple and its muzzle kept banging on my head on the bumpy road.'[17]

successful speeches, Kerensky made direct appeals to 'his' people:

> Comrades, do you trust me? [*Chorus of voices shout 'Yes!'*]
> I am speaking from the depths of my heart, comrades. I am ready to die, if that will be necessary.
>
> I cannot live without the people, and in that moment when you suspect me, kill me!

One observer was disconcerted to see that tears ran down Kerensky's face as he spoke. After his ascendancy to the premiership and the attempted Bolshevik rising in July, his tone became increasingly authoritarian. Where once he had appealed directly to the goodness of the people, now he called for the preservation of the state. Despite this, it is difficult to find strong evidence for his much-reported egotism and power mania. Kerensky was the only moderate prepared to take on the responsibility of leading Russia; he faced opprobrium from across the political spectrum when he was unable to avert the Bolshevik seizure of power and subsequent descent into civil war. Nikolai Sukhanov was a 'convinced political opponent of Kerensky's from the day of our first meeting', but still presented a relatively sympathetic portrait of him:

> [Kerensky had] supernatural energy, amazing capacity for work, and inexhaustible temperament. But he lacked the head for statesmanship and had no real political schooling. Without these elementary and indispensable attributes, the irreplaceable Kerensky of expiring Tsarism, the ubiquitous Kerensky of the February–March days could not help but

Olga Kerensky and her sons, *c*.1910. Photograph from *Voina i revoliutsiia*: *c*.1918.

General's daughter Olga Baranovskaia married Kerensky in 1904. Their two sons – Oleg and Gleb – both became engineers and lived in Britain. Oleg Kerensky was made a CBE for designing many British road bridges and structures.

X.802/4756.

Novyi Satirikon (New Satiricon), no.19, July 1917, cover.

The situation in the country by June 1917 was perceived by many as anarchy, and this is the interpretation suggested by artist Nikolai Remizov (Re-Mi). He fled Russia in 1918, and from the 1940s made a name in Hollywood as an artistic director. The 1917 cartoon was probably the source for the anti-Bolshevik poster *That is how the workers' question has been solved in the Soviet Russia (Tak razreshen rabochii vopros s Sovdepii)*, 1919.

L.B.31.c.900.

stumble headlong and flounder into his July–September situation, and then plunge into his October nothingness, taking with him, alas! an enormous part of what we had achieved in the February–March revolution ... he was a sincere democrat and fighter for revolutionary victory – as he understood it ... [but] by conviction, taste and temperament he was the most consummate middle-class radical.[19]

The June Offensive

On the global stage, the June offensive was the linchpin of Kerensky's policies as minister of war. The offensive had been promised to the Allies, and was initially part of a plan for a joint offensive with the French. The big question was whether the disparate Russian troops would be capable of reforming and going on the attack. Kerensky himself is widely attributed with having made the offensive possible at all. He toured the front tirelessly, giving impassioned speeches to the troops and often receiving rapturous responses from the listening crowds. The newly revolutionary members of the army were being asked to sacrifice their lives, not from a collective order but as individuals choosing death of their own volition. Shklovsky described his own attempts to propagandise in favour of the June offensive among front-line troops:

> One soldier said to me 'I don't want to die'. With desperate energy, I spoke to him about the right of the revolution to our lives. I didn't despise words then, as I do now. Comrade Anardovich told me that my impassioned speech had made his hair stand on end. The audience was deciding the question of its own death, an immediate death, and the necessity of ordering men to renounce themselves, the silence of this sad crowd of thousands and the vague uneasiness caused by the proximity of the enemy stretched nerves to breaking point.[20]

The offensive began on 1 July (18 June), and after initial success was hailed as a great victory. This was premature, however, as reserves refused to relieve the men in new forward positions, and the endless meetings endemic on the front were renewed every time officers gave an order. Richard Boleslavskii, an officer in a Polish cavalry regiment that fought with the Russians, described his experience of the June offensive, in which soldiers who obeyed orders and attacked were threatened by their own comrades from behind:

> Along the front of the trench stood a line of shock troops, in perfect order, calmly firing their rifles. In the entrance to the dugouts back of them lounged soldiers of the Izmailovsky Guards. They were taking no part in the shooting. Right in front of me was a Sergeant with a grey beard on a young face. He had a whistle in his mouth. The end of his ear was shot off. From time to time he wiped the blood off his ear with a dirty handkerchief held in his left hand. In his right hand he was holding a big German ten-shell Mauser. The Mauser was pointed not towards the enemy but down his own trench. In front of him was a machine gun propped up on two empty shell boxes and also pointed along the trench. I asked him what the trouble was. Almost hysterical, he exploded: 'These cowards! The sons of bitches! They won't move! They threaten they won't allow the shock troops over the top. I'm standing here and I've got to guard the backs of my men while they're fighting. Otherwise these dogs would shoot them in the back.'[21]

The June offensive proved to be a turning point in the fortunes of the army. Soldiers were alienated from the committees that they had elected, who had supported the offensive and the Provisional Government initiatives. This contributed to the disenfranchisement of the soldiers, whose interests were no longer represented by the bodies that they had elected to represent them.

Maria Botchkareva

An uneducated peasant woman from Siberia, Maria Botchkareva received a special dispensation from the tsar to join the active army in 1914. She won a series of military honours with her brave and doughty conduct on the front lines, and became a stalwart supporter of the Provisional Government. She was an iconic figure in 1917. Kerensky authorised her to establish a 'women's battalion of death', made up of patriotic women volunteers. Botchkareva recalled her appeal for volunteers in May 1917: '"Men and women citizens!" I heard my voice say. "Our mother is perishing. Our mother is Russia. I want to save her. I want women whose hearts are crystal, whose souls are pure, whose impulses are lofty. With such women setting an example of self-sacrifice, you men will realise your duty in this grave hour!"'[22]

Around 2,000 women joined the battalion. One of their first experiences on signing up was to have their heads shaved. This was presented as a part of the women's transition from civilian to soldier, but it also represented an attempt to de-sex the female recruits, thus distinguishing them from other women active in the army, including nurses and auxiliary staff, who were associated with sexual licentiousness. While Botchkareva's unit did see front-line service, its primary function was to shame men into serving in the army. This unit was one of the 'shock batallions' formed in early 1917 in an attempt to galvanise morale and commitment among the Russian army.

The shock battalions were made up of individuals or regiments who volunteered to lead the attack. Though the concentration of loyal forces did enable them to spearhead attacks effectively, they faced unusually high casualty rates because they were leading the assaults. As a result the core of the Provisional Government's most loyal forces were wiped out. Kerensky had hoped to inspire a move towards the shock-battalions by offering a special insignia to be worn on the sleeve, but there was little real enthusiasm for the scheme; many shock battalion personnel were loyalist officers eager to escape the pressures of their unruly troops.

Soldiers' Wives

The First World War defined Russia's experience in 1917 more than any other factor. Around 15 million men were mobilised into the army between 1914 and 1917, of which 7 million were killed or injured. The mobilised men who joined the armed forces formed a disparate but influential interest group in 1917.

Maria Botchareva. Photograph in Maria Botchkareva, *Yashka: My Life as Peasant, Officer and Exile*, 1919.
010795.aaa.10.

They were not the only powerful social force to emerge from the war. A bewildering array of interest groups emerged from the social dislocation caused by the conflict.

Refugees, orphans, prisoners of war, invalids and the disabled all formed associations and clamoured to have their visions of the February revolution heard. With the exception of the soldiers themselves, soldiers' wives comprised the largest and most vocal of these groups. Just like the soldiers, they encapsulated a diverse array of social, ethnic and national groups. Soldiers' wives were unified by their common grievances, which were locally defined. Their demands tended to crystallise around household issues – such as demands for lower produce prices at the market, for an increase in the allowance with which they were provided by the state, for free or subsidised fuel, and for help with working their fields. The dramatic inflation of the war years meant that the real value of soldiers' wives allowances plummeted, leaving many in states of destitution.

Despite low levels of formal organisation, and the systematic marginalisation of women by the predominantly male political hierarchies, soldiers' wives made a significant mark on revolutionary politics at a local level. They generally failed to secure formal representation in the plethora of democratically elected committees that sprang up across the empire, and they did not forge a strong national presence. However, soldiers' wives did act collectively at local level in a range of ways that publicised their grievances and simultaneously destabilised local government. As well as writing huge numbers of statements and

Orphan refugees of the First World War, *c.*1916. Photograph from *Voina i revoliutsiia, c.*1918.

X.802/4756.

petitions to local and national government about their plight, the women also took direct action to pressurise local government.

In Kazan province, soldiers' wives presented their demands directly to the provincial administration, sometimes with open hostility. In May 1917 a meeting of soldiers' wives demanded that their allowance be increased from 7 to 20 roubles per month, and that they be supplied with sugar and white flour. All the participants of the meeting then marched to the gates of the palace where the city soviet was in session, and effectively besieged it, before marching around the centre of town with banners and placards to make their voices heard. Though soldiers' wives in many respects inhabited the margins of political power in 1917, they nevertheless used their new-found revolutionary freedoms to present their demands to local government. In so doing, they destabilised local government and demonstrated their collective identities and motivations.

The Grain Crisis
One of most profound challenges for the Provisional Government and for the subsequent soviet administration was supplying the country with sufficient grain. The overall crop yield for 1916 was not far down on former years, but problems arose because although the yield increased in Siberia and the north, it decreased markedly in European Russia.

A major factor in the February revolution was the grain shortage afflicting urban areas. Russia's transport system was unable to cope with the demands of 1917, meaning that good crops in the north were not accessible to the major conurbations of Petrograd and Moscow. In 1917 Petrograd received only 44.1 per cent of the grain it had received in 1913 by rail, and such shortfalls became even more marked as 1917 progressed. The challenge was not restricted to the capital, but was manifested all over Russia. Some parts of the empire, such as Arkhangelsk in the north and Nizhegorod province in the centre, always had to import grain to meet the food needs of their residents. Other regions, such as Tambov and Kazan, had a grain surplus that they were able to sell.

The Provisional Government responded to the food crisis in two key ways. Firstly, they sought to intervene in the market, and secondly they organised democratically elected local committees to administer these interventions. All grain produced was to be at the disposal of the state. A grain monopoly was established in an attempt to prevent grain merchants from driving prices up, and to assure the supply of grain to the cities and the army. A fixed price was established and producers were obliged to surrender all grain not for their own needs.

Food-supply committees were established to ensure the effective local organisation of the grain monopoly. They had wide-ranging duties, from ensuring the appropriate use of land

and protecting it from damage and destruction to ensuring that the peasants were adhering to Provisional Government policy and surrendering all their grain. The food-supply committees were difficult for the Provisional Government to monitor, let alone control. They were elected by local people, and accountable to them. If central policy was seen to be at odds with local needs, the committees responded to their constituents. If they did not, local communities ignored, assaulted or deselected them. The Kadet newspaper *Russkie Vedomosti (Russian Record)* published a lengthy and panic-stricken report about the food crisis on 6 September (24 August) 1917:

> The food crisis has become extremely acute. The grim spectre of hunger faces the country. Popular discontent mounts with frightening force. Riots provoked by the food situation are a common occurrence throughout the length of the country. On the whole, the picture everywhere is the same. A riot starts because of food and the mob arbitrarily begins a search of stores and houses. Or they march on the food supply boards with the demand for bread and food. They force their way into the premises, commit violence. Intense discontent, irritability, heightened nervousness and suspicion are favourable psychological ground for all sorts of rumours, and the mob falls under the power of irresponsible agitators who conduct all sorts of violent agitation

Novyi Satirikon (New Satiricon), no.21, June 1917.
The way politicians tackled the food crisis was criticised in the liberal press. In this caricature, the politician campaigning in front of the bread line incoherently declares: 'Here is our turn ... Actually, it is our turn to talk to this breadline ... To summarise: the sugar queue has already voted for us. We cannot believe that the united bloc of bread and milk queues will not support us ...'
In Russian there is one word for 'turn', 'queue' and 'line'.

LB.31.c.900.

— Граждане! Теперь пришла и наша очередь... Т. е. теперь пришли мы и къ вашей очереди... Однимъ, словомъ сахарная очередь уже подала свои голоса за насъ — неужели же промолчитъ блокъ хлѣбной съ молочной?

against Jews, against the bourgeoisie, and also against the intelligentsia. And recently counterrevolution finds it place here also … The officials and food supply delegates report from everywhere about their helplessness to do anything. The population refuses to listen to them, throws them out, beats them unmercifully and hides the grain.[23]

Reports of attacks on provisions administration came in from across those regions that had food deficits. Ordinary people were frustrated by the apparent failings of the committees that they elected, and the councillors were often accused of corruption. These attacks were characterised by collective action, as local people gathered, often on market day, and made various demands, usually focusing around the immediate distribution of foodstuffs and the resignation of the administration, alongside threats of violence against administrators. In Gorbatov town, in Nizhegorod province, demonstrators gathered from all over the region to protest against the provisions administration for four consecutive days.

The government and the Petrograd Soviet tried to coax the rural population into meeting national expectations through appeals calling on them to protect freedom and the new Russia. The Petrograd Soviet made this appeal directly to peasants on 6 May (23 April) 1917:

Peasants! Your brothers and your children are soldiers and workers in the towns. By shedding their blood they have won the freedom which will bring benefit to the peasantry and will resolve the land question. But this freedom is in danger. Its enemies, supporters of the overthrown Tsar, are taking advantage of the bread shortage in the towns – [a situation] which they themselves have brought on – in order to undermine your freedom and ours. They are saying that it was supposedly the revolution that left the country without bread. They are slandering when they say that peasants are not bringing grain to towns because supposedly they are against freedom, against workers and soldiers.

Peasants! If you want to preserve freedom, if you want to throw off the yoke of land captains, village police, and small landlords for all time – save the revolution! Know this: the revolution will be destroyed if the army on the front and in the towns is left without bread, if your and our enemies succeed in killing the new-born freedom by starvation. And without freedom there will be no land!

We will insist on the most determined confiscation, at a fixed price, of grain reserves, hoarded and accumulated by small landowners and merchants. But we both have a common task. We will solve it together, through our voluntary efforts.

The demands of the crowd were 'Give us grain. You will make us starve'. The crowd would not accept explanations from members of the administration. A voice was heard from the crowd, cursing foully, and threatening administration members with murder. At that moment several administration members ran away. The crowd, with the intention of lynching him, seized the president of the administration, but the commissar and armed soldiers persuaded the crowd to leave him untouched. He was then arrested by the militia, together with another administration member Sokolov, who had his beard pulled by the crowd on the way to the guardhouse, and the key of the provisions warehouse was taken.

Report on events in Gorbatov, Nizhegorod province, in regional paper Narod (The People), *no.61, 3 September 1917.*[24]

Bring as much grain as possible to the mills and wharves at once. Every sack of grain now is a firm stone in the foundation of the building of a new Russia – a Russia in which the toiling people will be their own master. Let this building be built by the invincible hands of workers, peasants and soldiers.

Your brothers in the towns and on the front are waiting for your help. Time does not wait. Every day is valuable. Take the grain to the mills, the railroad stations, the wharves![25]

Blaming the crisis on the former administration, as this appeal did, was possible early in 1917, but the argument became increasingly difficult to sustain as the year wore on and the provisions crisis actually worsened. The appeal captures the naïve innocence of both the Soviet and the Provisional Government, who imagined the rural population to be simple, untutored people who only needed to be told 'the truth' for them to conform to state expectations. Such naïvety left the national government horribly exposed. Russia's ordinary people were not simple children, to be instructed on their futures, and the grain crisis was not the fault solely of a handful of speculators.

The depth of the crisis was not easily resolved, and the credibility of both Soviet and Provisional Government was gravely undermined by their inability to resolve this problem. In an attempt to stimulate the release of grain, the Provisional Government doubled the fixed price of grain in August. This failed to have a significant impact. The stark alternative to appeals was forcible seizure of grain reserves from producers. The Provisional Government threatened such measures, but lacked both the will and the military force to implement them. Lenin quickly resorted to these measures once in power, and much of the civil war was a conflict between competing ruling powers and local populations over the control of food resources. The Bolshevik promise of bread was a fallacy.

Land Control

The vast majority of Russia's population in 1917 made their living in agriculture as small farmers. For many rural dwellers, the 1917 revolution offered the opportunity to resolve perceived injustices in local land use and ownership. All over Russia the norms of private ownership were transgressed as the rural population took local power into their own hands. They grazed their cattle in privately owned fields, took their carts and axes to the forests to harvest timber for building and fuel, seized arable land and in some places forcibly removed gentry landowners. Every locality across the great expanse of the empire experienced its rural revolution differently. A broad range of locally defined features determined land relations, including the types of agriculture that were practised there and personal antagonisms between local landowners and rural communities.

Both the Provisional Government and the Petrograd Soviet appealed repeatedly to peasants to wait calmly for the convocation of the Constituent Assembly before the land question could be resolved. This extract from the Provisional Government's appeal issued on 6 May (23 April) 1917 encapsulates the tone of many such appeals in 1917:

> A great disaster threatens our native land should the native population take upon itself the reorganisation of the land question without waiting for the decision of the Constituent Assembly. Such arbitrary actions carry the threat of general ruin. The fields will remain unsown and the harvest will not be gathered. Destitution and hunger will descend on the country.
>
> But this will not happen. Conscious of our great responsibility for the future of our native land, let us calmly prepare for the arrival of the true organizer of the Russian land – the national Constituent Assembly – which will find an equitable solution to the land question and will establish a new land system.[27]

'Water is yours, light is yours, the land is yours, the wood is yours.'

Declaration at Moshtaushsk village meeting, Kazan province, by Kronstadt sailor-agitator, Khalapsin, 26 (14) June 1917.[26]

The Socialist Revolutionary Party was widely recognised to be the party supported by Russia's rural population. The most central tenet of its political programme was the socialisation of land, whereby those who worked the land would reap the rewards of its produce. In 1917, though, like the other moderate socialist groups, the Socialist Revolutionary Party appealed to all working people to support the Provisional Government and to wait for the land question to be settled by the Constituent Assembly. An editorial in the party newspaper *Delo Naroda (People's Cause)* on 29 (16) March ended with a shrill appeal to all toiling people:

> Guard the sacredness and success of the revolution! Do not turn the great work into a reign of arbitrary rule and violence!! Do not confuse the socialisation of land with its arbitrary seizure for personal gain!! Do not tolerate any pogroms! Fight against them! Organise and be prepared for the elections to the Constituent Assembly which must give the people both land and *freedom*!!![28]

These appeals were ignored. The norms of private ownership were repeatedly transgressed in the countryside during 1917 as peasants seized land and wood. Yet the rural population was not a random and arbitrary violent force in 1917. Where local communities infringed on private owners, they often sought to couch their actions in the new revolutionary language and appealed to revolutionary justice. The rural revolution is not

АГРАРНОЕ.

Помѣщикъ: — Что это ты, мужичекъ, на одной ногѣ стоишь?
Крестьянинъ. — Да другую, вишь, поставить некуда: вездѣ вашей милости землица. Боюсь, еще за потраву судить будете...

easily categorised – forms of action depended on local factors, including the historic relationship between landowner and peasants and the forms of agriculture in the region. In some regions, there was neither significant land hunger nor high levels of non-peasant land ownership, so there the land question was less prominent than in national discourse.

Much of the rural revolution concerned disputes among peasants. Wealthier individuals who had separated from communal landholding were reintegrated, sometimes forcibly, into communal structures. Neighbouring villages disputed the fair use of common and noble land. Violence was often threatened but less often deployed, as rural people sought to validate their actions with the support of the new revolutionary norms and avoided actions that brought them into open conflict with authority. When peasants of Seitovo village in the Kazan region were involved in an incident of illicit woodcutting and the regional authorities challenged them, for example, they issued a detailed apology:

> We the undersigned citizens of Seitovo village acknowledge that we are guilty in the unauthorised theft of wood which formerly belonged to citizen Pauluchchi, and which is now NATIONAL property. And in order to wash this stain from ourselves, [which was made] THROUGH IGNORANCE, and which we cannot with honour leave on ourselves, we ask the provincial commissar to take from us this fine gathered voluntarily from those guilty of wood theft, and use the money for the needs of a school. We have gathered the fine at 50 kopeks for every one of us guilty of stealing wood. Altogether 280 roubles have been gathered.[29]

The peasants of Seitovo recognised that the new freedoms of 1917 were balanced against requirements to uphold the law and maintain the state. This example of peasants withdrawing from their initial cause is unusual. The pseudo-legal justifications used by peasants to support their claims showed that they engaged with the language of revolution, and used such language to support their own interpretations of the new order.

Regional administrators recognised that regulation rather than unenforceable prohibition was the best way to deal with peasant actions, and they were forced by practical exigencies to negotiate a course between demands from peasants and demands from central government. In Kazan, the peasant soviet decreed that all privately held land in the region was transferred to the land committees in May 1917. Peasants all over the region used this decree to vindicate their seizure of land. Local government in Nizhegorod province waited until October 1917 to overrule national policy guidance and transgress norms of private ownership. Mikhail Sumgin, the Nizhegorod provincial

(opposite) *Novyi Satirikon (New Satiricon)*, no.17, May 1917, cover.
The situation with the 'land question' is satirised here. The landlord asks the peasant why he is standing on one leg. The peasant replies that there is no room for his other leg – he is afraid of being prosecuted for trespassing on the landlord's property.
L.B.31.c.900.

commissar, declared to the Ministry of Internal Affairs on 5 November (23 October) 1917 that he had to take extraordinary measures:

> The anarchy which exists in most of the province is manifested absolutely everywhere in the seizure of grain; cutting of wood continues along with arson of property. I am taking these measures, on the one hand actually transferring all land and woods to the keeping of the land committees to show the population the undoubted victories of the revolution, and on the other hand using ranks of soldiers to cut short counter-revolutionary calls to burn and rob.[30]

Local government had their options dictated to them by the actions of their constituents, as did the national government. After their seizure of power in October 1917, the Bolshevik government issued a land decree that authorised the transfer of all privately held land into the hands of local land committees for the use of working people. This decree merely legitimised a process that had already gone on in the course of 1917, and showed how local actions could define national policy alternatives.

Whose Freedom?

'Land and freedom' (*Zemlia i volia*) was the rallying cry of Russia's largest and most popular political party, the Socialist Revolutionary Party. Meanings of freedom in the slogan were convoluted and uncertain, and this uncertainty contributed to its popularity: it could mean whatever you wanted it to mean. The slogan is often interpreted by historians as representing freedom from outside interference, and freedom to govern life without restriction from the state. It could also be interpreted more straightforwardly as referring to political freedom and the destruction of autocracy.

Freedom in 1917 had a multitude of meanings and implications. The challenge of trying to pin a concrete meaning on the use of freedom in this context is a useful illustration of the challenge in understanding what freedom could mean in practice, even as the old state collapsed and the emerging one presented itself as the implementer of freedom. The challenges of reconciling these differing visions of freedom – against the backdrop of a state at war and in economic collapse – were beyond the means of any government.

What did freedom bring to the Russian soldier in 1917? The spread of democratisation in the army's ranks subverted military discipline. Soldiers formed committees, which they used to debate the orders that they were given and to make collective decisions about whether these orders should be obeyed. Such freedom in the heart of an active army was

Itō Chūta, cartoon describing Russian events in 1917, from *Ashura-jō* (*The Book of Demons*), Tokyo, 1920–21.

The original caption, inaccurate in places, explains the changes in Russia to the Japanese public: 'The Romanov dynasty which, for 304 years from 1613 when Tsar Michael I ascended the throne had ruled one-sixth of the globe and been revered as God's representatives by their 200,000,000 subjects, finally came to a sad end. What led to this momentous event? After the re-elections of 1915, popular sentiment was inspired by the idea of overthrowing the government. With this sudden change in popular feeling, holding authority as God's representatives counted for nothing.' Japanese architect, architectural historian, artist and cartoonist Itō Chū-ta produced a total of approximately 3,700 postcard-size illustrations on national and international events during his lifetime. About 500 of these cartoons, produced between 1914 and 1919, were later compiled into a five-volume set, known as *Ashura-jō* (*The Book of Demons*), reflecting the violence and turbulence of the period.

ORB.30/757.

profoundly destabilising. When given the order to advance during the Russian offensive in June 1917, individual regiments debated this order. Some of them chose to advance, but others refused to obey the orders. This led to an effective collapse of the offensive.

What did freedom mean for Russia's industrial workers? They, like the soldiers, elected and served in committees and participated in local government. Some of them joined the ranks of Bolshevik supporters as 1917 wore on, and some took up arms to seize state power in October 1917. Their privileged position within the revolutionary state ensured that they were well placed to enjoy the new freedoms of 1917. These freedoms failed to improve living conditions, however, and proved unable to protect job security in the face of the burgeoning economic crisis.

In 1917 more than 80 per cent of Russians were peasants. What did they do with their freedom? They voted. They elected provisions committees and land committees, and other bodies of local government. However, these freedoms, far from being used to support and defend the state, were used to support and defend local interests. Elected food committees either met the demands of their constituents to secure grain reserves for the local community, or were forcibly removed and re-elected. Land committees were responsive to their local constituency. In Kazan the regional committee responded to local demands and needs,

Novyi Satirikon (New Satiricon),
no.22, June 1917.

The general disillusion in the achievements
of the revolution can be seen in this
caricature, where a poor man supports
the revolution because he gets copious
quantities of cigarette papers.

L.B.31.c.900.

using pseudo-legal measures to appropriate privately owned
land and transfer it to the hands of peasant communities.
This was in direct violation of Provisional Government policy.

In practice, political freedom frayed the threads that
connected the centre to the periphery in the Russian Empire.
By the end of 1917, these threads snapped altogether in some
places.

The process of political freedom and democratisation
did not resonate with the centralised state. As one peasant
community declared to their elected representative, 'We elected
you – you must listen to us!'[31]

NOTES

1. Maria Botchkareva, *Yashka: My Life as Peasant, Officer and Exile*. Frederick A. Stokes: 1919.
2. Robert Browder and Alexander Kerensky (eds), *The Russian Provisional Government 1917: Documents, Vol. II*. California: Stanford University Press, 1961, doc. 942.
3. Victor Shklovsky, *Sentimental Journey: Memoirs, 1917–1922*. New York: Cornell University Press, 1970.
4. Eduard M. Dune, *Notes of a Red Guard* (trans and ed by Diane Koenker and Steve Smith). Chicago: University of Illinois Press, 1993.
5. William Thomas Allison (ed.), *Witness to Revolution. The Russian Revolution Diary and Letters*. Praeger: 2002.
6. Robert Browder and Alexander Kerensky (eds), *The Russian Provisional Government 1917: Documents, Vol. I*. California: Stanford University Press, 1961, doc. 11.
7. V. V. Shul'gin, *Memoirs of a Member of the Russian Duma, 1906–1917. The Years*. Hippocrene Books: 1991.
8. Victor Shklovsky, *Sentimental Journey: Memoirs, 1917–1922*. New York: Cornell University Press, 1970.
9. Mark D. Steinberg and Vladimir M. Khrustalev, *The Fall of the Romanovs: Political Dreams and Personal Struggles in a Time of Revolution*. New Haven and London: Yale University Press, 1997.
10. Ibid.
11. N. N. Sukhanov, *The Russian Revolution 1917: A Personal Record* (ed by Joel Carmichael). New Jersey: Princeton University Press, 1984.
12. Victor Shklovsky, *Sentimental Journey: Memoirs, 1917–1922*. New York: Cornell University Press, 1970.
13. Ibid.
14. Maria Botchkareva, *Yashka: My Life as Peasant, Officer and Exile*. Frederick A. Stokes: 1919.
15. Sarah Badcock, 'Politics, Parties and Power: Sormovo Workers in 1917', in S. Pirani, D. Fitzler, W. Z. Goldman and G. Kessler (eds), *A Dream Deferred: New Studies in Russian and Soviet Labour History*. Peter Lang: 2008.
16. Robert Browder and Alexander Kerensky (eds), *The Russian Provisional Government 1917: Documents, Vol. II*. California: Stanford University Press, 1961, doc. 1187.
17. V. Sukhomlinov, *Vospominaniia*. Minsk: Kharvest, 2005.
18. George Buchanan, *My Mission to Russia and Other Diplomatic Memories*. Cassell and Company Ltd: 1923.
19. N. N. Sukhanov, *The Russian Revolution 1917: A Personal Record*, ed by Joel Carmichael. New Jersey: Princeton University Press, 1984.
20. Victor Shklovsky, *Sentimental Journey: Memoirs, 1917–1922*. New York: Cornell University Press, 1970.
21. Richard Boleslavskii, *Way of the Lancer*. Bobbs-Merrill: 1932.
22. Maria Botchkareva, *Yashka: My Life as Peasant, Officer and Exile*. Frederick A. Stokes: 1919.
23. *Russkie Vedomosti*, no.193, 24 August 1917, p.1, cited in Robert Browder and Alexander Kerensky (eds), *The Russian Provisional Government 1917: Documents, Vol. I*. California: Stanford University Press, 1961, doc. 552.
24. *Narod*, no.61, 3 September 1917.
25. *Izvestiia*, no.48, 23 April 1917, p.1, cited in Robert Browder and Alexander Kerensky (eds), *The Russian Provisional Government 1917: Documents, Vol. I*. California: Stanford University Press, 1961, doc. 542.
26. Sarah Badcock, *Politics and the People in Revolutionary Russia: A Provincial History*. Cambridge: Cambridge University Press, 2007.
27. Robert Browder and Alexander Kerensky (eds), *The Russian Provisional Government 1917: Documents, Vol. II*. California: Stanford University Press, 1961, doc. 470.
28. *Delo Naroda*, 29 (16) March 1917.
29. Sarah Badcock, *Politics and the People in Revolutionary Russia: A Provincial History*. Cambridge: Cambridge University Press, 2007.
30. Ibid.
31. Ibid.

3 Cursed Days: The 'Russian' Civil Wars

Jonathan Smele

The events that took place in the wake of the October revolution have often been demoted to a coda to the main event of 1917. This is an unbalanced view. The October revolution, although sporadically violent, was brief and relatively bloodless. It was neither the beginning nor the end of a prolonged process experienced by Russians and non-Russians across (and beyond) the borders of a former empire that had encompassed one-sixth of the land surface of the globe. In fact, it was the subsequent events, taking place through the following decade, that were almost unprecedentedly sanguinary. Between 1917 and 1921 alone, at least 10,500,000 people lost their lives during the civil war. Of these, some 950,000 were Red Army fighters and 650,000 were members of the White Armies or of nationalist forces. Around 2 million deaths were due to the Red and the White Terror – atrocities that both sides frequently emphasised in their propaganda.

Millions more were maimed, orphaned or widowed, and at least 2 million former subjects of the tsar went into exile abroad. Then, as the most active fronts of the struggles began to die down, in 1921–1922 another 5 million people perished in a horrendous famine across the Volga–Urals region and some other areas. The famine had, in large part, been precipitated by the previous years of chaos. Indeed, between 1917 and 1920 hunger had been among the chief enemies within the Soviet zone, which tended to consist largely of food-consuming rather than food-producing regions. The Whites were anxious to emphasise this situation in propaganda issued from their food-rich encampments in Ukraine, the North Caucasus and Western Siberia.

Several tens of thousands of others then perished in anti-Soviet uprisings – mostly in Transcaucasia and Central Asia – before the upheavals reached a temporary quietude around 1926. Consequently, the first complete Soviet-era census, which was conducted that year, identified 147,027,915 citizens of the newly founded USSR. Without world war, revolution and civil wars

> The next day after our counter attack colonel Zhebrak, who had lost one leg [in previous battles], was found dead. The Reds cut off his other leg and poked his eyes out. One army cadet was burnt alive. Our retaliation was brutal – using machine guns, we shot dead over 3000 prisoners. Tonight, we had a long discussion about whether there was any difference between us and the Bolsheviks when it comes to executions. The majority agreed that we tortured people less and not so often. However, all sorts of things happened. There was no Cheka, but there were some 'chekists' among us, too.
>
> *Nikolai Raevskii, 27, an officer in the Volunteer Army in South Russia, diary entry, June 1921.*[1]

(above) *Otstupaia pered Krasnoi armiei, belogvardeitsy zhgut khleb* (*Retreating, the Whites are burning the crops*), Soviet propaganda poster, *c*.1918–20.

Cup.645.a.6.

(right) *Tak khoziainichaiut bol'sheviki v kazach'ikh stanitsakh* (*That is how the Bolsheviks feel at home in Cossack villages*), White propaganda poster, *c*.1918–20.

1856.g.8 (28).

(opposite) *Vashi rodnye i blizkie stonut pod igom bol'shevistskihk komissarov. Oni mrut ot nasiliia i goloda, oni zovut vas. Idite zhe spasat' ikh!* (*Your loved ones are groaning under the Bolshevik commissars' yoke. They are dying of terror and famine. They are calling you, Go and save them!*), White propaganda poster, *c*.1918–20.

1856.g.8 (17).

Schastlivyi rabochii v Sovdepii (*A happy worker in Soviet Russia*), White propaganda poster, *c.*1918–20.

1856.g.8 (10).

(and taking into account the loss of the former imperial lands of Finland, the Baltic provinces, Poland and Bessarabia), it might have expected to have found at least 175,000,000.

In addition to the physical losses, the psychological scars inflicted on the participants in the struggles of this period remain incalculable. Such destruction and loss of life were undoubtedly the greatest cataclysm to engulf Russia since the Mongols had emerged from Asia, in 1237–1240, to overrun Kievan Rus'. It took Russia half a millennium to recover from that event. Today, a century after the events with which we are here concerned, it could be argued that the Russian Federation and the other successor states to the USSR are still coming to terms with the civil wars that inspired, and were inspired by, the revolutions of 1917 – hence the currently strained relations between Moscow and the Baltic states, the Transcaucasian republics of Azerbaijan, Armenia and (especially) Georgia, and, of course, Ukraine.

Chronology and Geography

Although all the major works on the subject routinely use the term, there never was such a thing as a unitary 'Russian Civil War'. Rather, as the Russian Empire collapsed and the USSR was constructed, a complex of wars erupted across and beyond the formal imperial space. Almost all of them, naturally, involved Russians, but in many cases the issues were local and chiefly concerned non-Russians – or they involved conflicts between Russians and non-Russians. For example, one of the most fought-over cities of the period was Lemberg (now called Lviv). The city had been in Austrian Galicia until November 1918. Never part of the Russian Empire, it was to be incorporated (as Lwów) into Poland. Since the Second World War, it has been part of Ukraine.

The Red–White struggle forming the main focus of most works on the period needs to be supplemented by a consideration of the wars of independence waged by the Baltic states, the Finnish Civil War, the Soviet–Polish War, the Soviet–Ukrainian War, the Ukrainian–Polish War, the Polish–Lithuanian War, the Armenian–Azeri War, the Georgian–Armenian War and so forth. Persia, Sinkiang and Mongolia also experienced contemporaneous turmoil, unleashed as violence and disorder leached across the borders of the former Russian Empire. There were further waves of unrest within the Soviet zone, not to mention interventions by both the Central Powers and the Allies.

Incontrovertibly, however, all the wars were about the fate of the former Russian Empire as it disintegrated during and after the First World War. Russian nationalists strove to rebuild it, while Bolshevik internationalists sought to use it to spread socialist revolution into Europe and Asia. Non-Russian nationalists sought to seal its fate by achieving independence, and Socialists Revolutionaries (SRs) and Mensheviks sought to transform it into a democratic confederation. Even within the Russian and Ukrainian heartlands, peasant rebels (sometimes termed 'Greens') sought local autonomy. Unsurprisingly, therefore, although tensions had been building across the empire for decades, it was amidst the destruction, disruption and chaos of the First World War that the seeds of the civil wars were planted.

This is not how accounts of the civil wars have usually been framed, chronologically. Seeking to portray their domestic opponents as little more than the lapdogs of the Allies, historians working within the strictures of anti-imperialist Soviet ideologies (especially during the Cold War) tended to cite the revolt of the 35,000-strong Czech Legion on the Volga and in Western Siberia in May–June 1918 as the origin of the conflicts.

The Legion consisted mainly of former soldiers of the Austro–Hungarian army who had either been captured by Russian forces or had deserted to them, and who, in 1917–1918, had been fashioned into an Allied unit prior to their aborted attempt to leave Russia, via Vladivostok, to fight on the Western Front. Certainly the Legion's revolt (provoked by Bolshevik attempts to disarm them and the Legionnaires' fear that they would not be repatriated subsequent to the Brest-Litovsk Treaty) was important in inspiring further revolt against Soviet power in the east. Over the following year the Legion became such a fixture in Siberia that its headquarters began publishing periodical publications in Czech. From the autumn of 1918, however, the Czechs confined themselves to garrisoning duties in the rear of the White forces in Siberia.

Similarly the Japanese, the only other numerically significant Allied force that landed in Russia in 1918, remained ensconced at Vladivostok and sent no forces to the front.

In the north, the British and US interventionists largely confined themselves to protecting Russian White forces and undertook few significant offences. In South Russia, the 40,000 French and French colonial forces who disembarked at Odessa and in the Crimea in December 1918 had been driven out by the Reds by April of the following year. The Soviet historians' emphasis on the Allied intervention as the cause of the civil wars always sat oddly with the obvious fact that extensive fighting took place in Ukraine, South Russia, the Urals and Siberia over the winter of 1917–1918, and that Lenin himself had referred to this as a 'civil war'.

Some Western historians adopted spring 1918 as a starting point for the civil wars; others opted for the morrow of the Bolshevik seizure of power in 1917, implying that 'civil war' was caused by the Bolsheviks' actions. If, however, the wars are re-conceptualised as not being only about the Bolsheviks' attempt to build socialism, but also about issues of nationalism, decolonisation, recolonisation and identity, it is necessary to

Image taken by a Japanese photographer, showing Japanese troops marching in Vladivostok, c.1920.

S.T.54/13.

extend the chronology backwards. If it is accepted that the First World War was the trigger for the revolutions and civil wars that destroyed the empire of the tsars and begat the USSR, it is to that era that we should cast our eye.

Certainly the destruction of normal channels of authority and the normalisation of violence that were preconditions for the civil wars can be identified in the first days of the First World War. One climactic event, however, stands out as the starkest signifier of what was looming – the revolt in Russian Turkestan of June 1916, precipitated by the tsar's order to mobilise the previously exempt Muslim menfolk of the region for war work at the front. In the subsequent repressions and punitive actions 88,000 rebels were killed and a further 250,000 fled into China. Yet even this did not stay the conflict, which rumbled on through 1917, culminating in the Muslim intelligentsia's establishment of an anti-Soviet government at Kokand (the 'Kokand Autonomy') at the end of 1917. It would then develop into a region-wide guerrilla resistance, the Basmachi movement, which was strongly influenced by the Muslim clergy. The Red Army was

The Civil Wars: an overview

1916   Summer: Anti-tsarist rebellions engulf Central Asia, pre-dating the February 1917 revolution and signalling the onset of the civil wars.

1917   August: The Kornilov affair.

October: The Bolshevik revolution.

November: Formation of the first White force, the Volunteer Army, in South Russia.

1918   January: Dispersal of the Constituent Assembly in Petrograd and the declaration of Ukrainian independence in Kiev, which initiates the Soviet–Ukrainian War.

January–April: Finnish Whites victorious in the Finnish Civil War.

February: The first Allied (British) interventionist forces land in North Russia, followed by Japanese landings at Vladivostok in April.

February–September: Formation of the Red Army under war commissar Leon Trotsky.

March: The Brest-Litovsk Treaty takes Soviet Russia out of the First World War and invites the intervention of the Central Powers in Ukraine and South Russia.

May: Declaration of independent Azeri, Georgian and Armenian republics in Transcaucasia.

Summer: Anti-Bolshevik socialist administrations founded on the Volga, in Siberia, North Russia and elsewhere (the 'democratic counter-revolution').

November: End of the First World War facilitates further Allied intervention in Russia, inspiring declarations of independence by the Baltic states and initiating their 'Wars of Independence'.

November: A right-wing coup at Omsk topples the democratic counter-revolution and proclaims a military dictatorship under 'Supreme Ruler' Admiral Kolchak, subsequently recognised as such by other White leaders but not the Allies.

1919   January: Opening of the Paris Peace Conference.

March–December: White advances from Siberia, South Russia, North Russia and the Baltic are defeated by the Red Army.

1920   January–March: Defeated White forces are evacuated from South Russia and North Russia; others are interred in Estonia.

April–October: Red Army defeated in the Soviet–Polish War.

November: The last White forces in European Russia are evacuated from Crimea.

1920–21 The Red Army invades Ukraine and Transcaucasia, while crushing internal peasant rebellions across the Soviet zone and suppressing the Kronstadt rebellion (the sailors' anti-Bolshevik uprising in the naval base of Kronstadt)

1921   Peace treaties with Poland, the Baltic states and Finland secure Soviet Russia's western border. Treaties with Turkey, Persia and Afghanistan secure the southern border. Anglo-Soviet Trade Agreement opens the way to international recognition of the Soviet state.

1921–26 Soviet forces battle Muslim rebels (the Basmachi) across Central Asia.

1922   November: The last White forces in the Far East are evacuated in the wake of the withdrawal of Japanese interventionist forces.

December: Formation of the USSR.

1924   January: Death of Lenin.

August: Major anti-Soviet uprising crushed in Georgia.

1925   Trotsky is removed as war commissar.

1926   June: In Central Asia the last active Red front is closed, as the Red Army contains the Basmachi, bringing the civil wars to a close.

only able (at great cost) to tame, but never entirely extinguish, this resistance by 1926.

Prominent and numerous among the Basmachi, not surprisingly, were those who had fought the Russians in 1916 and who had lost their livelihoods and their families to the Russians' 'pacification' of the region. As Edward Dennis Sokol explained in his book on the revolt of 1916, it 'sounded the first rumble of the oncoming disaster and in it there participated in one form or another the eleven million native peoples of Russian Central Asia … [It] was both the prelude to the Revolution in Russia proper and the catalytic agent which hastened the alignment of forces in Russian Central Asia'.[2]

The events of 1917 – from the February revolution, through the July Days and the October revolution to the closure of the Constituent Assembly by the Bolsheviks in January 1918 – might be seen not as a preliminary to civil war, but as a stage in it. It was a period of phoney civil war in which political lines were drawn, embryonic military forces gathered, and peasant and national autonomies asserted.

The key event of 1917 was the Kornilov affair, in which conservative generals seemed to be conspiring to topple the Provisional Government and to establish a military dictatorship under the commander-in-chief of the Russian army, General Kornilov. What really mattered, however, was not the much-debated conspiracy itself, but the changes that emerged from it. On the one side, Red Guard forces that were to play a key role in the October revolution (and were then deployed to stifle any advance on Petrograd by counter-revolutionary forces) became the nucleus of the Red Army, formed in early 1918 in line with a series of orders issued by war commissar Leon Trotsky. They were then despatched south to capture or reinforce key urban centres such as Kharkov, Rostov and (briefly) Kiev. On the other side, several future leaders of the White Army were placed under arrest as 'Kornilovites'. Among them were Kornilov himself and General Denikin, who later became White commander in South Russia.

Kornilov's successor at the head of the old army, General Alekseev, created an underground network of officers (the Alekseev Organisation), primed to resist any deepening of the revolution and committed to restoring order in the country. In the wake of the October revolution, the arrested generals escaped to the Don territory, where they were soon joined by Alekseev and members of his organisation, as well as by leading Kadets – thereby creating the nucleus of the Whites' Volunteer Army and its political leadership. Lenin certainly saw it this way, noting that 'the Kornilov revolt was a political conspiracy supported by the landowners and capitalists led by the Cadet [Kadet] Party, a conspiracy by which *the bourgeoisie has actually begun a civil war*' [emphasis added].[4]

I described to [Olia] the new life that we are fighting for. This bright life will come when we crush all the bourgeoisie. And that is why I joined the Red Army … Olia listened to me and nodded. Although she is a priest's daughter, she understands that there was no justice before, when the rich oppressed the poor … 'It's not the right time for love now,' I continued. 'First, we have to defeat all the enemies of the revolution, and after that one can fall in love … I wonder whether we will see each other again?

Filipp Golikov, 18-year-old Red Army soldier, later Marshal of the Soviet Union, diary entry, 18 January 1919.[3]

1918: Intervention and Counter-Revolution

By the spring of 1918 a series of conflicts were well underway between the Soviet government and its many opponents – around Novocherkassk, against the Don Cossacks; in the North Caucasus, against the Volunteers; around Orenburg, in the southern Urals, against the local Cossacks; around Tomsk, against proponents of Siberian autonomy; around Irkutsk and Chita, against the forces of the local warlord Grigorii Semenov; in Central Asia, where the pro-Bolshevik Tashkent Soviet engaged with the Kokand Autonomy; around Kiev against the newly proclaimed Ukrainian National Republic (UNR); in Belorussia (Belarus) against an uprising of the 1st Polish Army Corps; and in Finland, where Russian Red Guards assisted the Finnish Reds in their battles against the White Finns. All these battles of 1917–1918 (except for that in Finland, which the Whites decisively won) would drag on over the coming years and must be regarded as integral to the 'Russian' civil wars.

Nevertheless, a prominent place in deepening the civil wars must be accorded to the Soviet government's signing of the Brest-Litovsk Treaty with the Central Powers on 3 March 1918. Apart from adding to the general chaos in the former empire by detaching from it all of Russia's territorial gains in Eastern Europe since the early seventeenth century and those in Anatolia made since 1878 – together with more than one-third of the old empire's population (56 million people), one-third of its railway network, half of its industry, three-quarters of its supplies of iron ore, nine-tenths of its coal resources and much of its food supplies – the signing of the treaty had several other important consequences.

Firstly it invited both Austro–German and Turkish intervention in Russia, as well as the counter-intervention of the Allies. This, in turn, raised the issue among all combatants in the nascent civil wars of 'orientation' – whether to seek the assistance of the Central Powers or the Allies in the struggle for or against Bolshevism. This would have important consequences once the Allies won the conflict. The Whites, Poles and Baltic nationalists chose the Allies and were rewarded, if not with the dispatch of huge numbers of troops to Russia, then at least with political support as well as weapons and ammunition. This aid did not arrive in sufficient quantities to allow the Whites to triumph in Russia, but it was sufficient to safeguard the winning of Baltic and Polish independence.

The Ukrainians (governed from April to December 1918 by a conservative dictator, Hetman Pavlo Skoropadskyi) and the Georgians (under a Menshevik government) accepted German protection following the Brest-Litovsk Treaty. Consequently scorned by the Allies, they had their putative independence crushed by the Reds in December 1919–March 1920 and February–March 1921 respectively. In general, the question of

Svetit, da ne greet (*It shines, but doesn't give heat*), Allied propaganda poster aimed at Russian soldiers, 1918.

The celebration of the Brest-Litovsk Treaty by the generals round the table in the lit-up room will not warm up the miserable folk who are freezing outside.

Cup.645.c.12.

'orientation' caused great consternation among the Bolsheviks' opponents. The Volunteers and the Don Cossacks, for example, although both consisting of bastions of the old regime, were not the natural allies it had been assumed. The Cossacks were more interested in securing autonomy for the Don region and in limiting the flood of Russian settlers in the Cossack territory than in ousting the Reds from Moscow, and in summer 1918 sought alliance with Germany, while the Whites were overtly pro-Allies. Such differences would bedevil relations between the Cossacks and the Whites in South Russia throughout the civil wars, severely hampering the anti-Bolshevik cause. In 1919 the White leadership even felt obliged to execute several leading members of the Kuban Cossack parliament in response to their campaign for the independence of the Kuban.

A second important consequence of the treaty was that it exacerbated pre-existing tensions on the Soviet side. Coming as it did during the revolt of the Czech Legion, this temporary disruption in the Soviet ranks caused the Red Army – which was otherwise transforming from a disorganised rabble into an effective force in the first nine months of 1918 – to founder over late spring/summer, as almost all their opponents gained stronger footholds.

It was only through a combination of blackmail (threatening to resign), distortion and gerrymandering that Lenin was able to force the Bolsheviks' acceptance of the treaty, which enraged the left of his party who viewed it as a surrender to world imperialism. Even more outraged was the party of Left Socialists Revolutionaries, the Bolsheviks' former partners in government. They had resigned from the government in March 1918 over the treaty, and staged an uprising in Moscow in July. This proved all the more dangerous because it coincided with other revolts in the provinces, including those funded by Allied diplomats in Moscow. The revolts were crushed but the Red front was weakened, allowing the Czechs and the People's Army of Komuch (an abbreviation for the SR-dominated Committee of Members of the Constituent Assembly, and the chief manifestation of the so-called 'democratic-counter-revolution') – to capture Kazan and other Volga cities in August–September 1918. As Trotsky recognised from his vantage point on the opposite bank of the Volga, with Kazan in their hands and with Red forces in such disarray – actually in 'a state of psychological collapse', as the war commissar put it – the road to Moscow lay open before the People's Army by September 1918 and 'the fate of the revolution was hanging by a thread'.[5]

What Trotsky could not see was that, for all the SRs' long-standing popularity in the Volga provinces, the People's Army of Komuch had established only a fragile hold over the region. The Soviet government's Decree on Land of 8 November (26 October) 1917 had essentially implemented the SR programme on the redistribution of the estates of large landowners among the peasantry, leaving Komuch with little to offer the villages. Consequently, volunteers for the People's Army were few and even mobilisation netted less than 35,000 recruits. Meanwhile Komuch's political initiatives rarely got off the ground, as members of the fissiparous SRs argued among themselves and with their own more conservative military leaders in the area. Moreover, the regimes established by the SRs and Popular Socialists were continually fighting on two fronts – the Red Army, and the rightist forces that were gelling into the White Armies. Komuch was consequently pressed into an uneasy alliance with the more conservative anti-Bolshevik Provisional Siberian Government at Omsk. The Directory – the putative All-Russian Provisional Government established there – was then quickly overthrown by the Siberian army and local Kadets (with the probable support of the British mission). A military dictatorship under 'Supreme Ruler' Admiral Kolchak was proclaimed at Omsk on 18 November 1918.

Meanwhile, at Arkhangelsk, the socialist Supreme Administration of North Russia was overthrown by officers on 6 September. In isolated Central Asia the process was more extended. The SR–Menshevik Transcaspian Provisional Government, established in July 1918 following an anti-Bolshevik Ashkhabad uprising (sponsored by British forces), gave way in January 1919 to a more conservative Committee of Social Salvation. Six months later, in July 1919, the Committee accepted its subordination to the White forces in South Russia, thereby marking the end of the 'democratic' episode of the civil wars.

In contrast, White forces in the south fared well in the second half of 1918. After a disastrous campaign in the spring (the First Kuban campaign, known as the 'Ice March', February–April 1918), during which many White units suffered 100 per cent casualties on the frozen steppe of the North Caucasus, a Second Kuban campaign saw the Volunteers' combined cavalry and infantry attacks snaring a string of railway towns before finally securing the port of Novorossiisk, the Kuban Cossack capital of Ekaterinodar, in August 1918. General Kornilov, the commander of the army, was killed in the battle and General Denikin succeeded him. The capture of Novorossiisk allowed scattered White forces in Crimea and South Russia to move across the Black Sea to reinforce the Volunteers. Among them was General Wrangel, who then led a grinding cavalry campaign across the Kuban and Terek regions to cut the local Reds' rail communications with the north and subsequently to annihilate pro-Soviet forces and institutions in the North Caucasus by mid-November. The White success here also tempered Cossack suspicions of the Whites sufficiently to allow for the formation of the Armed Forces of South Russia (AFSR), uniting the

Portrait of General Denikin, *c*.1918.
Portraits of Generals Alekseev, Kornilov and Denikin appeared in numerous brochures and leaflets. This portrait is part of a series of posters of White military commanders.
1856.g.9.

Volunteers and the Don, Kuban and Terek Cossack Hosts under Denikin's command in January 1919.

Meanwhile, the victories in the south were echoed by Admiral Kolchak's Siberian army's capture of Perm, in the northern Urals, the following month.

Western Territories of the Empire between Self-Determination and Sovietisation

The stage was now set for the major Red–White military clashes of 1919, but the situation was made complicated by the ending of the First World War. In the wake of the armistice of 11 November 1918 the Germans withdrew from Ukraine, where the UNR re-established itself under socialist and later moderate nationalist leadership, while nationalists of a liberal stamp also emerged from the underground (or German prisons) in Estonia, Latvia and Lithuania to proclaim the independence of the Baltic states. Thus, somewhat perversely, the presence of the Central Powers in the Baltic and in Ukraine had acted to preserve the moderate socialist–liberal cause in those regions, whereas it had been stamped out in the east and north, where Allied interventionists were predominant. The Soviet government's response was to invade all these regions, but with little success.

In Ukraine, the Red advance netted Kiev on 5 February 1919, obliging the UNR government to resettle far in Ukraine's rural south-west. Further battles in March/April 1919 entirely shattered the Ukrainian army, which retreated into former Austrian territory. By May 1919 all Ukrainian territory that was part of the Russian Empire, including the Black Sea coast, was in Soviet hands. However, Red efforts in Ukraine were undone by the attempts of local hardline Bolsheviks to impose extreme versions of Soviet economic policies – the prohibition of all private trade, grain requisitioning and even collectivisation – upon a reluctant Ukrainian peasantry. The Ukrainian Bolshevik leadership also initially refused to work with non-Bolshevik radicals in Ukraine, notably the *Borotbists* (literally 'Fighters', essentially Ukrainian Left SRs), but they were forced into an alliance with them in the face of a string of peasant rebellions against Soviet power in the region.

Against the inclinations of the Red Army main commander Jukums Vācietis, the commander of Red forces in Ukraine Vladimir Antonov-Ovseenko insisted on taking the military campaign across the Dnepr into south-west Ukraine, thereby severely overstretching his thin resources. In fact he was obliged to rely upon unstable alliances with a variety of Ukrainian warlords, and was unable to counter the sudden revolt against Soviet Russian power by the 20,000-strong Trans-Dnepr Brigade led by Nykofor Hryhoriiv. On 8 May 1919 the Brigade proclaimed a 'Soviet Ukraine without Communists'. Hryhoriiv also forged an alliance with the anarchist commander Nestor Makhno, leader of

(below) Postcard of anarchist commander, Nestor Makhno, c.1918–20.

Private collection.

(opposite) Nestor Makhno by 'Kukryniksy' (the artists Kupriianov, Krylov and Sokolov). Caricature from *Pervaia Konnaia: albom* (*First Cavalry Army: An Album*), designed by A. Rodchenko and V. Stepanova, Moscow, 1938.

L.R.276.c.5.

Leader of the Revolutionary-Insurgent Army of Ukraine, Makhno crossed the Romanian boarder with a small squad in the summer of 1921, living abroad thereafter. He died in Paris in 1934. In Soviet Russia, Makhno's image in propaganda and popular culture was especially grotesque and anecdotal.

НЕСТОР МАХНО
ръководител на свободното селско и работническо движение (повстаничество) в Украйна.

a very powerful (if amoebic) force, the Revolutionary-Insurgent Army of Ukraine, which was at that time fighting the Whites, the Reds and the Ukrainian Army. In the following month Makhno had Hryhoriiv executed when the latter proposed an alliance with the Whites.

With Hryhoriiv gone and Makhno temporarily on their side, some problems faced by the government in Moscow were solved. However, this would prove to be insufficient for Soviet Ukraine to withstand the next onslaught, which came from the Whites.

Meanwhile, in Belarus and Lithuania, Bolshevik progress was blocked by the Poles, and the putative Lithuanian–Belorussian Soviet Socialist Republic (Litbel) had to be disbanded. In Estonia the Soviet Estonian Red Army was defeated by a 75,000-strong nationalist force, based on Estonian divisions mustered in 1917. In Latvia more progress was made, supported by the Latvian Riflemen, who formed the spearhead of the Red advance. A Latvian Soviet Socialist Republic was proclaimed in January 1919. But, as in Ukraine, extremist Bolshevik tactics had negative results and the Soviet regime proved to be spectacularly unpopular. In response to local resistance, a wide-ranging campaign of repression against all enemies, real and perceived, was instituted. This contributed to a cooling of the Latvian Riflemen's ardour for Bolshevism. Faced by an unlikely combination of nationalist, White Russian and German forces (still lingering in the region as a bulwark against Bolshevism, in accordance with the terms of the Treaty of Versailles), the Latvian Soviet government was driven from Riga on 22 May 1919.

All this was symptomatic of a wider malaise. In general the national communist leaderships of the Soviet republics that were established, at Moscow's behest as the Red Army advanced, to coat the pill of Sovietisation with a sugary national façade, actually proved less flexible than Moscow in reaching accommodations with local nationalists, even those of a socialist stamp. They tended to regard merger with a larger state entity (Soviet Russia) as representing not a retrograde subjugation but a progressive internationalisation, thus abhorring the notion of national self-determination and strongly emphasising the merit of proletarian internationalism – which was not Lenin's line on the national question at the time.

White Defeat

The tenuous hold of the Soviet government on the periphery regions was revealed most glaringly during 1919, as the regions were overrun by the Whites. Kolchak's grandly named and 140,000-strong Russian army, consisting for the most part of unreliable peasant conscripts, advanced across the Urals in April 1919. It came within 30 miles of the Volga by May/June, before being repulsed and destroyed by December 1919. Its successors in the Far East, notably the afore mentioned Semenov's Far

on to Moscow

*On to Moscow, c.*1919.

This watercolour is unlikely to have served as propaganda, as it has a caption in English.

1856.g.8(56).

Eastern (White) Army, were first contained and then driven into China by late 1922. Denikin's 'Moscow Offensive', proclaimed in May 1919, saw the somewhat smaller but officer-heavy forces of the AFSR reach Orel – just 200 miles from Moscow – in mid-October, before a Red counter-attack drove them back to the North Caucasus and into the sea in March 1920.

General Iudenich's small North-West Army from Estonia reached the suburbs of Petrograd itself in mid-October – before the arrival of Red reinforcements drove them back into Estonia, where the nationalist government disarmed and interned them. Advances of the White Northern Army towards Petrozavodsk in May 1919 were almost entirely reliant upon Allied support, collapsing immediately once British and American forces evacuated the region in the autumn. None of this, of course, had prevented the ever-optimistic Whites from dreaming of hearing the Kremlin bells, and of clearing that and other symbolic sites of the Bolshevik 'rabble' and sending Lenin and his followers to hell in retribution for their defilement of Holy Russia (see poster on page 23).

The reasons for the White collapse have been widely debated and most versions contain at least a germ of truth. Their advances were uncoordinated and tended to be launched without sufficient preparation (particularly in the case of 'Supreme Ruler' Kolchak, who wished to impress the Allies and gain official recognition in order to win a seat at the ongoing Paris Peace Conference, where he feared that 'others are deciding upon our fate without us'). Moreover, local White commanders tended to ignore orders from the high commands, or in some cases even acted directly contrary to them. Many terrorised the local population, driving them into the arms of Red partisans. Furthermore, the Whites' nationalist outlook alienated the non-

Russians on whose territories they were based. Their politics, although far from being as reactionary as portrayed by the Bolsheviks and in many histories of the period, were muddled, and their promises of reform were not delivered. This in particular alienated the peasant population, who were generally opposed to Bolshevism and wished only to be confirmed in possession of the lands they had seized in 1917–1918.

The White leaders made inept and unwilling politicians – they favoured a policy of 'All for the Front', neglected the rear and disdained propaganda. With regard to the last, they never once attempted to capitalise on the distinctly non-elitist backgrounds of their leaders – Denikin was the son of a serf, for example, while Kolchak's father was an engineer – in order to counter Bolshevik portrayals of the Whites as a gang of debauched aristocrats. However, White propaganda efforts were severely undermined by a lack of resources, in contrast to the relative abundance of such material commanded by the Reds. The Reds' budget even stretched to the deployment of agitation trains and

(above) 1,000-rouble banknote, in circulation in territories under General Iudenich's control, 1919.

One of the security levels on Russian imperial banknotes was the use of signatures of bank managers and treasurers. Banknotes issued by the Field Treasury of the North-West Army's front were designed with Iudenich's signature and printed in Sweden. Convinced that their advance into Petrograd would be a success, the manifesto of the North-West government promised to exchange paper money for bills issued by the Central Petrograd Bank within three months after taking the city.

National Library of the Czech Republic – Slavonic Library, T-BAN 2-2- S 207.

(left) Map visualising the population's moods, presented by the Propaganda Department of General Command of the Armed Forces of South Russia, March 1919.

Blue indicates the territories where peasants supported the Bolsheviks; red indicates the territories where they were not welcome.

Add MS 54475 f. 142.

(below left) *Za edinuiu Rossiiu* (*For united Russia*), White propaganda poster, *c.*1918–20.

1856.g.8(19).

(below right) *Mir i svoboda v Sovdepii* (*Peace and freedom in Soviet Russia*), White propaganda poster, *c.*1918–20.

1856.g.2(46).

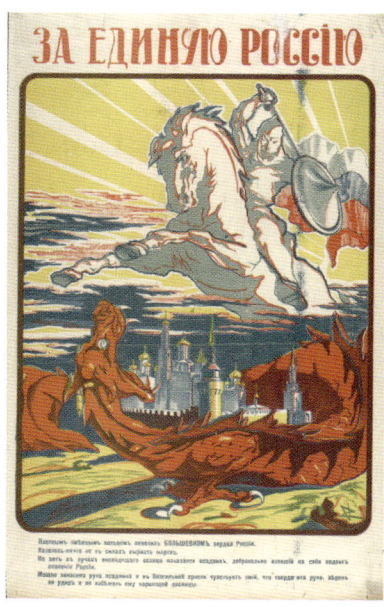

He explained that Osvag was the Information Bureau of the Department of Propaganda of the General Command of the Armed Forces of South Russia. 'Actually, you won't understand until you stay here for a while. Have you seen these strange pictures with didactic maxims about "great and united" and the generals' portraits with their quotes? This is what Osvag is.' ... In these pictures one could see the Moscow Kremlin lit with the rising sun, Trotsky as a devil, and a ginger Englishman, pulling behind himself a bunch of toy battleships and canons, saying: 'My Russian friends! I will give you all you need for victory!'

Georgii Villiam, journalist and writer, from his memoir The Defeated.[6]

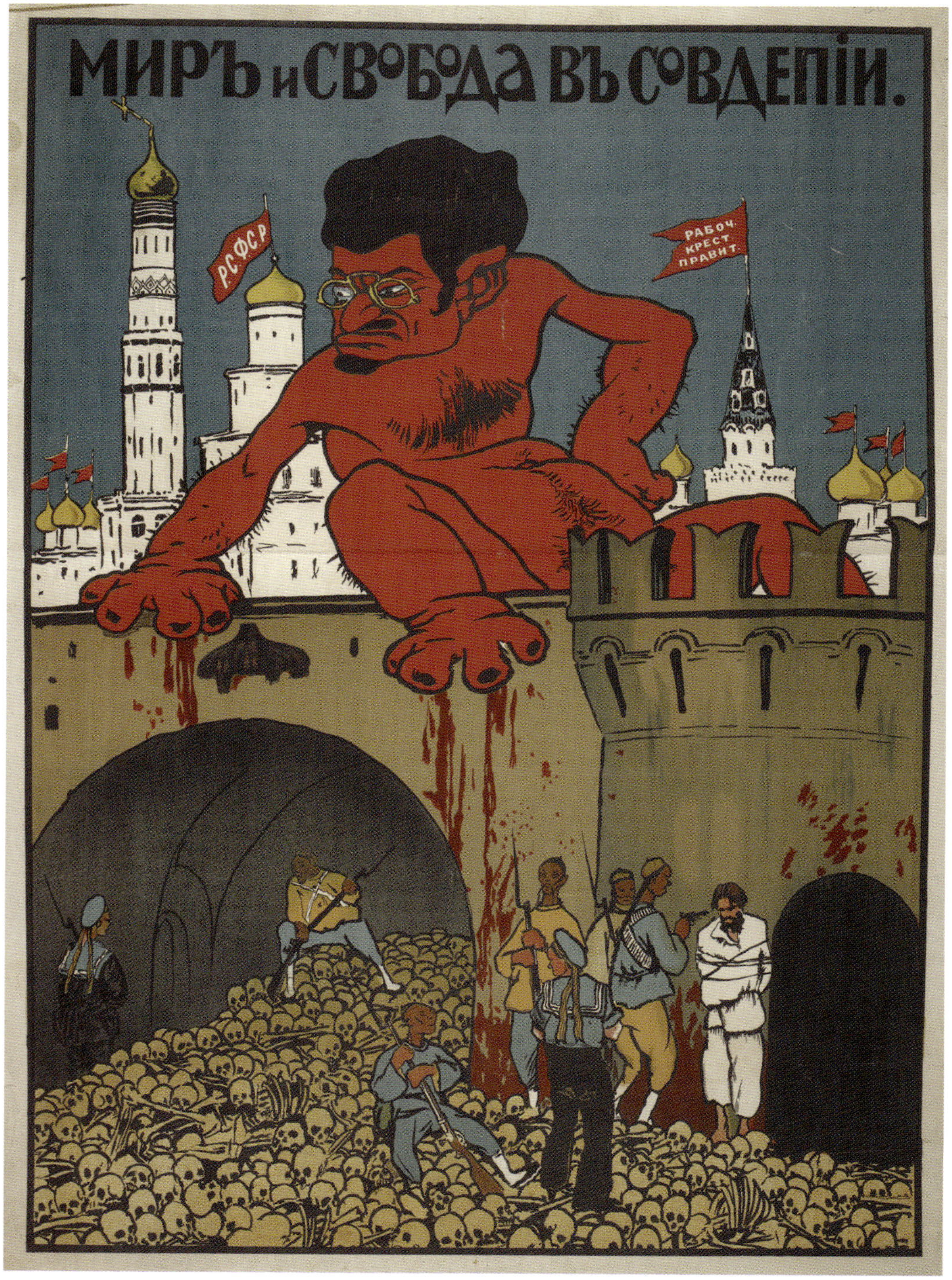

agitation barges – one of them commanded by Lenin's wife, Nadezhda Krupskaia – that toured the rivers and railways of the Soviet zone. Trotsky's own train not only provided a mobile base for the military command, but also housed a telegraph station, a radio station, an electricity-generating wagon, a printing house (with presses), a library, a secretariat wagon, and even a special wagon for transporting a collapsible small aircraft. As it spread the revolutionary word it made 36 visits to the front and travelled 75,000 miles in the course of the civil wars. For Trotsky, 'The Train', as it was known, was the cement that bound the Red fronts to the Red rear.

The Whites' base territories were economically underdeveloped, lacked communications networks and were sparsely populated. Their handling of the one industrial region that they held for more than a few months – the Urals – was so careless and disastrous that its governor sent a letter of resignation to Kolchak as early as March 1919, even as the admiral's armies were initiating what at first seemed to be a successful offensive across the Urals. The Whites were also overly reliant on foreign support, which was given only reluctantly. The Allies were suspicious of White politics, unsure whether the Whites' ambition to restore a 'Russia, One and Indivisible' was necessarily a good thing in the age of self-determination (although *Realpolitik* also played a part here, especially regarding Britain, who feared recreating its chief rival in Asia). They had myriad other concerns too, domestic and foreign, in the

Photograph of agitation train, *c.*1918–20. Special Collections, Leeds University Library, LRA Hayes MS 783/24–25.

aftermath of the First World War. The White leaders, stubbornly committed to just such a restoration, also tended to alienate potential allies among the new border states. This was best exemplified when General Denikin, upon entering Kiev in the summer of 1919, issued an address 'To the People of Little Russia' – the name for Ukraine preferred by Russian nationalists, but one regarded as an insult by many Ukrainians. Likewise, during his struggle, Denikin's efforts were constantly undermined by conflicts with putative non-Russian states in his rear.

This last point may have been critical. Had either Finland or Poland come to the Whites' aid, the outcome of the civil wars might have been very different. As it was, Admiral Kolchak refused to negotiate with either Helsinki or Warsaw over disputed territories and other issues. The Finnish regent, Gustav Mannerheim, withdrew his offer of May 1919 to capture Petrograd for the Whites, while the Polish leader, Józef Piłsudski, maintained an informal armistice with Moscow from mid-1919. Piłsudski breached this only in April 1920, once the AFSR had been disposed of by the Reds, thereby triggering the active stage of the Soviet–Polish War. General Wrangel then attempted to take advantage of that conflict to burst out of Crimea in July–August 1920, but the Bolsheviks, roundly beaten by the Poles, agreed an armistice with Warsaw in October. They promptly focused the now 5-million-strong Red Army on quashing the meagre 35,000 men that Wrangel (who had by now been abandoned by the Allies) had been able to mobilise. In November 1920 the Red Army drove the last Whites from Crimean ports into the sea.

Wars in the East

With the Whites mostly crushed and Allied forces withdrawn, from the spring of 1920 the Red Army could turn its attention to its remaining and less powerful enemies. In Transcaucasia the weak, and weakly led, army of the Democratic Republic of Azerbaijan (few Muslims had gained command experience in the Imperial Russian Army) was also engaged in a bloody conflict with Armenia over border regions. It was swept aside and an Azeri Soviet Socialist Republic proclaimed at Baku on 28 April 1920. Next the Democratic Republic of Armenia, struggling with terrifying refugee problems as a consequence of its ongoing war with Turkey, was subjugated in December 1920. Finally a Bolshevik coup was staged at Tiflis in February 1921 and the Democratic Republic of Georgia overthrown – although a series of rebellions (mostly coordinated by the Georgian government-in-exile) would challenge Soviet power in the country over the following years. This culminated in the August uprising of 1924, which saw at least 4,000 Georgians killed in three weeks of fighting. Subsequently around 10,000 nationalist prisoners were executed by the infamous Cheka, a Soviet state security organisation, with possibly as many as 20,000 deported.

I was visited by a relation of my wife's, a former officer, who said that he too wanted to take part in the defence of Petrograd. 'I must tell you straight,' he said, 'that by conviction I am a monarchist, but I can't let the Finns take Petrograd.' [The tsarist officer was duly assigned to a construction team.] The next time I saw him he literally roared with laughter. 'Do you know where you sent me?' he said. 'In that construction team we are all monarchists. I've fallen in with my own set, as it were.'

Aleksandr Il'in-Zhenevskii, a pro-Bolshevik officer, chess-player, memoir.[8]

(opposite) Recruitment poster in Russian, Arabic and two local languages (Circassian and Nogay), 1919.

This recruitment poster in four languages invites Caucasian Muslims to join voluntarily the Mountain-Muslim Cavalry Brigade under Colonel Pukovskii's command, which had become part of the Armed Forces of South Russia by 1920. Andrei (born Shir-Khan) Berlandnik-Pukovskii survived the war; from 1927 he lived in France where he died in 1964.

1856.g.8.(30).

Only the Amur and Maritime Provinces, in the Far East, were now outside Soviet control. Unwilling to challenge the 40,000 or so Japanese forces that remained in the region, Moscow decided to create a buffer state. At Blagoveshchensk on 6 April 1920 a nominally independent Far Eastern Republic (FER) was proclaimed. The FER had a coalition government, included SRs and Mensheviks in its administration, and possessed its own armed forces, the People's-Revolutionary Army, but its self-government proved a chimera. The FER was always and entirely controlled by Moscow through the Bolsheviks' Far Eastern Bureau, as was its army, into which were incorporated forces from the Red Army's recently disestablished Eastern Front. Still, the 'independence' of the FER was a useful fiction, as the Allies also sought to wash their hands of their former White protégés, now rendered embarrassing through failure.

In reality the Allies were starting, albeit uneasily, to normalise relations with this strange new regime in Moscow, and negotiations with the FER were sometimes used as a stepping-stone to that end. Even the Japanese signed a treaty with the FER in 1920, although at that point Tokyo refused to acknowledge its claim to sovereignty over Vladivostok and the nearby region, the Maritime Province. Over the next two years, however, the FER's forces drove back the remaining White formations in the region (while the Japanese gradually abandoned them). The FER also contrived to expand operations into Mongolia, where a pro-Soviet government was established in July 1921 and a Mongolian People's Republic proclaimed in November 1924. When in October 1922 the Japanese evacuated Vladivostok, the White regime there – under the reactionary, monarchist and antisemitic General Diterikhs – collapsed, and its forces fled into in China. Some isolated pockets of resistance remained, notably at Iakutsk, where a small White force held out until April 1923, but with Vladivostok and the Pacific coast in Red hands, the struggle of Red against White had essentially reached an end. Consequently in 1922 the FER petitioned for union with the Russian Soviet Federative Socialist Republic – a request immediately granted by Moscow – thereby extending Soviet power to the Pacific coast. Meanwhile, the Red Army celebrated its fifth anniversary.

As Kolchak's Eastern Front collapsed in late 1919, thereby allowing the Red Army access to Central Asia, Soviet power was soon firmly established in the ancient cities of Khiva, Bukhara and Tashkent. However, across the vast expanse of Central Asia it was far from secure. Hiding out across the region (and sometimes over the borders in Persia and Afghanistan), were relatively small but seemingly inexterminable groups of guerrilla fighters, whom the Soviet government termed *Basmachi* ('raiders'). The Reds' battle with these Muslim rebels, previously much neglected by historians, came under renewed scholarly attention in the West after the Soviet invasion of Afghanistan in 1979 provoked new generations of anti-Communist Muslim guerrillas into action. Although evolving through a series of relatively distinct chronological phases and played out in one of the most remote reaches of the former imperial space, and although the Muslim rebels were prone to internecine vendettas and rarely united in purpose, the Reds' struggles against the Basmachi were an integral part of the 'Russian' civil wars. As one pioneering study of the phenomenon concluded, 'In the history of the Turkestan's war of liberation, the Basmachi must be seen not only as a mere uprising but as an armed *civil war* against Soviet supremacy'.[7]

Even as the 1916 revolt in Central Asia can be regarded as the opening stage of the 'Russian' civil wars, the Red Army's battles against the Basmachi can be regarded as their conclusion. During these last battles of the conflict, which ranged long after the usual dates suggested as an endpoint in 1921 or 1922, it is thought that over half a million Red soldiers were killed, compared to rebel losses of around 50,000. Famine and disease accounted for several hundred thousand further deaths across Central Asia. The struggle only came to an unquiet end in June 1931, with the Reds' capture and execution of the Basmachi leader Ibrahim-bek, although small pockets of resistance held out until at least 1934, and possibly beyond that. However, from the mid-1920s Soviet forces had been engaged in only relatively minor security operations. These were skirmishes, police actions and border-control events, not warfare. Significantly, the last active civil-war front of the Red Army to be closed was the Turkestan Front – on 4 June 1926. It was replaced by the peacetime administration of the Central Asian Military District. This can, therefore, best serve as the terminal date of the 'Russian' civil wars – albeit in a region that is considerably closer to Mumbai than it is to Moscow.

The Red Army

The reasons for the 'Red Victory' largely mirror the reasons for the White defeat cited above. The Reds had more unity of purpose in their drive to build socialism, as well as the will and the means to deliver it both at home and abroad. Their base territory was better supplied with communications (the telegraph system, railways, canals and rivers), facilitating the movement of men and weaponry from one front to another. 'Sovdepiia', as the Whites called it (literally 'the Land of the [Workers' and Peasants'] Deputies') was relatively well developed economically and, vitally, housed most of the resources of the former Imperial Russian Army and government from arsenals to artists, secretaries to doctors and vets. The Reds' base was also more populous. Despite losing vast peripheral regions in 1918, the Soviet government retained 30 provinces of European Russia,

which, with a population of some 60 million, made it the largest state in Europe even when at its most embattled and restricted.

Key to their success, however, was the creation of the Red Army. This was remarkable as, like most socialists, the Bolsheviks generally despised militarism and regarded the standing army as the chief instrument of state oppression of the working class. For them, especially the left Bolsheviks, one of the essential purposes of the revolution was to destroy the army and to replace it with a democratic militia system. In line with this, the Soviet government had issued an avalanche of decrees cancelling all ranks and titles, permitting the election of officers, expanding the competences of soldiers' committees and ordering the demobilisation of successive classes of conscripts. All this culminated in the order for a general demobilisation of the old army in January 1918. However, the disintegration of the old army did not necessarily imply the creation of a new one.

As advocates of the untapped potential for revolutionary creativity of the proletariat, the left Bolsheviks further considered that any subsequent conflict, either domestic or international, would be conducted according to quite different principles of organisation and strategy – a concept they dubbed 'revolutionary war'. This system would rely on the unstoppable and incorruptible élan of the workers-in-arms, rather than military training or experience. However, the militia system failed at the first hurdle. During the German invasion of Soviet territory in February 1918, occasioned by the initial reluctance to accept the peace terms tabled at Brest-Litovsk, it had been expected that at least 300,000 recruits would come forward for this partisan army. In the event, only around 20,000 were mustered.

This had an immediate impact upon Trotsky, who became the people's commissar for military affairs on 14 March 1918. Dedication to order, routine, hierarchy and discipline were central to his character and style as a revolutionary, and he soon began to impose such maxims on the Red military. Within a week of becoming war commissar, he was telling the Moscow Soviet 'Comrades! Our Soviet Socialist Republic needs a well-organised army'. But how was such an army to be organised and led? Certainly, as Trotsky knew, such a task would be beyond his own capabilities.

In a leap of faith that must be regarded as a key moment in the civil wars, Trotsky grasped the nettle. In his address to a Moscow city conference of the party on 28 March 1918, he focused on what he termed the 'sore point' in ongoing party discussions that, for him, had to be at the heart of the new army: 'the question of drawing military specialists (*voenspetsy*), that is, to speak plainly, former officers and generals, into the work of creating and administering the army'. Within a few weeks, more than 8,000 *voenspetsy* had joined the Red Army – either willingly, as Bolshevik sympathisers, or because their families

Zapis' v Krasnuiu Armiiu (*The Red Army Enrolment*), poster, *c.*1918.

The visual message of the poster is supported by a poem that describes how a *kulak* (wealthy peasant) laments that he had to give away two rifles (hidden under a mattress 'just in case') and a horse.

Cup.645.a.6.

were being held hostage, or in the mistaken belief that the Soviet government might re-enter the war against the Central Powers.

By the end of 1918, 30,000 *voenspetsy* were employed, a disproportionate number being *genshtabisty* (graduates of the imperial Academy of the General Staff). Debates around this issue would become particularly vitriolic at the Eighth Congress of the Bolshevik Party in March 1919, where concessions had to be made to Trotsky's opponents in order to defuse a sizeable 'military opposition' within the RKP(b) – the Russian Communist Party (Bolsheviks), as Lenin's party was then called. This loosely organised group was demanding that military commissars (usually party members) be afforded greater decision-making within the army. They wanted party institutions to assume a larger role in directing a Red Army that was increasingly being commanded by former tsarist officers and manned by conscripted peasants who, according to the Bolsheviks, were innately hostile to socialism.

Although it was claimed at the time, by Trotsky, that only 5 out of 82 *voenspetsy* army commanders ever deserted, a more recent investigation of materials in the Russian archives has established that some 549 highly valued *genshtabisty* deserted from the Red Army in the period 1918–1921 and that, in total, almost one in three *voenspetsy* managed to flee to the enemy. Yet, despite this debilitating and dangerous haemorrhage, and despite the lingering qualms of the leftists, at least the principle of utilising officers and experts had been firmly established. With the civil wars winding down after 1920, the majority of officers in the Red Army (including 613 *genshtabisty*) remained at their posts before being shifted from command posts into teaching, as a new network of Red Army military academies was producing more Red commanders.

Left Bolshevik irritations were at least partly salved by a second, truly revolutionary aspect of the new army – the appointment of the above-mentioned military commissars to all units. This was the second great innovation of the Bolsheviks in military affairs. According to an order signed by Trotsky:

> The military commissar is the direct political organ of Soviet power in the army ... The commissar takes part in all the work of the military leaders, receives reports and dispatches along with them and counter-signs orders. War Councils will give effect only to such orders as have been signed not only by military leaders but also by at least one military commissar.[9]

Both the relative rarity of desertions by the *voenspetsy* and the motivational advantage of Red forces over their opponents (especially the Whites) can be attributed in no small part to the commissars' efforts. These efforts were redoubled as Trotsky made clear to the commissars that they would be held personally responsible for any acts of collective insubordination, cowardice or desertion in the Red Army, and that the sentence would be death, with no right of appeal.

Soviet propaganda could turn military figures into a legendary hero. Vasilii Chapaev was a Red Army commander who died in a battle in September 1919. His fictionalised biography was written after the war by Dmitrii Furmanov, a young journalist and writer who served as military commissar in Chapaev's brigade. The biography was made into the film *Chapaev*, which Stalin apparently watched over 30 times within the first two years of its release in 1934. A lot of USSR citizens also watched the film repeatedly. It played an important role in the mythmaking process, helping to shape the new Soviet identity at a time when the cult of the 'Civil War' was created in the Soviet Union. In the notes for the book Furmanov wrote:

> In the whole area, one can hear about Chapaev and his glorious unit. They call him simply – Chapai. This word terrifies the Whites ... His personality is quite legendary. Chapai is very independent, he hates any kind of planning, combinations, strategy and all sorts of other 'art of war wisdom'. He has only one strategy – a flaming and mighty blow ... He is not very politically conscious. He has an intuitive feeling that he has to fight to protect the poor, but doesn't go further than that.[10]

Leftists within the Bolshevik Party would have been, at least initially, less sanguine about another of Trotsky's initiatives – the Red Cavalry. As a symbolic and aristocratic bastion of the old regime, the cavalry was regarded as a likely nest of

Photograph from *Pervaia Konnaia: albom (First Cavalry Army: An Album)*, designed by A. Rodchenko and V. Stepanova, Moscow, 1938.

The *tachanka* – a cart with a heavy machine gun installed in the back – became a symbol of the Russian civil war. It was primarily used in the western territories, and became an important feature of the Makhno army and of both sides in the Soviet–Polish war.

L.R.276.c.5.

Весной 1920 г. Конная Армия начала свой исторический переход на польский фронт.

counter-revolutionaries. Moreover, the Bolshevik leadership was modernist to a man when it came to matters of engineering and technology; they regarded the horseman as obsolete in the dawning age of tanks, armoured trains and aerial warfare. Despite such views, the major raids that Denikin's cavalry and other White forces had conducted suggested there might still be a place for them in combat. Consequently, in October 1919, Trotsky gave the order 'Proletarians to Horse!' and soon was born the 15,000-strong 1st Red Cavalry Army under the ruthless Semen Budennyi.

However, the Red cavalrymen tended not to be proletarians at all. They were mostly radicalised Cossacks who, beneath their Bolshevised exterior, brought with them into their service many traditional Cossack tropes – not least a vehement strain of antisemitism that was unleashed against the Jews of eastern Poland during the Soviet–Polish War of summer 1920. The horrors faced by the Jews in that region were captured in the story cycle *Red Cavalry*, authored by the Bolshevik journalist (and Jew) Isaac Babel. Red Army commander Budennyi condemned Babel as 'a literary degenerate', but he was not punished immediately – he died in the Stalin purges in 1940, having been accused of being a Trotskyist and foreign spy.

In 1919 at least 50,000 and possibly as many as 200,000 Jews were slaughtered in the region, with the worst perpetrators being the Ukrainian Army of the UNR. But while the Red Cavalry was not the worst of the many agents of pogroms in this brutal war, the disorder and indiscipline engendered by such activities weakened it sufficiently for it to be routed by Polish forces between 30 August and 2 September 1920 at the Battle of Komarovo (Komarów). The greatest cavalry battle since the Napoleonic era, it was the last significant cavalry battle of the twentieth century.

Nevertheless the Red Cavalry remained one of the most lauded of all Red formations of the civil wars. Its commander, Budennyi, was one of the few Red heroes of the civil wars who did not to fall victim to Stalin's purges of the 1930s. He evolved into a folklorish figure in the USSR – a decorative accoutrement and counterpoint to the grey men of the post-war Soviet leadership, and something of a museum piece. Present at all important military parades and state occassions, bedecked with magnificent moustache, medals and orders, Budennyi became a living relic of the heroic days of the civil wars until his death in 1973.

After a series of rather unsuccessful experiments in army administration in the first half of 1918, a permanent and winning structure for the Red Army was eventually reached. On 6 September 1918 the Supreme Military Council of the Republic (RVSR or *Revvoensovet*), chaired by Trotsky, was established. The Army was divided into five armies, each with eleven divisions of

It so chanced that I was billeted in the house of a red-haired widow who smelled of grief and widowhood ... Right under my window some Cossacks were trying to shoot an old silvery-bearded Jew for spying. The old man was uttering piercing screams and struggling to get away. Then Kudrya of the machine gun section took hold of his head and tucked it under his arm. The Jew stopped screaming and straddled his legs. Kudrya drew out his dagger with his right hand and carefully, without splashing himself, cut the old man's throat...

Isaac Babel, diary.[11]

(above) Isaac Babel, *Rudá jízda (Red Cavalry)*, Prague, 1928. Cover designed by Czech avant-garde artist Karel Teige.

The first stories from Babel's book *Red Cavalry* were published in magazines in 1923–24. Red Army high command claimed the stories were nothing but slander. The last edition of *Red Cavalry* in Babel's lifetime appeared in 1933. Banned in the Soviet Union until Babel's rehabilitation in the 1950s, the book has been translated into more than 20 languages, one of the earliest being Czech.

YA.1999.a.3948.

(opposite) Photographs and collages from *Pervaia Konnaia: albom (First Cavalry Army: An Album)*, designed by A. Rodchenko and V. Stepanova, Moscow, 1938.

Leading constructivist artists Rodchenko and Stepanova designed the album *The First Cavalry Army* for the 20th anniversary of the Red Army. The first luxury edition is now extremely rare. Containing images and citations of Bolshevik leaders that were proclaimed enemies of the people, copies were almost immediately destroyed or mutilated. In the second edition, published several months later, the 'enemies' had vanished. Budennyi appears in several photographs in the album. The photograph of his mother (bottom left) is the only portrait of a civilian in the book.

L.R.276.c.5.

between six and nine regiments (plus reserve units); these were grouped around three fronts (the Northern Front, the Eastern Front and the Southern Front), and the Western Fortified Area. The coordinating organs of the Red Army were then topped-off, with the formation of the Council of Workers' and Peasants' Defence, chaired (*ex officio*) by Lenin.

The directives of the Council of Defence were considered to be the equivalent of state laws. The Council played no part in the formation of military strategy, but sought instead to direct and coordinate the work of all government bodies and institutions with a stake in the defence of Soviet Russia. In the circumstances of a confusion of civil wars, it managed that task with relative success (certainly the scattered Whites were never able to create anything remotely similar in their zones). Thus the structure of the Red Army that would eventually emerge victorious from the wars was essentially in place before the end of the first year of serious conflict.

From May 1918, the nascent Red Army could also begin to draw upon a steadier stream of recruits, as a general mobilisation was instituted, stretching even into the Muslim lands of the North Caucasus. The volunteer principle was abandoned, although the registration of those eligible was rudimentary and the non-appearance and desertion of mobilised men remained a problem. By late 1918 the Red Army was still a long way from resolving this issue, but was much closer to doing so than its rivals. Signs were becoming apparent that a solution acceptable to both sides of this bargaining process – the citizens and the state – was achievable.

A recent investigation concludes that retention rates were significantly improving in the Red Army over 1918–1919. In July 1918 a decree was passed that linked citizenship to military service and obliged all healthy men aged 18–40 years to come forward. The Bolsheviks managed to created a system in which soldiers acquired rights when they performed their national duty. In particular, they were assured that their families would be cared for and that they, as soldiers, would be respected by the state and would acquire privileges above those granted to other citizens.

Tied to this, though, was a degree of flexibility in the approach of the state. The Red Army could, of course, unleash Terror against those who deserted, and by April 1919 its Anti-Desertion Commission had established numerous branches at local level. However, commanders actually used a 'two-pronged' approach to desertion by, for example, offering short amnesties for absentees who voluntarily returned to their units. This was accompanied by a nationwide propaganda campaign to convince shirkers and deserters that they could not hide and would be punished, while the Red Army Central Desertion Commission urged that repression be mixed with 'proof of concern for the families of Red Army soldiers'.

ПЕРВАЯ КОННАЯ

Мать первого командарма Красной конницы Меланин Никитична Буденная.

I. V. Stalin nad frontakh grazhdanskoi voiny, 1918–1920 (Stalin at the fronts of the civil war, 1918–1920), 1940.

In his role as member of the All-Russian Central Executive Committee, during the war years, Stalin visited most of the major fronts. At various points he was responsible for food supply in the south of Russia, and was involved in the defence of Petrograd and the Soviet–Polish war. In some cases his decisions had disastrous consequences for military operations, but once he became incontestable leader of the party and state, his participation in the civil wars was turned into a triumph that he delivered almost single-handedly. This propaganda map visualises the legend.

Maps CC.6.a.80.

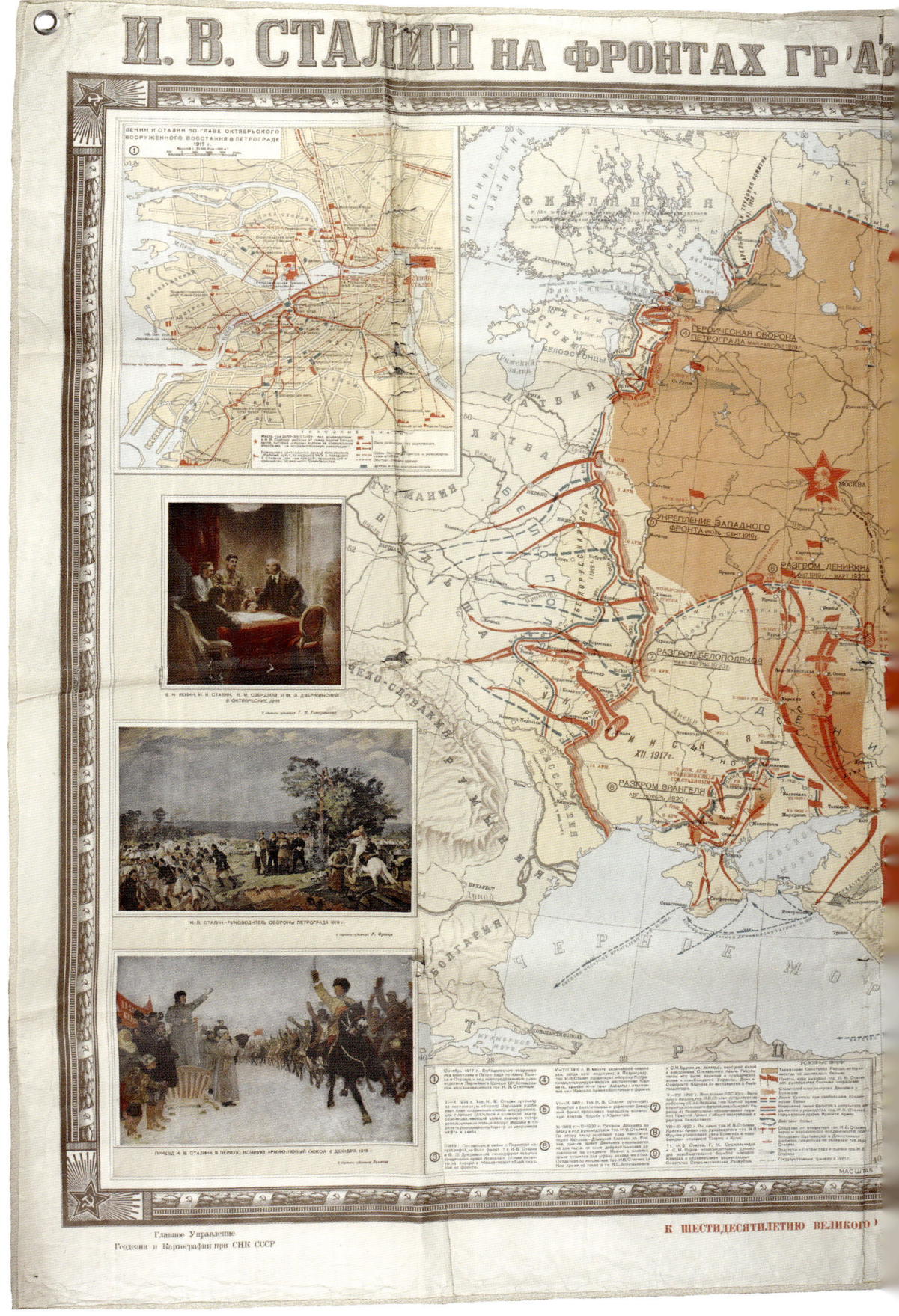

Finally, an intensive and extensive 'verification' campaign throughout 1919 seems to have been particularly effective. During the campaign all men of draft age in the Soviet zone were required to attend meetings at which their eligibility for military service would be checked. Of course, given the ongoing chaos, this was never applied universally, but in the second half of 1919 over 2 million men attended such meetings and 272,211 of them were then enrolled in the armed forces. Kitted out in their distinctive *budenovka* hats (named after Budennyi), they were dispatched to their units.

(opposite) Draft note by Trotsky on the organisation of the Red Army, with annotations by Lenin (?), March 1918.

In this note Trotsky asks if questions relating to the creation of the Red Army and related legislation – such as compulsory universal military training for men between eighteen and forty, the establishment of local military administrative units, and the approval of salaries for professional staff – could be included in the agenda for the next government meeting. The comment below agrees that this should be done. It is highly probable that the pencil comments are by Lenin. The PS comment says that the 'Left' (Left SRs in the Soviet government in early 1918) 'quite rightly' stress the class nature of the new army and insist on (a) isolating the 'rich' from all military activities and (b) replacing all ranks, including top commanders, with proletarians. This demonstrates that there was little unity in the cabinet on the question of the creation of the army.

Special Collections, Leeds University Library, LRA Ransome 2/B/50.

(left) *Budenovka*, Red Army uniform hat, 1918 to mid-1930s.

The design for the Red army uniform was selected in a competition announced by the Soviet government in 1918. The shape of the *budenovka* hats (named after Budennyi) is based on old Slavonic helmets as depicted in 19th-century Russian art.

Polish Army Museum.

By August 1920, a further 470,106 men were recruited by this means. Certainly the White forces never came close to emulating this, although their failure to do so had as much to do with a lack of administrative resources in the peripheral areas in which they operated as ignorance of the importance of such systems of social control. On the Red side, the results were clear – a Red Army consisting of 800,000 men in January 1919 would in a year's time become one of 3 million. This was ten times larger than the White and nationalist forces ranged against Soviet Russia (if the Polish and Finnish armies are excluded). In such figures, the basic cause of the 'Red Victory' is laid bare.

Beyond The Civil Wars

On the face of things, then, the Bolsheviks were the clear victors of the 'Russian' civil wars. They had been able to see off, one by one, their White enemies in Siberia and South, North-West and North Russia; they had been able to convince the Allies that armed intervention in Soviet Russia was a lost cause; and, with the Anglo–Soviet Trade Agreement of 1921, they had begun to normalise relations with the capitalist world. The series of peasant uprisings against Soviet power that were a feature of the years 1920–1921 had been successfully quelled, sometimes through the deployment of tanks, aircraft and poison gas against the rebel villagers; and the uprising in favour of 'Soviets without Communists' staged by the sailors of the Baltic fleet in March 1921 (the Kronstadt rebellion) had been dealt with swiftly and mercilessly. Thereafter, through the introduction of the New

Today the Red Army in Simbirsk is celebrating its anniversary. Last night, soldiers wandered about the city and tried to distribute some paper red stars, asking to 'donate to the Red Army'. A young pretty soldier approached me and I gave him one rouble. He attempted to give me a star. 'What do I do with it, my dear?' – I asked. 'Whatever,' – he answered. I took his star and shovelled into the purse. How mean is it to make soldiers beg! I watched them beg last night – nobody gave them anything. Poor soldiers!

Alexander Zhirkevich, 61, lawyer, poet and journalist, diary entry, 23 February 1919.[12]

Economic Policy (NEP) in 1921, which entailed legalising private trade and replacing the requisitioning of foodstuffs from the countryside with a progressive tax in kind, the Soviet government had brought (or bought) an end to peasant resistance. The Red Army had – piecemeal, and when the time was ripe – reconquered Ukraine, Transcaucasia, the Far East and Central Asia. The USSR had become an established state, which from 1924 was recognised by other world powers, and which would have a profound influence on international affairs for decades to come.

Nevertheless, several qualifications have to be made when describing the Bolsheviks as 'victors' in the civil wars. For one thing, some important territories of the former Russian Empire remained outside the Soviet imperium at the close of the wars – notably the strategically and economically important lands of independent Finland, the Baltic states and Poland, while grain-rich Bessarabia had been incorporated into Romania.

Secondly, although peasant resistance to Soviet power had been broken and its recrudescence in armed form contained by the NEP, it had not altogether been extinguished and would resurface in what amounted to an economic war between the hungry cities and relatively prosperous villages of the USSR in the mid-to-late 1920s. Lenin was therefore right to have termed NEP a 'peasant Brest' – just as the treaty of 1918 had not brought (and was never intended to bring) a permanent peace between Soviet Russia and imperial Germany, NEP was regarded by most Bolsheviks as a temporary breathing space. Once the civil wars were finally over in 1926, the Soviet state, increasingly under the sway of Stalin, would again turn on the peasants in the collectivisation campaign that was intended finally to extend Soviet rule into the countryside and to break peasant resistance forever. Indeed, a case can be made for regarding the collectivisation campaign of 1928–1932 as a second round of the civil wars.

Thirdly, although the Allies had withdrawn from Soviet Russia, they would welcome their former enemy into the League of Nations in 1934 and were grateful for the Soviet contribution to the subsequent struggle against Hitler. The enmity between East and West that would characterise the post-1945 period was demonstrably born in the period immediately following the October revolution of 1917. Thus, the 'Russian' civil wars continued to shape the Soviet Union's internal and international policies years after they officially finished and, it can be argued, their profound impact can be traced in our modern world.

NOTES

1. Nikolai Raevskii, 'Dnevnik gallipoliitsa', in *Prostor* (Alma-Ata), nos 1–2, 2002. Quoted from: http://prozhito.org/person/58. Access date: 22 October 2016.

2. Edward Dennis Sokol, *The Revolt of 1916 in Russian Central Asia*. Baltimore: John Hopkins Press, 1954.

3. F. I. Golikov, *Krasnye orly (iz dnevnikov 1981–1920 gg.)*. Moscow: Voeizdat, 1956. Quoted from: http://prozhito.org/person/28. Access date: 22 October 2016.

4. V. I. Lenin, *The Russian Revolution and Civil War*. Quoted from Lenin's *Collected Works*, vol. 26. Progress Publishers: 1972.

5. L. D. Trotsky, *My Life: The Rise and Fall of a Dictator*. London: Thornton Butterworth, 1930.

6. G. Villiam, *Pobezhdennye*. Berlin: 1922.

7. Baymirza Hayit, *Turkestan im XX Jahrhundert*. Darmstadt: Leske, 1956.

8. A. F. Ilyin-Zhenevsky, *The Bolsheviks in Power: Reminiscences of the Year 1918*. London: New Park Publications, 1984.

9. Jonathan Smele, *Historical Dictionary of Russian Civil Wars, 1916–1926*, in 2 vols. Rowman & Littlefield: 2015.

10. D.A. Furmanov, *Sobranie sochinenii v chetyrekh tomakh. Tom 4. Dnevniki. Literaturnye zapisi. Pis'ma*. Moscow: 1961. Quoted from: http://prozhito.org/person/82. Access date: 22 October 2016.

11. Isaac Babel, *1920 Diary*, trans by H. T. Willetts, ed by Carol J. Avins. New Haven: Yale University Press, 1995.

12. A. V. Zhirkevich, *Potrevozhennye teni ... Simbirskii dnevnik*. Moscow: Eterna-print, 2007. Quoted from: http://prozhito.org/person/34. Access date 22 October 2016.

КАК ИЗ ХЛЕБА

4 The New World is Born

Ekaterina Rogatchevskaia

Will the Bolsheviks Maintain Power?

The struggle for the new Soviet government started in Petrograd, against a backdrop of chaos and confusion across the country. Four million inhabitants of Petrograd and Moscow tried to make sense of the shooting in the street. The Moscow-based 34-year-old avant-garde theatre director Yevgeny Vakhtangov recorded the confusion in his diary:

> Shooting started in Moscow on 27 October ... We hear guns, pistols and cannons. We have not been out for two days. No bread delivery today. We eat what is left. At night we block the windows, so that light cannot be seen from outside. No newspapers. We don't know who is shooting at whom. We cannot make outgoing telephone calls, and those who call us know nothing either. It is not clear who is winning: the Bolsheviks or the government troops. Trams don't work. We still have water and electricity supply. When will it finish?[3]

Meanwhile, 22 million urban citizens all over the country were waiting for newspapers from the capital, and 7.5 million people at the front lines and military districts located in the rear were struggling to understand contradicting wires. The rest – over 130 million people in rural areas – were entirely unaware of developments happening miles away from their homes.

The Second All-Russian Congress of Soviets of Workers' and Soldiers' Deputies, where the Bolsheviks formed the majority, opened as the October uprising was unfolding. After the fall of the Provisional Government in the early hours of 8 November (26 October) 1917 it became the supreme governing body, and ratified the revolutionary transfer of state power. In his *History of the Russian Revolution*, Trotsky wrote:

> The outward appearance of the Congress proclaimed its make-up. The officers' chevrons, the eye-glasses and

In the newspaper 'The Russian Word', I saw a prayer about us, Russians, which was being read in English churches on command of their senior clerics. The prayer is very touching. But I was reading it with tears in my eyes, tears of sadness and shame: they pray for us as if we were dead, as if we were some barbarians who had forgotten God, Jesus Christ, conscience, and all moral norms.

Alexander Zhirkevich, 59, lawyer, poet and journalist, diary entry, 6 November (24 October) 1917.[1]

On Friday, everybody in our *gymnasium* was talking about the strike, and there were very few students there. I went to school, but the porter told me that there were no classes.

Kira Allendorf, 12, schoolgirl, diary entry, 12 November (30 October), 1917.[2]

neckties of intellectuals to be seen at the first Congress had almost completely disappeared. A grey colour prevailed uninterruptedly, in costumes and in faces. All had worn out their clothes during the war. Many of the city workers had provided themselves with soldiers' coats. The trench delegates were by no means a pretty picture: long unshaven, in old torn trench-coats, with heavy *papakhi* on their dishevelled hair, often with cotton sticking out through a hole, with coarse weather-beaten faces, heavy cracked hands, fingers yellowed with tobacco, buttons torn off, belts hanging loose, and long unoiled boots wrinkled and rusty.[4]

The immediate aim of the Congress was to elect the new government and the All-Russian Central Executive Committee that would act between congresses. The Central Executive Committee was composed of 62 Bolsheviks, 29 Socialist Revolutionaries (SRs) and 10 Mensheviks, which roughly mirrored the representation of these parties at the Congress. Although change of power did not surprise anyone, and Lenin and his party had been actively preparing for it, there was little

Vladimir Serov, *Lenin provozglashaet Sovetskuiu vlast'* (*Lenin is Proclaiming the Soviet Power at the Second Congress of Soviet*), 1947 (left) and 1962 (right).

The first painting was created for the 30th anniversary of the revolution. Stalin and two other Bolsheviks (Dzerzhinsky and Sverdlov) are behind Lenin. The painting was presented to Mao Zedong. Its whereabouts is now unknown, but the image remains on postcards and stamps. During the short period of de-Stalinization under Nikita Khrushchev, the artist re-painted the work, removing Stalin, Dzerzhinsky and Sverdlov. Two copies of the second variant (dating from 1955 and 1962) are known – one is at the Tretyakov Gallery, Moscow, and the other was sold at auction in London in 2014.

agreement even among the Bolsheviks on how they could secure their political survival. Yet the implementation of Lenin's idea of party-building with its strict hierarchy and discipline allowed the Bolsheviks to look (if not to be) more organised and decisive than the more moderate socialists, who left the Congress in protest at the Bolshevik-dominated Presidium.

Although in the cause of the Congress the left-wing Socialist Revolutionaries were the Bolsheviks' allies, they refused to form the first revolutionary government together, and thus the first government became a one-party cabinet. As the word 'minister' sounded too bourgeois, the term 'commissar' (derived from the word 'commission') was adopted. The Council of People's Commissars (*Sovnarkom*) was given a mandate to execute power until the All-Russia Constituent Assembly – a democratically elected body to decide the form and system of government in Russia and give it a new constitution – was appointed.

In her memoirs *Lenin in Sovnarkom in 1917* Elizaveta Koksharova, a secretary of the first Bolshevik government, gives a colourful reminiscence of the early days of the new power:

> For quite some time two machine guns guarded by soldiers were placed at the Secretariat window. Red Guards always stayed on duty at the door to Vladimir Ilich's office. Later the Latvian Riflemen replaced them. It was a disquieting time: not once did counter-revolutionaries plot an attack on Smolnyi ... Vladimir Ilich very carefully managed his time, and therefore demanded strict time-management from all members of *Sovnarkom* ... On 29 December 1917 *Sovnarkom* set up a fine for late-comers: 5 roubles for coming half an hour late and 10 roubles thereafter.[5]

To provide some context for the policy of fines introduced by *Sovnarkom*, in December 1917 white flour cost 150 roubles per

The first Council of People's Commissars, 1917.

In the centre of the photograph is Alexandra Kollontai, the first woman to hold a ministerial post. As Soviet Ambassador to Norway, she was also one of the first female diplomats. She was the author of articles and fiction focused on a 'new woman' character, devoted to her class and not restricted by the ties of marriage. On Kollontai's left is Koksharova, author of the book *Lenin in Sovnarkom*, published in 1917.

(opposite) *V bor'be obretesh' ty pravo svoe* (*Through Struggle You Will Attain Your Rights!*), Socialist Revolutionary election poster, 1917.

The name of the Socialist Revolutionary Party is written in art nouveau style letters at the top of the poster. A soldier and a labourer beckon crowds of workers and peasants to leave their factories and villages, and experience for themselves the promised land. The text on the globe reads: 'Land and Liberty'. The Constituent Assembly election campaign produced very few examples of powerful political art. Election materials were poorly produced and visually boring; limited access to printing facilities did not help. Images created in the style of illustrated magazines and advertising had very little connection with the revolutionary impulse and did not convey the notion of entering a new era.

Private collection.

pood (16.3 kg), rye bread cost 2 roubles 50 kopeks per pound (409.5 g), a basic pair of boots cost 100–150 roubles, and a bottle of vodka cost 50–60 roubles.

Although the Bolsheviks had to take into account the existence of other parties, their desire to rule alone was quite obvious to all involved in the political process. Many scholars agree that, at the same time, the contradictory responses to the October uprising were determined by the complex contradictions among the Bolsheviks themselves. Lieutenant-General Budberg, later a White Army officer, wrote in his diary on 19 (6) November:

> [Today] I received a whole bunch of decrees, produced by the Bolshevik government. They are very attractive to the masses ... The wording and the decisiveness of the decrees, that are supposed to cut the most tangled knots of social and political life, give an impression that it was done by a crowd of barbarians, who managed to get possession of some previously unseen objects and tried using them in their barbarian manner.[7]

The first Soviet laws – such as decrees on the Land, Peace, an Eight-Hour Working Day, Abolition of Classes and Civil Ranks, insurance for the sick and unemployed, and on civil status (which significantly simplified the divorce procedure) – were issued in parallel with decrees on Press, the Arrest of Leaders of the Civil War Against the Revolution, and state monopoly on newspaper advertising that restricted various forms of freedom.

The Constituent Assembly elections took place on 25 (12) November 1917, as had been planned by the Provisional Government. This was two months after they were originally meant to occur. The next day, Moscow governor Vladimir Golitsyn wrote: 'I looked through the papers, played with the grandchildren, but I kept feeling terribly upset and tormented ... Our only hope now is the favourable outcome of the Constituent Assembly elections that took place yesterday. But will the present rulers obey the voice of the people?'[8]

It is likely that Lenin and other leading Bolsheviks were not quite clear whether the Constituent Assembly could help them to compete for overall control. In their view, however, the inability of the Provisional Government to call the elections justified their seizure of power. Having initially supported the idea of the All-Russia Constituent Assembly, in the course of 1917 the Bolsheviks and other socialists started accusing the Provisional Government of deliberate delays in conveying the Assembly. One of the reasons for dismissing the government, as they presented it, was to take the initiative and deliver what the Provisional Government, apparently, had failed to deliver. Thus revocation of elections would be a U-turn that was far too risky. With the turnout of just under 50 per cent of the population, the

elections yielded a convincing victory for the socialists and
a spectacular defeat of the liberal Kadets, who polled less than
5 per cent. The Bolsheviks' share in the national poll was less
than 25 per cent.

The Bolsheviks did well in large industrial cities and received
support from sailors of the Baltic fleet and soldiers of the
Northern and Western fronts, but they were defeated in the rural
areas by the Socialist Revolutionaries – the party that was initially
based on the philosophical foundation of Russia's populist

(narodnik) movement. The titles of their main newspapers – *Cause of the People; Will of the People; Labour, Land and Liberty; Banner of Labour* – all show clear reference to this ideology.

Fearing that they would not be able to keep control over the Assembly, the Bolsheviks authorised the recall of all elected deputies, arrested the members of the electoral commission of the Constituent Assembly, and declared the Kadet Party a 'party of enemies of the people'. Following coverage of events in the press Nikita Okunev, a 53-year-old employee of a steamship company, recorded in his diary:

> The members of the electoral commission of the Constituent Assembly have been arrested. The reasons are still a mystery, but it looks like the Bolsheviks would disrupt the Constituent Assembly. They are already saying that if the Soviets are ruling, there is no need for the Constituent Assembly, especially if there are more SRs and Kadets in it than the Bolsheviks.[9]

Writing his notes in a prison cell, doctor, politician and statesman Andrei Shingarev, one of the leaders of the Kadet Party and one of the first arrested 'enemies of the people' commented: 'I have not read anything more shameless and stupid than the articles in *Izvestiia* and *Pravda* about some "monarchist plot" organised by the Kadets. During the search [at my place] they discovered a draft of a bill ... It is impossible to understand why it is called a "monarchist plot".'[10]

The opening of the Constituent Assembly was postponed until 18 (5) of January 1918. A few days before the opening, Arthur Ransome wrote for Britain's newspaper, the *Daily News*:

> In five days' time the Constituent Assembly meets. It now seems probable that it will contain a majority against the Bolsheviks by some other necessarily weaker government, which will offer the German generals an antagonist infinitely less dangerous to them than Trotsky. Efforts are being made to secure street demonstrations in the Constituent Assembly's favour. If these efforts are successful, the result will be anarchy, for which the Germans could wish nothing better.

It was clear to the Bolsheviks that the Constituent Assembly was opposed to the Soviet government, so they were prepared to dissolve it by force. Although all the delegates supported the Bolsheviks' suggestion and sang the 'International', this symbolic sign of loyalty to the ideals of revolution could not fool anyone. As expected, the Bolsheviks' decrees were rejected by the majority, and the Bolshevik delegation stormed out of the meeting in protest, followed by the left-wing SRs. A Bolshevik

(opposite) *L'Unique séance de la Constituante, le 18 Janvier 1918 (The Only Sitting of the Constituent Assembly, 18 January 1918).* Plate by Boris Zvorykin in Henri de Weindel, *Histoire de Soviets*, Paris, 1922.

The caption for this image suggests that this artistic impression was based on the testimony of Osip Minor, an old revolutionary, SR and former member of the Constituent Assembly. The red banner in the picture conceals a huge empty frame that used to hold a portrait of Nicholas II.
1854.g.15.

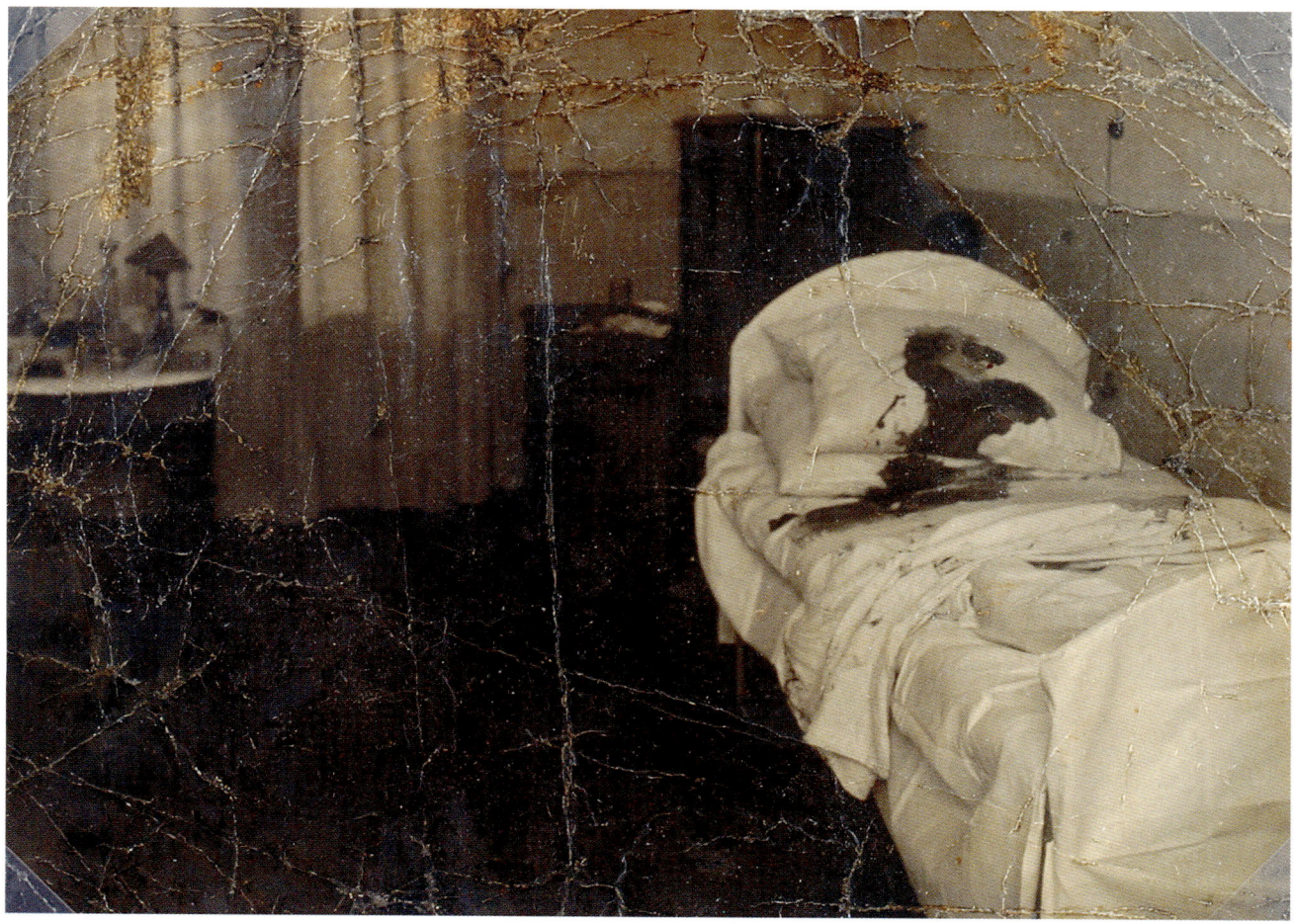

Murder scene photograph, showing the room in Mariinskii hospital where Fedor Kokoshkin was murdered in 1918.

In his diary on 23 (10) January 1918, economist Vladimir Sitnikov of the provincial town of Saratov wrote: 'Shingarev and Kokoshkin – the leaders of the Kadet Party – have been killed in the [prison] hospital by some unknown sailors. The Constituent Assembly has been dissolved. The 3rd Congress of the Soviets of Workers' and Soldiers' Deputies has been opened.'[11]

delegate, and later Red Army officer and diplomat, Fedor Raskolnikov, left his witness account of what happened on the first and last day of the Constituent Assembly's existence:

> In the Ministerial wing Vladimir Ilyich, wearing a black overcoat with an Astrakhan collar and a hat with earflaps, gave us our last instructions. 'I am leaving now, but you must keep an eye on your sailors,' said Comrade Lenin to me, with a smile. 'There is no need to disperse the Constituent Assembly: just let them go on chattering as long as they like and then break up, and tomorrow we won't let a single one of them come in.' ... Choking with laughter he [People's Commissar of naval affairs Dybenko] told us, in his booming bass voice, that the sailor Zhelezniakov had just gone up to the chairman of the Assembly, placed his broad hand on the shoulder of Chernov numb with astonishment, and said to him in a peremptory tone: 'The guard are tired. I propose that you close the meeting and let everybody go home.[12]

On 21 (8) January British newspapers reported that the Assembly had been 'dissolved by sailors', that a dozen demonstrators in support of the Assembly had been killed and 50 people wounded in Petrograd, and that bloodshed had occurred in Moscow. In fact about 50 people died and over 200 were injured in Moscow during the protests. The numbers of people who were willing to raise their voices in defence of the Constituent Assembly are still debatable, but it is estimated between 10,000 and 100,000. The funeral of the victims symbolically took place on 22 (9) January – the thirteenth anniversary of Bloody Sunday, a peaceful demonstration in 1905 that had ended in bloodshed.

The lack of reaction provoked by the closure of the Assembly in the rest of the country shows that the 'masses' did not feel properly represented, and were indifferent to large political issues that did not immediately translate into local politics. However, restoration of the Assembly became one of the unifying aims of the White movement, and in various territories under the control of the White Armies the former delegates established several governments, which for a short period of time were united into the Ufa Directory. In autumn 1918 the Directory was dissolved.

Many people at the time were confused by movements on the political scene, and in a situation where information was scarce they had to rely on rumour and gossip. Yurii Got'e, historian and director of the Rumiantsev Museum in Moscow, wrote in his diary on 2 July 1918: 'Some kind of SR government flying the flag of the Constitutional Assembly has been formed in Samara. Forgive me, Lord, for they know not what they do, and deliver me from my pessimism, which torments me.'[13]

Having split into right and left factions back in November 1917, the Socialist Revolutionaries were divided in their attitude to the Bolsheviks' tactic and aims. The right wing joined the White movement, while the left SRs remained allies of the Bolsheviks until the July 1918 uprising (which some historians think to be a Bolshevik provocation). As a result of the 'uprising' the left SR leaders were executed, some party members joined the Bolshevik Party, and the rest split into further factions. The party disintegrated in 1922 after a show trial in which 12 SR leaders were accused of plotting against the Soviet state and were sentenced to death. Under international pressure this sentence was postponed, depending on the 'good behaviour' of the remaining party members. The Bolsheviks had already employed the tactic of punishing hostages, but this was one of the first times when such a tactic was revealed to the outside world. By the mid-1920s all parties representing political opposition to the Bolsheviks had been formally banned, and the foundations of a single-party state had been laid. The Council of People's Commissars was relegated to a role subordinate to the Bolshevik Party Politburo, as all the Politburo members held posts in the government, soviets and other executive and legislative bodies.

The Sun of the Dead

> If light goes out – I see nothing,
> If a man is a beast – I hate him,
> If a man is worse than a beast – I kill him,
> If my Russia is over – I'm dying.
> Zinaida Gippius, 'Esli' ('If'), February 1918.[14]

Consolidation of power in the hands of the Bolshevik Party and an ongoing fight for survival were ideal conditions for constructing dehumanised images of the enemies of the new state. Domestic and international bourgeoisie, priests and *kulaks* were designated as primary enemies. The category of 'capitalists' or 'bourgeoisie' was broadened to include almost everyone from nobility, industrialists and entrepreneurs to merchants, bureaucrats, junior civil servants and professionals. Similarly *kulaks*, a term initially applied to landed farmers, was expanded to encompass any peasants who resisted handing over their agricultural produce to special food brigades, which had been set up to confiscate grain for urban populations and the Red Army.

These enemies were visually represented as the 'dark force', but very soon the tendency to portray them as obese caricature types or as parasites, spiders and waste, which should be wiped off the Soviet land and the entire world, prevailed.

The task of cleansing the country was given to the so-called Emergency Committee – the infamous Cheka, led by a Polish aristocrat and Russian revolutionary Felix Dzerzhinsky. The Committee, first organised in December 1917, was reorganised under a new name in 1922 and thereafter went through several reincarnations, such as the Stalin People's Commissariat for Internal Affairs (NKVD), the late Soviet Committee for State Security (KGB) and the post-Soviet Federal Security Service of the Russian Federation (FSB). Initially created as an Emergency Commission to fight counter-revolutionaries, saboteurs and financial speculators with 23 staff, it soon turned into a secret police department with regional apparatus and about 40,000 combatants, organised in squads. In July 1918 Red Army soldier Filipp Golikov wrote in his diary (and therefore privately): 'The Cheka are arresting suspicious individuals. We are helping them ... But in my view, Vania Petukhov was arrested for nothing. We were schoolmates. He is a modest and hardworking person, and we never heard anything bad about the Soviet power from him. Vania is not a bourgeois.'[15]

The number of Cheka victims remains controversial, but many researchers accept the estimate that between 10,000 and 30,000 people were killed in the years of the Red Terror (1918–1922) – a campaign of mass and systematic oppression. Although capital punishment in Russia was abolished straight after the Bolshevik uprising in 1917, it was officially reinstated

(opposite) *Bor'ba krasnogo rytsaria s temnoiu siloiu* (*The Fight of the Red Knight with the Dark Force*), poster by Boris Zvorykin, 1919.

Although the poster supports the Soviet cause, its aesthetics are associated with pre-revolutionary neo-Russian style – a movement within Russian modernism that based its visual language on stylisation of national heritage.

Cup.645.a.6.

(above) 'Rabochii podmetaet kriminal'nye elementy iz respubliki' ('A Worker Sweeping Criminals out of the Soviet Land'), from *Russian Placards 1917–1922, 1st part,* by Vladimir Lebedev, Russian Telegraph Agency ROSTA, St Petersberg, 1923.

This and other posters in the album were created in the constructivist style, born in the early 1920s. Constructivism was an art movement that aimed to be practical for social purposes of the new era.

C.191.a.13.

in June 1918. 'Bourgeois' courts were abolished and replaced with revolutionary tribunals, a term that referenced the terminology of the French Revolution. The tribunals were established in December 1917 following the 'Decree of the Soviet of Peoples' Commissars Concerning the Courts No. 1'. Revolutionary tribunals implemented the Red Terror in close relations with the Cheka.

However, renunciation of the justice system was soon adopted as a principle of Cheka operations, and execution without trial became standard. This was when the notorious *troikas* were first introduced to decide the fate of enemies of the state and issue verdicts without right of appeal. Initially a *troika* comprised a chekist, a local Bolshevik Party secretary, and a representative of the state power. However, soon all formalities were abolished and *troikas* began to comprise just chekists. The horror and disgust that people experienced when they had to come in contact with the Cheka was expressed by the writer Mikhail Prishvin in his diary:

> the invasion of a chekist; the terror of this situation is that he suddenly intrudes, catches you off-guard in the middle of your secret private life and looks at you as if you are just another element of the public space; he behaves as if he is in a public place: he doesn't take off his hat and spits out sunflower seeds hulls ... but actually, he came with a mandate to nationalise musical instruments. He needs to get a grand piano for a musical club, for the people, and you have to feel towards your own grand piano as he feels – it is not yours, it should serve society.'[16]

The Cheka is associated with the period of war communism – the internal policy introduced by the Soviet state in 1918–1921, which aimed to secure its survival in the face of civil war and foreign intervention. There was no agreement between the Bolsheviks themselves (nor is there any among researchers today) on to what extent the policy was a direct and haphazard response to current economic problems, inherited in large part from the previous governments, an inevitable transitional period to socialism or a rushed attempt to fix the economy according to ideal communist views on how the victorious proletariat state should be run.

During 1918 the Bolsheviks nationalised most of the industries and the financial system, centralising their management. They introduced state control of foreign trade and the railways, established rationing of food and commodities, implemented obligatory labour duty, and banned workers' strikes and private enterprise. Agricultural supplies, confiscated from peasants for nominal fixed prices, became subject to centralised distribution in the Red Army and in towns and cities. Here shortages reached their peak, not only because of

DÉTENU CONDUIT AU TRIBUNAL RÉVOLUTIONNAIRE

Dessin' de ZVORYKINE

the lack of supply, but also because of the deficiencies in the
entire infrastructure of the country, which lay in ruins. This
policy was referred to as *Prodrazverstka* (obligatory deposited
portion of food). Similar policies had been introduced as
wartime measures by the tsarist government in 1916, and by
the Provisional Government in 1917, but only the Bolsheviks
promoted *Prodrazverstka* as a principle and took it to the extreme,
with devastating results.

'Détenu conduit au tribunal révolutionnaire'
('Detainee accompanied to the
revolutionary tribunal'). Plate by Boris
Zvorykin in Henri de Weidel, *Histoire des
Soviets*, Paris, 1922.

In this drawing Zvorykin depicts an arrest,
which had become a routine event.

1854.g.15.

Как из хлеба сделать ситец ?

А это очень просто и можно из хлеба делать не только ситец, но и многое другое, что нужно крестьянину в его хозяйстве. И сумеет это сделать прежде всего сам крестьянин. Для этого необходимо взять весь излишек своего хлеба и сдать его на семенной пункт по твердой цене. Отсюда хлеб попадет прямо на фабрики и заводы в руки тому самому товарищу-рабочему, который выделывает все то, что нужно крестьянину.

Для того, чтобы рабочий исправно работал, он должен быть прежде всего сыт, а накормить его может только крестьянин.

Вот и выйдет дело так, как нарисовано здесь: в один конец фабрики крестьянин всыпет свой лишний хлеб, а из другого конца фабрики к нему вылетит все, что нужно ему.

Крестьяне, в организованном товарообмене залог вашего благополучия!

Крестьяне, весь свой лишний хлеб сдавайте по твердой цене на семенные пункты!

Kak iz khleba sdelat' sitets (*How to Make Chintz out of Bread*), poster, 1920.

Published by the People's Commissariat of Food, this poster shows ideal relations between workers and peasants, as seen by Bolshevik theoreticians.

Cup.645.a.6.

In 1921 the Bolshevik Party and the Soviet government, prompted by the revolt of soldiers and sailors in their stronghold at the navy base of Kronstadt, replaced war communism with the so-called New Economic Policy (NEP). This was in essence a state capitalism. For many hardcore Bolsheviks and recent converts the policy was a major disappointment – a betrayal of the revolutionary principles. For Lenin and the Politburo, however, the NEP was a controversial survival strategy. Peasants were allowed to sell their produce on the market after having given away some of it in tax, so the policy was called *Prodnalog* (food tax). But the change of direction did not prevent an outbreak of severe famine that affected nearly 90 million people in 1921–1923. *Prodrazverstka* left most peasants with no crops to sow for the following season. After a dry summer in 1921 peasants were left not only without a new crop, but also with no emergency grain. The number of victims who died is estimated at around 5 million. Graphic and powerful descriptions of the tragedy were created by writer Ivan Shmelev in his book *Solntse mertvykh* (*The Sun of the Dead*), published shortly after the famine, when he was in exile:

[The cow's] sides are all fallen in, and her flank-bones projecting, and the lines of her spine sharpened to a knife-

Рр
Рр

РАБОЧЕМУ КРЕСТЬЯНИН – ДРУГ.
В ОБМЕН НА ХЛЕБ ПОЛУЧИТ ПЛУГ.

Page with letter 'R', in Dmitrii Moor, *Azbuka krasnoarmeitsa* (*Alphabet for the Red Army Solider*), Moscow, 1921.

The letter to learn is 'R' for *rabochii* (worker). Seen on the left, he looks much younger, brighter and more energetic (compare the two triangles formed by the worker's and peasant's legs) than the shabby peasant dressed as a fairy-tale character.

Cup.401.g.25.

edge, with the back half eaten away with the blood-sucking of gnats and gadflies, and the sores on her back exuding pus as a cluster of young grubs irritates the heat-festered wounds, and the udder below blackened and drawn in, and the teats so dry and wrinkled that even the most skilful housewife could never again wring thence a drop of milk. 'Tamarka, I have nothing whatsoever for you. Away, I say!' But she will not believe me, for she has known that mighty power of man, and refuses to understand why she is not fed by him. I too, Tamarka, cannot understand it. I too cannot understand how any-one or anything has benefited through this country of ours having been turned into a blood-soaked wilderness.[19]

Homeless children whose parents had died as a result of the war were joined by those orphaned by the famine. According to various sources, in 1921–1922 the number of children who lived on the streets was between 6 and 7 million. At the same period 540,000 children lived in orphanages. As this situation was identified as 'extraordinary', the Cheka was tasked to resolve it, which was done by the mid-1930s.

January. A horse costs 20 million; a cow – 20 million; rye flour – 1,200,000; millet – 950 000 per pound [c.0.4 kg]; barley – 900 000; oats – 500 thousand; hay – 200 thousand per pood [c.16.3 kg]; meat – 30,000 for a pound; boots – 4,000; fabric – 1,200,000 per yard.

Nestor Belous, 33, Ukrainian peasant, diary entry, 1 January 1922.[20]

Homeless children playing cards, 1925.

The number of homeless orphans grew rapidly due to military conflicts, famine and the Red Terror. At the same time, according to the new ideology, the entire family institution was under scrutiny. The new state took full responsibility for its children – their wellbeing and upbringing. Children's deviant behaviour was thought to be a manifestation of counter-revolution, so the solution was to bring in the Cheka.

Photographs of victims of the famine, in *Zritel' (Spectator)*, no.1, 1922.

High Commissioner Nansen visited Soviet Russia and Ukraine several times in 1921–23. To attract public attention to the crisis, Nansen and the international organisations working with him (such as the Save the Children International Union and the International Red Cross) took photographs and distributed them in the news media. Some were used on postcards to raise funds for the relief effort. These photographs of a couple who became ill from eating grass and of children dying of severe malnutrition were published in this arts and theatre magazine. Creating a disturbing contrast with these graphic images, the text on the same page is a short story, unrelated to the famine appeal.

P.P.7500.b.

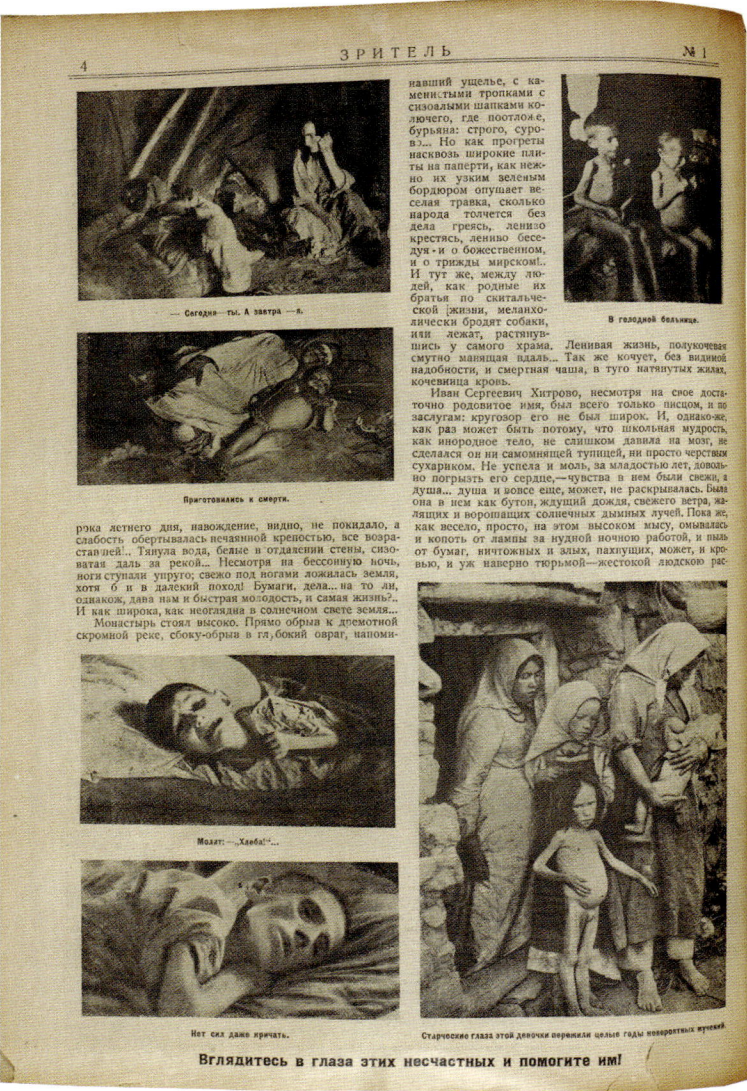

The disaster was so frightening that the state had to accept international aid from the capitalist world. The Norwegian explorer Fridtjof Nansen, in his role as League of Nations High Commissioner for Refugees, was instrumental in organising help, although quite a few national delegations were reluctant to send humanitarian aid to the Bolshevik government.

In Soviet Russia the Famine Relief (*Pomgol*) Central Commission was founded on the initiative of Sergei Prokopovich, an economist, liberal politician and minister in the Provisional Government, and his wife Ekaterina Kuskova, also a liberal politician and activist. Although led by the Soviet government, *Pomgol* was associated with prominent public figures, including another ex-minister Nikolai Kishkin, the writers Maxim Gorky and Vladimir Korolenko, veteran of the revolutionary movement Vera Figner and many others. Most of them were arrested by the Cheka and accused of various counter-revolutionary activities. It was expected that the arrested *Pomgol* activists would be executed, but Nansen intervened and instead of execution they were sent into exile abroad or in Russia.

The Soviet government started looking for solutions to the famine by confiscating property and treasures held by the Russian Orthodox Church and other religious institutions, to be used as payment for imported food supply. On behalf of the Russian Orthodox Church the Patriarch of Moscow and All Russia, Patriarch Tikhon, suggested giving voluntary contributions, but the initiative was not approved by the government. The campaign turned into a violent appropriation of cult objects.

The Russian Empire was a multi-confessional state with Orthodoxy being the 'ruling and predominant' faith. Although only the Orthodox Church was part of the state establishment, other religions were also institutionalised, controlled and legitimised by state power. Therefore minimisation of the role and influence of faith institutions was an integral part of the demolition of the old 'world of oppression'. The Russian Orthodox Church was declared separate from the state and thus denied any role in governing the country. The land that the Church had owned was redistributed among peasants in the first months of Bolshevik rule.

Lenin himself wrote little on religion. On the one hand, he suggested that Marx's definition of religion as 'the opium of the people' was 'the cornerstone of the entire ideology of Marxism about religion'. He furiously opposed those who were seeking a new 'revolutionary' religion and proposing the idea of God-building – an agnostic movement popular at the beginning of the twentieth century among some prominent Marxists and Bolsheviks. On the other hand, he thought that it would be rash to expect that 'religious prejudices could be dispelled by purely propaganda methods'.[21]

Ostanovite etot potok golodnykh vashei tovarishcheskoi pomoshch'iu (Stop This Stream of Starving People With Your Comradely Help), poster. Moscow, 1921. Cup.645.a.6.(47).

Golod-pauk dushit krest'ianstvo Rossii (*Spider-famine is Strangling the Russian Peasantry*), poster, 1921.

The spider legs represent disasters such as epidemics, cattle disease and problems with transport. Streams of goods coming from the churches, the synagogue and the mosque are fighting the spider. The poster promotes the slogan: 'Gold from churches should be used for saving the hungry from dying'.

1856.g.8.(27).

Depriving religious institutions of their economic basis was intended to lead, sooner or later, to their entire elimination. In May 1922 *The Times* in London reported: 'Patriarch Tikhon, the Archbishop Nikon, and other high dignitaries of the Church in Moscow have been brought before the Revolutionary Tribunal on charges of obstructing the sequestration of Church property.'[22] A diary entry from the period observed: 'Religious ministers, i.e. the Patriarch and other priests and clergymen, don't have the right for rations, as according to the Soviet classification they are not "workfolk", and those who don't work, don't eat.'[23] Under pressure from the Cheka, Patriarch Tikhon confessed his counter-revolutionary sins and declared full support for the Soviet government. He died in April 1925 at the age of 60 and was canonised by the Moscow Patriarchate in October 1989.

In the new political climate of the post-Soviet era, the controversial debates about the family of the last Russian tsar

БЕЗЧИНСТВА БОЛЬШЕВИКОВЪ ВЪ ЦЕРКВИ

Beschinstva bol'shevikov v tserkvi
(*Thuggish Bolshevik Behaviour in a Church*),
poster, *c.*1919.

Issued as anti-Bolshevik propaganda, the poster reads: 'When he broke open the fifth seal, I saw underneath the altar the souls of those who had been slaughtered because of the witness they bore to the word of God. They cried out in a loud voice, "How long will it be, holy and true master, before you sit in judgment and avenge our blood on the inhabitants of the earth?" (Revelations, 6:9,10).'

1856.g.8(27).

Будь здоров!

Bezbozhnik (The Godless) 1923,
no.7, cover.

Under Stalin anti-religious propaganda soon became quite aggressive. In 1925 the League of Militant Atheists, a volunteer organisation that promoted anti-religious views, was formed. One of the periodicals they published was *The Godless* (*Bezbozhnik*). Dmitrii Moor (pseudonym of Orlov), the creator of the most striking images associated with the revolution and civil war, became its main contributor and artists director. In this picture the peasant is sneezing out his religious beliefs under the supervision of the worker.

P.P.8000.rs.

Ipatiev House in Yekaterinburg (Sverdlovsk from 1924 to 1991), postcard, after 1924.

In 1918 Soviet officials ordered the owner of the house, a mining engineer called Nikolai Ipatiev, to vacate the premises. A special fence was erected and the building was named the House of Special Purpose. Here Nicholas II and his family spent the last 78 days of their lives. The caption on the postcard reads: 'Sverdlovsk. The last palace of the last tsar'. The house was demolished in 1977.

Private collection.

also concluded in their being pronounced saints in 2000. Sent first to the town of Tobolsk in Siberia and then to Yekaterinburg in the Urals, the royal family and four of their servants, who chose to accompany them into exile, were murdered by a Bolshevik squad led by Yakov Yurovsky on 17 July 1918. Born to a large Jewish family, Yurovsky was a professional revolutionary who had joined the Bolshevik faction as early as 1905. He worked in the Cheka and the Soviet State Treasury, and later managed the Polytechnical Museum in Moscow. He died in 1938 of a peptic ulcer. In the same year his daughter Rimma Yurovskaia, a communist activist, was arrested and sent to a labour camp.

The executions of the royal family and their relatives (19 members of the Romanov family were killed between June 1918 and January 1919) were committed in secrecy. Many documents and artefacts were forged, hidden or destroyed; execution orders and the correspondence concerning potential escape from captivity were classified. Understandably this created an atmosphere in which rumours and myths mushroomed in the Soviet Union and abroad. The most productive pattern was the survival story, so that over 200 imposters (mainly of Anastasia and Alexei, the crown prince, but also of others, including Romanovs who never existed) provided material for a number of popular books, films, cartoons and other forms of artistic representation.

Ode to Revolution

> 'O'!
> O Beastly!
> O Childish!
> O Halfpenny!
> O Great One!
> What other names have you been given?
> What turns might you still take, O Two-Faced One?[25]

Yesterday the commander Yurovsky brought a box containing all our jewels and asked us to verify its contents. He asked us to sign a receipt for them and left them in our custody. The weather is cooler, and in the bedroom it is easier to breathe. Avdeiev and his assistant were not only guarding us, but also robbing us. And, speaking of property, they even kept for themselves the larger part of the goods brought for us from the convent. It is only now, after the new change, that we learned about that, because a large quantity of provisions was found in the kitchen. Lately, as usual, I have been reading a lot. Today I began the seventh volume of Saltykov. I like his writing very much, both his articles and his stories. The day was rainy. We walked for half an hour and returned home to dry off.

Nikolai Romanov (Tsar Nicholas II), diary entry, 6 July 1918.[24]

The need for change was so vital in Russia that for many it was morally justifiable. However, the realisation that the old Russia had gone forever was very difficult to articulate. It was also hard to accept the responsibility for what was happening. Almost everyone had been involved in rocking the frail boat of the tsarist regime, but the image of what should replace it was the one thing that divided society, and the Bolshevik version of the new reality appeared to be shocking.

The symbolist poet Alexander Blok was one of the first who responded to the trauma in poetry. Written in the beginning of 1918, the poem *The Twelve* conveys fascination and apprehension at the spontaneity of the revolution. A poet with a very distinctive individual voice, in this poem Blok hides it in the polyphony of voices from the street, the 'music of revolution' played by the 'orchestra of the people's soul'. This is a story of a prostitute Kat'ka, in whom we can see a symbol of the faulty, vulnerable but holy Russia. She dies in the revolutionary storm, killed by one of the Red Guards of the title. At the end of the poem the squad of twelve Red Guards are marching along the snowy streets of Petrograd led by Jesus Christ. Revolution must destroy the old world completely, without pity. No one will be spared, including those for whose sake revolution was started. A new world will be built from ground zero in an absolutely alien country. Neither the

I'm thrilled with the new tasks and I'm carried away with the wide and original ways of their implementation. I support how the government tackles the management of the country. I want to live, work and move toward the future. And despite all crimes, deficiencies and faults of gloomy and cruel communists, I want to be with democracy and work for democracy, and under the present circumstances it means to be with the communists. Of course, this does not exclude a possibility of disagreements and refusing to do things that are in acute conflict with my reason and moral imperatives.

Nikolai Druzhinin, 35, historian, diary entry, 1 January 1921.[26]

Illustration by Yurii Annenkov, from A. Blok, *Dvenadtsat'* (*The Twelve*), 1918.

This narrative poem was one of the first poetic responses to the revolution. The first print run of this book was only 300 copies, but 10,000 more copies were consequently printed and sold. The illustrations by prominent Russian avant-garde artist Yurii Annenkov combine small everyday details and wide overviews in a montage style to create an impression of chaos and free-fall.

L.45/732.

Bolsheviks nor their political opponents liked this ambiguity.

Destruction of the old culture, poetry and society was in the centre of the artistic programme of futurists. They saw the revolution as a natural environment and the means of its implementation. The Russian futurist Vladimir Mayakovsky glorified the change in his poems 'Ode to Revolution' (1918) and 'Left March' (1919). He wanted to participate actively in the changes and directed his creativity into making the Soviet propaganda.

Mayakovsky's play *Mystery Bouffe*, in which he shows the triumph of the new world, was created for the first anniversary of the Bolshevik revolution. It was staged by Vsevolod Meyerhold, who also worked in the forefront of the Russian avant-garde, as a busy grotesque show in colourful sets with acrobatics and circus tricks. Mayakovsky described the show as 'our great revolution, thickened by lyrics and theatrical performance' and 'a miniature of the world in the circus'. Although the play praised revolution, its real meaning turned out to be much deeper. The tragedy of death and destruction, hidden behind satire and extravaganza, suggested that the downfall of the present world in its entirety was a necessary sacrifice for the ideal future. Philosophical and artistic examination of revolution is one of the most fascinating features of the early years of the Soviet state. Revolution as a phenomenon presented artists with a wide range of existential questions and creative opportunities.

Many avant-garde artists were convinced that their aesthetic programme was the best way to deliver the Bolsheviks' message to the masses. It was probably the most effective ammunition to impress 'the revolution impulse' and 'the emotional experience' of the revolution on mass consciousness.

In the early days of being in power, the Bolsheviks referred to the events in October 1917 as a 'coup'. As their power developed, the term 'coup' was replaced by 'revolution' and very soon the official name 'Great October Socialist Revolution' was introduced. According to Lenin's version of Marxism, communism was the final and the most advanced stage of historical development, and socialism – the social order that, as the Bolsheviks stated, they were establishing in Russia – was an opening stage of this new communist era. In the Bolsheviks' concept of history the October revolution was interpreted as the new Creation, of the same importance as the biblical one.

Although it took some time to mature, the myth of the October revolution as a legitimate conclusion of the world history was born straight after its victory. One of the most effective dramatisations of the October mythology was Nikolai Evreinov's mass spectacle *The Storming of the Winter Palace*, staged in the Palace Square and Winter Palace in Petrograd in 1920. On the day of the festival 2,500 people took part in the show. Seven years later the epic picture was recreated and immortalised in the visual memory for future generations as Sergei Eisenstein's legendary film *October: Ten Days That Shook the World*.

Many artists were tempted to glorify the new power, or at least show it their loyalty, but the power was not grateful to those who were suspected of being disingenuous. Writer Ivan Bunin condemned and ridiculed those of his colleagues who fell into this trap of temptation. In his diary (later reworked into a book) he recorded the following episode:

(opposite) ROSTA poster, designed by Vladimir Mayakovsky, 1919. From *V. Maiakovskii: okna ROSTA i GlavPolitProsveta*, Moscow, 2010.

Creating a visual propaganda to keep up with the rapidly changing situation, Vladimir Mayakovsky introduced the distinct ROSTA (the Russian news agency) Windows format – a strip of 4–14 cartoons with short lyrics. Although the project was short-lived, between September 1919 and January 1922 over 1,500 titles were created. About 400 were designed by Mayakovsky. Printed manually, they were produced in 150–300 copies. Later Mayakovsky put some together in the book *Formidable Laughter*, which was published in 1932 (two years after his death).

YF.2012.b.305.

A labour festival in town ... After breakfast, I went for walk around the town ... Red banners are on all houses; carpets are hanging down from balconies. The new authorities ordered to hang carpets on balconies. Maybe, this is their way to find out who has a carpet, so that they could requisition it later ... On the Cathedral square there is a poster: a fat bourgeois is holding a worker by the collar – 1918, and next to it is a picture of a worker watching a bourgeois swiping the street – 1919 ... I went further – up to the monument to Catherine [the Great], which is wrapped in some grey robe ... along the boulevard and the Pushkin street – posters and more posters everywhere.

Vera Bunin, 37, housewife, diary entry, 1 May 1919.[27]

Yesterday the poet Voloshin visited us for a long time. He had gotten into trouble because he had approached the Bolsheviks to help 'decorate the city for the First of May'. I warned him: 'Stay away from them. It would not only be stupid but also base for you to come to their aid, since they are well aware that you were in the opposing camp yesterday.' But Voloshin replied only with nonsense: 'Art is outside of time, it is outside of politics. I will help decorate the city but only in my capacity as a poet and an artist.' Decorate what? Gallows, and his own to boot? But he took off to see them nonetheless. The next day *Izvestiia* reported: 'Voloshin came crawling to us ...' Now Voloshin wants to write a letter to the editor. He is full of righteous indignation. And he's acting even more stupidly than before.[28]

Mass performances of historical events that were chosen to form the Bolsheviks' narrative of the revolution soon became an integral feature of people's life in all parts of the country. Schoolboy Anatolii Starodubov wrote in his diary:

I went to the station square to watch the show of 'shooting the workers in Petersburg' [Bloody Sunday on 9 January 1905]. Red Army troops – artillery, cavalry and infantry – impersonated the old army. They pinned old badges and shoulder straps to their uniforms and covered their red badges with pieces of fabric. 'Workers' were played by the workers from the railway workshop. The railway station was dressed as the Palace. The demonstration of 'workers' with banners and pennants was met with shooting. They started falling down on the snow. After that there was a short speech.[29]

However, it soon became clear that the Bolsheviks could not leave artists to their own devices. Attempts to fantasise about the future put the revolution in the wider humanitarian context; testing or scrutinising various scenarios was not needed by the proletarian state. Evgenii Zamyatin, the author of *We* – one of the first Soviet dystopias (written as early as 1920, but not published in Russia until 1988) – feared that the Bolsheviks were trying to create a sanitised, rational and controlled future. Whether his vision had any grounding was not relevant to those who criticised and banned the novel. Any endeavour of independent thinking was greeted with suspicion and hostility. Although the new power needed artists to legitimise its place on the world's cultural scene, any artistic interpretation of the revolution would be too complex and ambiguous. Even *Proletkult* (Proletarian Culture), the Soviet artistic institution most loyal to the government, was not trusted, as it claimed artistic independence

(opposite) *Doloi negramotnost': burvar' dlia vzroskykh* (*Down with Illiteracy: A Primer for Adults*), Moscow, 1920.

This primer for new readers adapted extracts from the Bolshevik leaders' speeches and articles.

12975.n.15.

ИЗДАНИЕ Всероссийской Чрезвычайной Комиссии по ЛИКВИДАЦИИ БЕЗГРАМОТНОСТИ.

Долой НЕГРАМОТНОСТЬ.

БУКВАРЬ ДЛЯ ВЗРОСЛЫХ,

разработанный Д. Элькиной, Н. Бугославской и А. Курской.

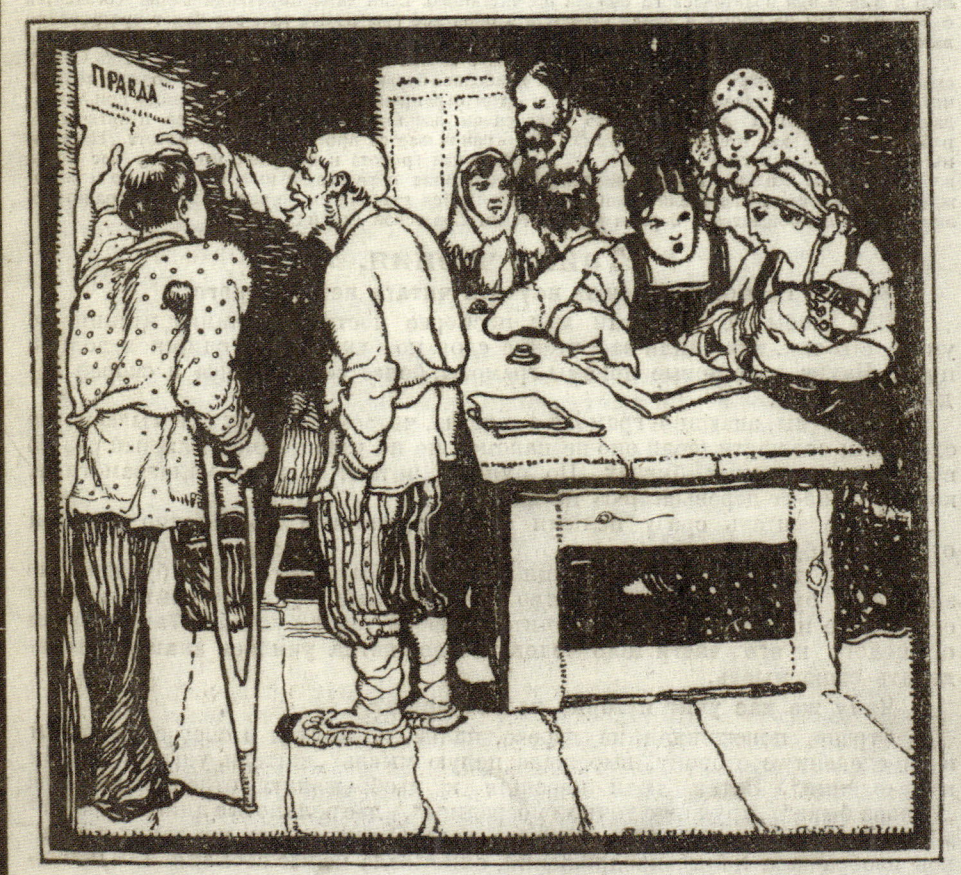

МОСКВА.—1920.

Ialtinskaia delegatka (The Yalta Female Delegate), hand-lettered wall newspaper, 1927.

The vogue for 'placard newspapers' emerged in Soviet Russia out of the shortage of print facilities and materials. Wall newspapers were used to disseminate official and local news, and very soon became a powerful propaganda tool. Small communities ('collectives', to use Soviet terminology) of co-workers or co-students formed editorial boards and periodically issued wall newspapers. This wall newspaper was issued by a local women's committee in Yalta. It contains reports on their joint achievements, amateur poetry and stories that were intended to inspire and promote new communist values, and artwork such as the multi-tasking woman shown in the detail.

Add. MS 57556.

from the party and Soviet bureaucracy. In 1920 this organisation was absorbed by the People's Commissariat of Education.

The shock of the Revolution revoked any possibility of returning to the pre-revolutionary state of play, be it in politics, the economy or personal life. The void had to be filled with a picture of an alternative utopian reality, as the actual reality was far too crude, cruel and chaotic to be faced. Successful creation of this parallel reality was the major achievement of early Soviet propaganda, tightly controlled by the party. This task was placed very high on the Bolsheviks' priority list, and Trotsky's book *Literature and Revolution* (1924) proves it:

To [Aleksandr] Blok the Revolution is a rebellious element: 'Wind, wind – in all God's world!' ... Elements, blizzard, flame, maelstrom, whirlpool ... The Revolution is above all the struggle of the working-class for power, for the establishment of power, for the reconstruction of society. It passes through the highest points, through the most acute paroxysms of bloody fighting, but it remains one and indivisible throughout its whole course – from its first shy beginnings to its final ideal moment when the state organised by the Revolution will become dissolved into a Communist society.[31]

Propaganda is effective when consumed in large quantities on a regular basis, so it was essential to form a receptive audience. Lenin thought that for his overwhelmed countrymen the most important media should be performing arts – 'film and circus'. At the same time, one of the first challenges set by the Bolshevik government was to eradicate illiteracy. The state literacy programme started in 1919, but not until the 1950s did the Soviet Union become a country with 100 per cent literacy. Most researchers agree that in 1897 the overall literacy rate in

Russia was just above 20 per cent, while by 1917 it was already over 40 per cent. Depending on how one approaches the definitions of functional and complete literacy the figures would be different, but it seems that despite special efforts the new regime did not change the global picture dramatically.

'The masses' were not only at the receiving end of propaganda; they had to participate actively in creating it. One form of such propaganda was the so-called 'placard newspapers', written and drawn by hand in schools, factories and offices. Originally they had a similar function to billboards. Apart from disseminating official information, which might not be obtainable in print due to various shortages, they very soon turned into communal forums.

Another vehicle of political propaganda was theatre. About 5,000 amateur workers' theatre companies were modelled on the example of the Blue Blouse troupe that had been founded in Moscow in 1923. By 1927 the movement included more than 100,000 members. The name comes from the artists' uniform – a loose style blouse. Their performances included elements of comedy, circus and gymnastics, and were sometimes referred to as 'live newspaper'.

Creating a revolutionary myth included sacralisation of the symbols of the revolution. The first signs of this process can be seen after the attempt on Lenin's life on 30 August 1918, when

Al'bom Siniaia Bluza SSSR (The Blue Blouse: An Album), no.71/72, 1928.
Images of the Blue Blouse troupe, in an eponymous album of photographs. ZA.9.d.615.

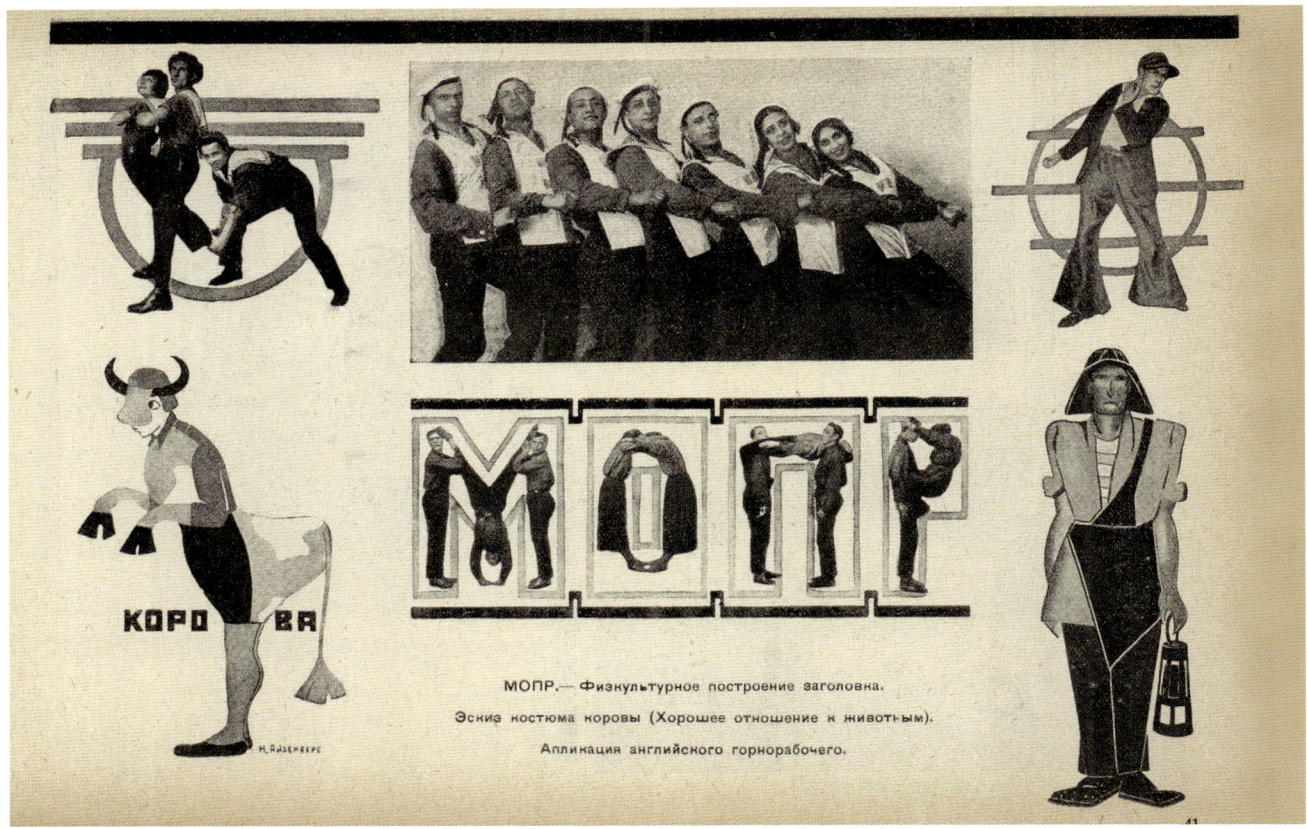

МОПР. — Физкультурное построение заголовка.
Эскиз костюма коровы (Хорошее отношение к животным).
Аппликация английского горнорабочего.

Председатель Совета Народных Комиссаров
Р. С. Ф. С. Республики
В. И. УЛЬЯНОВ (ЛЕНИН).

ЧИСЛЕННИКЪ

he was badly wounded. It is still unclear whether Fanny Kaplan, a member of the SR Party, fired a gun at Lenin, but apparently she took full responsibility and was shot without trial several days after her arrest. On the same day that Lenin was shot in Moscow, Leonid Kannegiser, another member of the SR Party, assassinated the head of the Petrograd Cheka, Moisei Uritskii. The Bolsheviks responded with the Red Terror and launched a propaganda campaign that laid the foundations of Lenin's cult. He was described as an ascetic and martyr, who sacrificed his life to the cause of the world proletariat. This rhetoric was deeply rooted in Christianity and popular culture. Although Lenin's wounds were thought likely to be fatal, he recovered in a couple of months, and this speedy recovery was deemed another proof of his sainthood. Although Lenin himself was not keen on being a subject of worship, he could not prevent it. By the time of his death in January 1924, Lenin was fully sacralised.

On the Other Shore

The displacement of the civilian population caused by the First World War was massive and created a series of refugee crises. For contemporaries it was difficult to cope with the abruptness and totality of the forced resettlement of millions of people. As Russia endured both external and internal conflicts, the immense scale of the country's crisis left it deeply traumatised. As with most global events, figures can only be approximate. It is estimated that around 5 million people had to move from the war zones to the eastern parts of Russia between 1915 and 1918, while in 1919–1923 around 2 million people left the Soviet republic. Many civilians, belonging to former privileged or middle classes, were evacuated with remnants of the White Armies. The refugee camps set up in Turkey (Istanbul, Gelibolu), Greece (Lemnos), Cyprus, Bulgaria, Egypt and Tunisia were under British and French administration. From the far east of Russia, refugees fled to China. Some people managed to escape directly to European countries. In 1922 the Soviet government deported a group of intelligentsia in the so-called 'Philosophers' ship', comprising intellectuals who were unwanted in, and deemed dangerous to, the young communist country.

In 1924, 500 Russian refugee children in Russian schools in Prague were asked to write essays about their experience. These recollections were collected and published in two books:

> There we lived in tents among rocks and thorns; there were no trees anywhere – just sea, rocks and thorns.

> Sometimes I didn't want to eat – I just was wandering around the desert recollecting my house ... evenings in spring ... horses in the fields – everything which was so sweet and dear.

(opposite) Soviet wall calendar, 1920s.
The design imitates popular traditional motives and the composition of the Resurrection from Christian icons.
Cup.645.a.6.(65).

(above) Wreath from the pupils of School No.2, from *Leninu: 21 ianvaria 1924* (*To Lenin: 21 January 1924*), Moscow, 1924.
The book was compiled immediately after Lenin's funeral and contains images and descriptions of about 950 wreaths, banners, ribbons and other objects laid on the coffin. Attached to this wreath from the pupils of School No.2 is a notebook with children's messages to Lenin.
10790.pp.9.

The Serbs greeted us very well. In the station they gave the cadets some presents; they also gave them some wine to warm up.

I reached Tuapse. But I could not find bread in this town – peas and peas everywhere.[32]

Reaching safety often seemed impossible and unrealistic after months of hunger, cold, fear and losses, as expressed in the diary of 16-year-old schoolgirl Nelly Ptashkina:

The night was almost a nightmare: there were three of us on the lower seat: we were all the time trying to invent more comfortable attitudes. Mummie suffered particularly ... By what route shall we travel? How shall we get to France? Is it really possible? ... It is strange: at one and the same time, life is so different around the world: Yalta, Paris, Kieff, Moscow, the war. It seems so remarkable.[33]

But reaching safety was not the end of ordeal. One of the fundamental problems faced by the refugees themselves, and the countries that had to deal with them, was their statelessness.

Theatre performance in a Russian refugee camp, early 1920s.

The remains of the defeated Volunteer Army lead by General Denikin were evacuated from the port of Novorossiisk in March 1920. Due to a combination of the Red Army offensive, panic and transportation shortages, only 33,000 people managed to escape. Hundreds of wounded soldiers, officers and their families died or were captured by the Red Army. The next evacuation took place in November, managed by General Wrangel. Around 146,000 military personnel and civilians were transported in 126 ships from the ports of Crimea. Russian refugee camps around the Mediterranean looked like a combination of a military site with amenities essential for civilian life, such as schools, theatres and workshops.

Special Collections, Leeds University Library, LRA MS 1500/617.

```
LIST OF RUSSIAN ROYAL FAMILY ON BOARD H.M.S. LORD NELSON.Z
          ( Passage YALTA to GENOA.).
The Grand Duke Nicholas of Russia & Grand Duchess of Anʧastasia.
The Grand Duke Peter & Grand Duchess Militsa.
Princess Marina & Prince Rohan. Dr. Malama.
Count & Countess Tyshkiewier.
Mr Boldyroff. (2) Counts Fierson.
Baron & Baroness Staal & Baroness.Mary.Staal.
          (8 maids & 3 menservants).


     2nd ROYAL PARTY ON BOARD H.M.S. LORD NELSON.
     Passage MALTA to ENGLAND. (YALTA to MALTA in" MARLBOROUGH".)


H.I.M. The Empress Marie Peodovrvna of Russia.
Grand Duchess Zenia.              Prince Obeliani.
Prince Dimitri.                      "   Wiasiesky.
    "    Rostislav.               ·M'dme  Erschoff.
    "    Wassily.                 .Princess's.Doloronky.
Princess Dolgoronky               M.Foguel.
    "    Wiasiesky.
Counyess.Z.Mengdon.               English Governess Miss Costa.
Prince Dolgoronky                 Nurse Mrs King
Mdsile Evireinoff
    "    Chatelain & child        Servants!- 13 Females )
    M.   Chatelain                              4 Male   )
Count & Countess .V.Mengdon.
```

According to Soviet decree many categories of Russian nationals were deprived of their citizenship. In July 1922 Fridtjof Nansen convened an Intergovernmental Conference that agreed to issue refugees with temporary travel documents, commonly known as Nansen passports. Some Russian émigrés and their children refused to apply for citizenship of the country of their residence until after the end of the Second World War or the collapse of the Soviet Union.

Large Russian communities settled in Belgrade, Prague, Riga, Berlin, Harbin and Paris. The political spectrum of those who left Russia spread from monarchists to Socialist Revolutionaries, but all of them believed that their exile was temporary. They tried to seek support from Western governments in their struggle with Bolshevism and to attract the world's attention to events in Russia. Such was the work of the Russian Liberation Committee, based in London. The governments of Czechoslovakia and Serbia established various support programmes for émigrés from Russia.

Not until the mid-1920s did it become clear that there was no going back. The question of preserving cultural identity became one of the most vital, despite the continuing

List of Russian royal family members being evacuated from Crimea on board British warships HMS *Marlborough* and HMS *Lord Nelson*, April 1919.

It is believed that certain British officials were given these lists to identify the passengers. This copy belonged to Marine J. Mitchell, who served on HMS *Lord Nelson*.

Private collection.

political debate. Various administrative, charitable, cultural and religious organisations were formed. The communities included people of different ethnic, social, political and cultural backgrounds, but the Russian language was one of the major bonds for them. Russian schools, publishing houses, journals, magazines and daily newspapers provided jobs and created the cultural environment for the communities. The term 'Russia Abroad' described the diaspora as a unique phenomenon, because its inhabitants not only aimed to keep their cultural identity, but also had a mission to preserve, pass on to future generations and transmit to the Western societies the values and accomplishments rejected by the Bolsheviks.

NOTES

1. A. V. Zhirkevich, *Potrevozhennye teni … Simbirskii dnevnik*. Moscow: Eterna-print, 2007. Quoted from: http://prozhito.org/person/34. Access date: 20 October 2016.

2. *Dnevniki sem'i Allendorf (Diaries of the Allendorf family)* on blog: *Skazki Olifanta (Olifant's Tales)* www.olifanpoff.ru Quoted from: www.prozhito.org/person/371. Access date: 20 October 2016.

3. B. E. Zakhava, *Vakhtangov i ego studiia*. Leningrad: Academia, 1927. Quoted from the digital edition: www.teatr-lib.ru/Library/Zakhava/vahtangov/. Access date: 20 October 2016.

4. L. D. Trotsky, *The History of the Russian Revolution*, trans by Max Eastman, 1932. Online edition: https://www.marxists.org/archive/trotsky/1930/hrr/ch47.htm. Access date: 20 October 2016.

5. E. K. Koksharova, *Lenin v Sovnarkome v 1917 godu*. Moscow: 1977.

6. V. I. Lenin, 'To Workers, Soldiers, and Peasants!' – spoken at the Second All-Russia Congress of Soviets of Workers' and Soldiers' Deputies. October 25–26, 1917 (November 7–8) in V.I. Lenin, *Collective works*, vol. 26, September 1917 – February 1918. Moscow: Progress Publishers, 1964. Quoted from: *Lenin Internet Archive* https://www.marxists.org/archive/lenin/works/1917/oct/25-26/index.htm. Access date: 20 October 2016.

7. A. Budberg, *Dnevnik belogvardeitsa*, Moscow: AST, 2001. Quoted from: www.prozhito.org/person/19. Access date: 20 October 2016.

8. V. M. Golitsyn, *Dnevnik 1917–1918 godov*. Moscow: Zakharov, 2008. Quoted from: www.prozhito.org/person/110. Access date: 20 October 2016.

9. N. P. Okunev, *Dnevnik moskvicha, 1917–1924: v 2-kh knigakh*. Moscow: Voenizdat, 1997. Quote from: www.prozhito.org/person/53. Access date: 20 October 2016.

10. A. I. Shingarev, 'Ispolinskaia nechaevshchina okhvatila Rossiiu' in *Druzhba narodov*, no.8, 1993. Quoted from: www.prozhito.org/person/79. Access date: 20 October 2016.

11. V. N. Sitnikov, *Perezhitoe; Dnevnik Saratovskogo obyvatelia 1918–1931*. Saratov, Slovo: 1999. Quoted from www.prozhito.org/person/103. Access date: 20 October 2016.

12. Fedor Raskolnikov. *Tales of Sub-Lieutenant Ilyin. The Tale of a Lost Day*, trans by Brian Pearce for New Park Publications Ltd. Quoted from: http://www.marxistsfr.org/history/ussr/government/red-army/1918/raskolnikov/ilyin/index.htm. Access date: 20 October 2016.

13. *Time of Troubles: The Diary of Iurii Vladimirovich Got'e*. Moscow, July 8, 1917 to July 23, 1922, trans, ed and introduced by Terence Emmons. New Jersey: Princeton University Press, c.1988.

14. Zinaida Gippius, *Stikhi, vospominaniia, dokumental'naia proza*. Moscow: Nashe nasledie, 1991.

15. F. I. Golikov, *Krasnye orly (iz dnevnikov 1918-1920 gg.)*. Moscow: Voenizdat, 1956. Quoted from: http://prozhito.org/person/28. Access date: 20 October 2016.

16. M. M. Prishvin, *Dnevniki, 1920–1922. Kniga tret'ia*. Moscow: Moskovskii rabochii, 1995. Quoted from: www.prozhito.org/person/56. Access date: 20 October 2016.

17. *Memories: From Moscow to the Black Sea* by Teffi, trans by R. Chandler. London: Pushkin Press, 2016.

18. 'Dnevnik E. K. Grachevoi' in *Umstvenno otstalye deti: istoriia ikh izucheniia, vospitaniia i obucheniia s drevneishikh vremen do serediny XX veka*. Moscow: NPO 'Obrazovanie',

1995. Quoted from: www.prochito.org/person/348. Access date: 20 October 2016.

19. I. Shmelev, *The Sun of the Dead*, trans from the Russian by C. J. Hogarth. New York: E. P. Dutton & Co, 1927.

20. N. M. Belous, diary. Quoted from: www.proxhito.org/person/87. Access date: 20 October 2016.

21. 'Socialism and religion' in V. I. Lenin, *Collective works*, vol. 10, November 1905 – June 1906. Moscow: Progress Publishers, 1965. Quoted from: *Lenin Internet Archive*: https://www.marxists.org/archive/lenin/works/1905/dec/03.htm. Access date: 20 October 2016.

22. *The Times*, London, 9 May 1922, issue 43026.

23. N. P. Okunev, *Dnevnik moskvicha, 1917–1924: v 2-kh knigakh*. Moscow: Voenizdat, 1997. Quote from: www.prozhito.org/person/53. Access date: 20 October 2016.

24. Kent de Price, *Diary of Nicholas II, 1917–1918, An Annotated Translation*. University of Montana: 1966. Quoted from: http://scholarworks.umt.edu/cgi/viewcontent.cgi?article=3084&context=etd. Access date: 20 October 2016.

25. Vladimir Mayakovsky, *The Ode to the Revolution*, 1918. Quoted from Vladimir Mayakovski, *Selected Poems*, trans from the Russian by James H. McGavran III. Evanston, Illinois: Northwestern University Press, 2013.

26. 'Dnevnik Nikolaia Mikhailovicha Druzhinina', in *Voprosy istorii*, 1995, nos 9–12; 1996, nos 1–4, 7, 9–10; 1997, nos 1, 3–4, 6–8, 10, 12. Quoted from: www.prozhito.org/person/134. Access date: 20 October 2016.

27. *Ustami Buninykh. Dnevniki Ivana Alekseevicha i Very Nikolaevny pod red.* Militsy Grin v 3-kh tomakh. Frankfurt-am-Main: Posev, 1977–1982. Tom. 1: 1881-1920.

28. Ivan Bunin, *Cursed Days*, trans from the Russian by Thomas Gaiton Marullo. London: Phoenix Press, 2000.

29. A. F. Starodubov, *Zapiski ochevidtsa: Ekaterinoslav 1924–1929 gg*. Dnepropetrovsk: Gaudeamus, 2001. Quoted from: www.prozhito.org/person/316. Access date: 20 October 2016.

30. V. Sudeikina, *Dnevnik. Petrograd, Krym, Tiflis*. Moscow: Russkii put', Knizhitsa, 2006. Quoted from: www.prozhito.org/person/67. Access date: 20 October 2016.

31. Leon Trotsky, *Literature and Revolution*, trans by Rose Strunsky, 1925. Quoted from: https://www.marxists.org/archive/trotsky/1924/lit_revo/. Access date: 20 October 2016.

32. *Vospominaniia detei-bezhentsev iz Rossii*, Prague, 1924, and *Vospominaniia 500 russkikh detei*, Prague, 1924.

33. *The Diary of Nelly Ptashkina*, trans by Pauline de Chary, London, 1923.

5 Russia and the World on Fire

Mike Carey and Nick Baron

At the beginning of the twentieth century, the world was far more connected than it had ever been before. Global economic ties, more sophisticated communications and transport, and a new wave of imperialist conquest and expansion by Western powers in Africa and Asia all meant that nations were growing increasingly interdependent. The era saw an explosion of warfare and revolutionary unrest affecting the whole world in which peasant movements, resistance to colonial expansion, nationalist aspirations and class struggle all played their part.

In the developed capitalist states, trade union movements and socialist parties were gaining in both strength and numbers. Of all the socialist groups united in the Second International (an international organisation of socialist and labour parties founded in 1889), Germany's Social Democratic Party was the most impressive, becoming the largest party in the country by 1912. Working-class movements which had once dreamed of revolution looked to the prospect of coming to power peacefully and legally.

However, unrest among the more militant sections was brewing even then. Syndicalist and Marxist currents sharpened their ideas in reaction to the growing moderation of socialism. Even in the United States, conflicts between organised labour and corporate power were growing in intensity, culminating in the Colorado Coalfield War (1913–1914) and the Ludlow Massacre (1914).

It was also an era in which modern, democratic and nationalist ideals symbolised by the American and French revolutions provided inspiration for rising mass movements striving to reform, if not overthrow, the power of established states and empires. The old Ottoman Empire had been shaken, but not yet felled, by the Young Turk Revolution of 1908. In Mexico a revolution began in 1910 which would outlast the decade. In China the Xinhai revolution of 1911 overthrew the Qing dynasty which had ruled China since 1644 (almost as long as the

House of Romanov had ruled the Russian Empire), and turned the empire into an unstable republic.

By the end of 1914, tensions raised by inter-imperialist rivalry had driven the great European powers to one of the bloodiest and most uncompromising wars in human history. After the assassination in July of French socialist Jean Jaurès, one of Europe's leading anti-war voices, the Second International found itself fragmented and unable to prevent the war; across the continent the majority of socialists supported their own national governments in pursuit of their war aims.

Despite the collapse of socialist internationalism, statesmen of all the belligerent nations quickly realised that their pursuit of 'total' war threatened to bring about profound political change. As British Foreign Secretary Edward Grey famously said: 'The lamps are going out all over Europe, we shall not see them lit again in our lifetime.' Just as states took measures to avoid social upheaval at home, they strove to foment unrest among the citizens, or subjects, of foreign powers. A rebellion against the British Empire by the Boers of South Africa in 1914/1915 was followed by the Easter Rising of 1916 in Dublin, in which nationalists proclaimed an Irish Republic. Both were crushed, as was a large-scale mutiny in the French army in April 1917.

It was not, then, the Russian Revolution that set the world on fire. Yet, in first overthrowing Europe's strongest autocracy three years into the First World War and then in defending and consolidating its power under the banner of global class war, the revolution became the brightest and hottest of flames. It symbolised the hopes and perils of the turbulent era for millions of people around the world.

Russian Experience

The February revolution came as a surprise to foreign onlookers, but not an unwelcome one. Statesmen from across the world, including most conspicuously the tsar's erstwhile allies, congratulated the new liberal regime with only a few misgivings. The form of political change was familiar and understandable – the Entente nations had not yet disowned the 'liberal' revolutions which gave birth to them. For many, 'February' called to mind not the working-class Paris Commune of 1871, but England's 'Glorious Revolution' of 1688, the American Revolution ending in 1783 and, above all, the French Revolution of 1789. They saw Russia emerging out of its backward, pre-modern absolutism to join the modern nations – if not yet as an equal, then at least as a recognisable member of the same family.

In a letter to the Russian translator Samuel Koteliansky, dated 1 May 1917, D. H. Lawrence wrote:

> I read unfathomable depths of gloom in your last letter, and concluded, alas, that the wrong things were happening in

Russia. Was that what cast you down so deep? Never mind, Russia is bound to run wrong at first, but she will pull out all right. As for me, I sincerely hope she will conclude a separate peace. Anything to end the war. – But tell me what news there *really* is, from Petrograd. – In the meantime, I keep my belief in Russia intact, until such time as I am forced to relinquish it: for it is the only country where I can plant my hopes. America is a stink-pot in my nostrils, after having been the land of the future for me.[2]

At first, the most pressing issue for the majority of observers was how the fall of the tsar would affect the war effort. On this question, people saw in the February revolution what they wanted to see. Many among the Entente had been concerned that the Russian state's faltering prosecution of the war had been due to 'pro-German' intrigues in the tsarist court; they hoped that the new Provisional Government would augur a turn of the tide. Citizens of the Entente countries were even told that the revolution occurred because the Russian people desired to fight more vigorously. The United States of America soon broke its neutrality and joined the war. The conflict could now be presented as a liberal crusade against Prussian militarism without the embarrassment of including tsarism as an ally – a kind of revolutionary war in its own right.

For pacifists and anti-war socialists on the other hand, the February revolution was a sign that the war would soon be over. They initially hoped that it would lead to a 'democratic peace without annexations or indemnities', a brokered end to the war without colonies or spoils, and were bitterly disappointed when the new Provisional Government appeared to renege on that aspiration.

French tennis player Jean Schopfer was in Petrograd in winter 1917, when the revolution broke out. Excitedly he recorded the popular reaction, although his first thought was the threat to France posed by the instability of its ally:

I thought of the Germans, of him who occupied the plains of Champagne and Artois, as well as the frozen banks of the Dwina. A revolution at this hour! Perhaps a civil war! At best, long months of anarchy, at a time when this country had need of all its forces to contend against the foreign foe. It was he who was triumphing to-day. Every shot fired in the streets of Petrograd was more harmful to Russia than a thousand bullets fired by the Germans on the front.[3]

A variety of foreign observers experienced the upheaval at first hand. Diplomats of the Allied nations, witnessing the fighting in the streets of Petrograd from the windows of the embassies above, were rather more cynical than the politicians

(above) Alexander Kerensky, in Claude Anet, *Through the Russian Revolution: Notes of an Eye-Witness, from 12th March–30th May*, 1917.

Claude Anet was a pseudonym for tennis player, Jean Schopfer. He was in Petrograd when the revolution broke out, recalling how 'everywhere extraordinary joy prevailed; people embraced one another; the soldiers were gay and triumphant'.

W48/5829.

(opposite) David Jagger, *The Bolshevik*, 1918.

This powerful work of art shaped and reflected Western fears of the demagogic – for many, demonic – power of the Russian revolutionaries. Reproduced in the British *Bibby's Annual* in 1918, the caption read: 'Posing as a righteous and single-minded advocate of democratic reform, [the Bolshevik] has succeeded, in a few months, in bringing his country into a state of helplessness and anarchy ... Instead of giving the country peace, bread and freedom, as promised, his half-baked theories have resulted in internecine war, hunger and famine. His methods of pillage, under the garb of freedom, have culminated in an orgy of murder and rapine. His contempt for the established order of Society has ended in selling his country to a relentless enemy. Our own idealists may study this picture with advantage, if only to remind themselves that no social changes can be effective which are not inspired by the desire for the welfare of all classes of the community.'

Beaverbrook Collection of War Art, CWM 19710261-0204, Canadian War Museum.

at home – both about the desire of the Russians to continue to fight, and about the possibility of a just peace.

French diplomat Louis de Robien expressed a fear that power would pass from the liberal politicians in the Provisional Government, such as Pavel Miliukov and Andrei Shingarev, to the socialist elements such as Alexander Kerensky. In his diary he refers to the 'Wilson plan' – not yet the famous 'fourteen points', issued only in January 1918, but President Wilson's previous idealistic overtures for a fair peace:

> I tremble for Alsace and Lorraine, which have already cost us so dear!!! What would happen, if the power slips away from the Milyukovs [*sic*] and the Shingarevs into the hands of the Kerenskys and their like, in the event of Germany wanting to make serious proposals on the basis of the *status quo ante bellum*. I very much fear that they would be received with enthusiasm here. As for America, she would inevitably agree, in view of the Wilson plan. There remain the Allies of the West ... The English will always get some colonies out of it ... But what about us? ... From this angle, the future looks very black, and the Russians have done us a terribly bad turn by having their silly revolution just at the moment when things were going a little less badly.[4]

The failure of the Provisional Government, leading to the Bolshevik seizure of power in October 1917, confirmed the worst fears of Entente governments. The new rulers of Russia had no desire to continue what they considered to be purely an imperialist war, nor any intention to halt the revolution at the stage of liberal capitalist democracy. Where the Provisional Government had been ideologically in line with the Entente states, the soviets of workers' and soldiers' deputies and the Bolshevik Party were alien and threatening, raising the 'spectre of communism' across Europe once more.

This spectre was vividly illustrated by British portrait painter David Jagger, in his 1918 work *The Bolshevik*. Three years later, American traveller Alice Ziska Snyder described the Bolshevik politician in the work as 'an unkempt, black-bearded orator, posed in front of a blood-red banner, his arms outstretched as he raves and gesticulates before a group of Russian soldiers. His dirty hands are clawing at the air; his face is transfigured by passion and from his mouth trickles saliva that besprinkles his long, ragged beard'.[5]

To the consternation of the Entente, the new Soviet government published the so-called 'Secret Treaties', outlining how the victorious nations planned to divide up territories after the war. Bypassing the ordinary channels of state diplomacy, the Bolsheviks issued an appeal to the world for an immediate and just peace. For the new People's Commissar for Foreign Affairs,

Výkřik (*The Scream*), 1919. Czech-language journal.

The Czech Legion had been formed from Czech national volunteers fighting for the Entente side, hostile to the Austro-Hungarian Empire. Towards the end of the First World War, the Czechoslovak Republic became one of the new states to emerge out of the dissolution of the Austro-Hungarian Empire. Politically aligned with the stream of revolutionary nationalism raised by the weakening of the old multi-national empires, the Czech Legion wandered the Trans-Siberian railway like Moses in the desert searching for his promised land. Despite having been drawn into the Russian civil wars on their journey to the new Czechoslovak Republic, they managed to produce cultural artefacts expressing their new sense of national awakening, like the journal *Výkřik*, in which they shared news, thoughts and artistic endeavours.

RB.31.c.832.

Leon Trotsky, this was foreign policy enough. He declared that he would 'issue a few revolutionary proclamations to the people of the world', and then 'shut up shop'.

In any case, the Russian army had already 'voted with its feet'. When a general European cessation of hostilities was not forthcoming, and after much internal controversy among the Bolsheviks, Soviet Russia acceded to a separate peace. The Brest-Litovsk Treaty (March 1918) left great swathes of the Russian Empire under the occupation of the Central Powers – a far cry from the 'just peace without annexations'.

Statesmen of the Entente nations, such as Winston Churchill, urged a vigorous response to the Bolshevik danger. Following the Bolsheviks' withdrawal from the First World War in March 1918, the Allies sent expeditionary forces to Russia to maintain a front against the Germans, with the aim of preventing them from transferring their forces to the Western Front. This brought many British, French, American and other soldiers – both officers and rank-and-file – into contact with Russians for the first time. Japanese troops also joined the intervention in Siberia, the great cost of which contributed to widespread food riots in Japan throughout 1918 and the resignation of its government.

One of the key sites of the British intervention in North Russia was Arkhangelsk. General Marushevskii, who was in charge of the White Russian troops there, left an interesting observation on the British-Russian interactions:

> The English responded to any Russian views, even those pronounced by people of the highest rank in imperial Russia, with benevolent condescension, back-slapping and that typical English joviality that makes interlocutors wonder if they are dealing with a very clever and cunning person or with a complete simpleton ... The outcome of this Russian–English exchange of opinions was always the same. The English always did everything in their own way, and always met with failure.[6]

Many British soldiers were war-weary and confused about the reasons for the intervention, especially after the end of the war. Great efforts were made to shield them from the Bolsheviks' anti-war propaganda campaign, which sought to appeal to the soldiers' class loyalties.

Revolutionary Russia was becoming a place of great intrigue to some. British spies such as R. H. Bruce Lockhart, Sidney Reilly and Paul Dukes sparred with the Cheka in the streets of Petrograd, attempting to gather information on the new regime and to assist in its overthrow. On the other hand, some on the left-wing of European politics saw in the Russian Revolution the inauguration of a new workers' state that would herald the (below) Frank Taylor, photograph of British soldiers, Murmansk, c.1919.

Taken on behalf of the Official Photography Section of the North Russian expeditionary forces, the photograph shows two heavily wrapped-up British soldiers changing guard by a makeshift 'Oxford Circus' in their camp in Murmansk.

Special Collections, Leeds University Library, LRA Frank Taylor Liddle RUS48.

The Author as

Joseph Afirenko

Sergei Ilitch

Alexander Markovitch

Alexander Bankau

Plate from Paul Dukes, *The Story of 'ST 25'. Adventure and romance in the Secret Intelligence Service in Red Russia*, London: Cassell & Co., 1938.

Disguises used by British spy Paul Dukes during his missions in Russia.

010290.ff.43.

Images taken by a Japanese photographer, showing medical staff of the Japanese Red Cross treating Russian patients, c.1920.

Foreigners providing aid amidst the terrible humanitarian disasters caused by war, revolution, disease and famine were not trusted by the Bolsheviks, as they saw them as potentially masking counter-revolutionary plots. They were also unpopular among many Allied statesmen, who thought they undermined the blockade aimed at spurring the regime to a total collapse. Despite this, the Quakers and J. Edgar Hoover's American Relief Administration, particularly, did much for the starving millions in revolutionary Russia.

S.T.54/13.

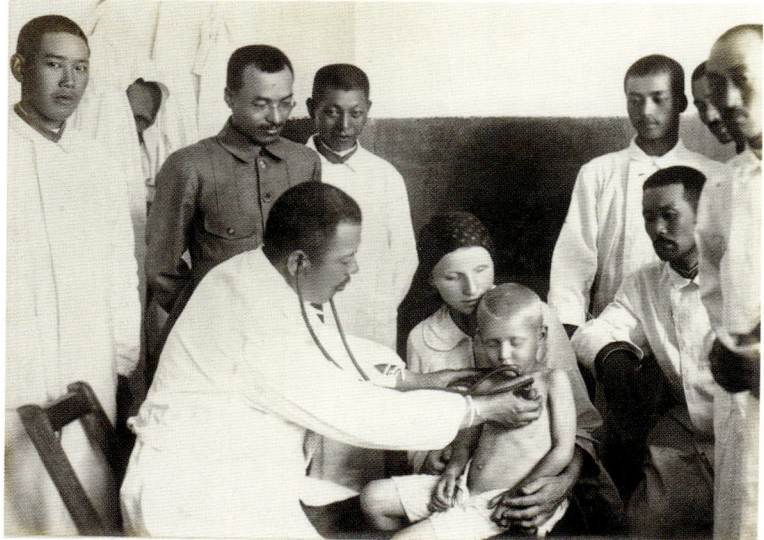

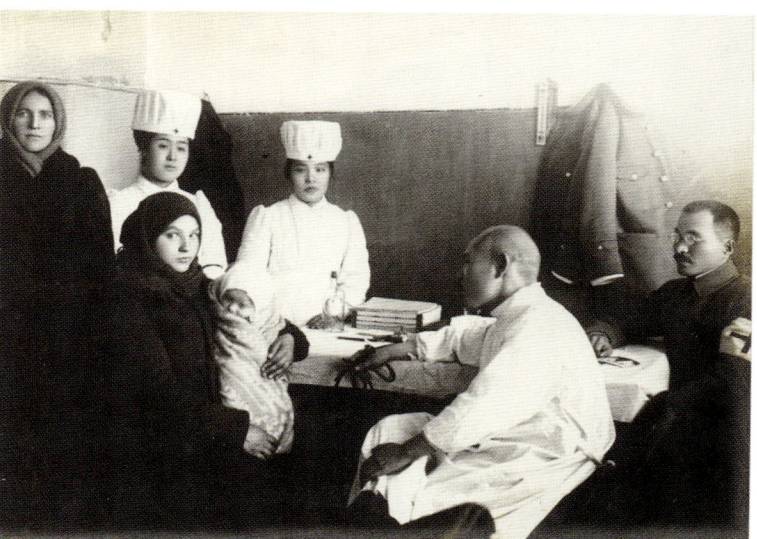

expansion of revolution – first across the continent and then worldwide. Anti-war socialists in particular saw the new regime as a powerful ally and inspiration. In 1918, at a time when the survival of the Soviet regime was uncertain, Arthur Ransome wrote this feverish report 'at a speed to break my pen':

> if they fail, [they] will fail only from having hoped too much. Every true man is in some sort, until his youth dies and his eyes harden, the potential builder of a New Jerusalem. At some time or other, every one of us has dreamed of laying his brick in such a work. And even if this thing that is being built here with tears and blood is not the golden city that we ourselves have dreamed, it is still a thing to the sympathetic understanding of which each one of us is bound by whatever he owes to his own youth.[7]

Leonid Andreiev, *Russia's Call to Humanity*, London, 1920.

Published by the Russian Liberation Committee, an anti-Bolshevik group of Russian émigrés based in London, this book appeals to the outside world to rescue Russia from Bolshevism. The cover is by the prolific British artist Frank Brangwyn.

W2/5898

Arthur Ransome's press pass to the Duma, 1917.

Known to many as the author of children's books such as *Swallows and Amazons*, Ransome was an early enthusiast for the revolution. This press pass dates from his days as a correspondent for the British radical newspaper, the *Daily News*.

Special Collections, Leeds University Library, Ransome 2/D/9.

In order to understand events, many foreign observers turned to earlier books about Russia, particularly those concerning the 1905 revolution and literary works by the likes of Dostoyevsky, Tolstoy and Chekhov.

A copy in the British Library of Tolstoy's *The Hanging Czar* from 1908 was annotated by W. J. Chamberlain, a leading conscientious objector in Britain. Pasted into the front is a 1919 poem by Ivy Litvinov, the wife of Soviet envoy Maxim Litvinov, which satirises what she considered to be the hysterical response of the press to the death of the tsar ('Mr Reuter says they baked him / With his daughters in a cake-tin'). Litvinov compares such reaction to the British newspapers' call to 'cut the cackle and hang the Kaiser!' Another British conscientious objector, Frank Westrope, wrote to his wife Myfanwy from Wandsworth prison on 21 November 1918:

The position in Russia is a great deal discussed in here, it makes my blood boil to hear that the allies are sending

Leo Tolstoy, *The Hanging Czar: An indictment of the Russian Government*, English version of *Ne mogu molchat'*, translated by L. and A. Maude, London: Independent Labour Party, 1908. This copy was annotated by British conscientious objector, W. J. Chamberlain.

8095.ff.64.

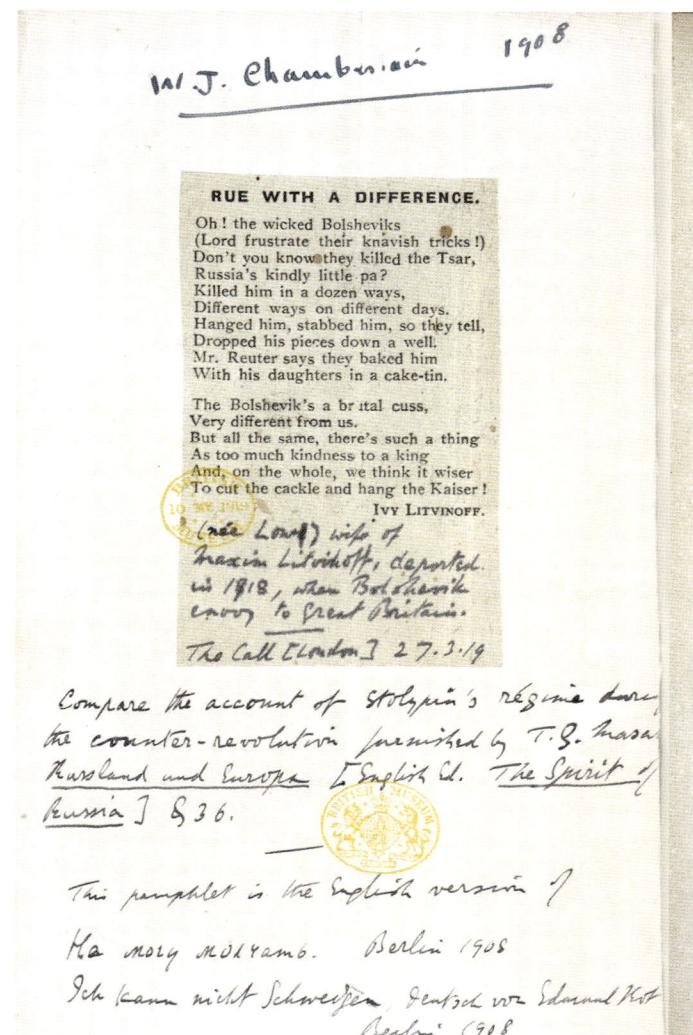

more troops, it would bring the position home to Craik if he were sent there, I would rather be shot ten times over. Have you read the constitution of the First Socialist Republic, the R.S.F.S.R. (Russian Socialist Federal Soviet Republic) it is issued by the Herald as a pamphlet & it is a historic document.[9]

The information reaching the outside world was notoriously inconsistent. Time after time reports that the Bolshevik government had collapsed turned out to be baseless. As future prime minister Ramsay MacDonald commented in 1919, 'The number of times that Kropotkin and other people whose names are known in Great Britain have been shot has become a joke'.[10]

Bolshevik leaders were presented as German Jews pretending to be Russians, secret agents acting on behalf of the Central Powers. Across the world newspapers thundered with anger that family life had been abolished by the new regime, and that Russia's women had been 'nationalised' by decree. Following the precedent set by the lurid reporting of the Great War and the many fictional atrocities attributed by each side to the other, the revolutionaries were presented as monstrous caricatures. With equal inaccuracy, ardent supporters of the Bolshevik revolution painted Russia as a near realised utopia, suffering only because of the Allied intervention and economic blockade, and envisaging the whole of Europe to be on the brink of its own socialist revolution.

Two of the most famous figures to visit revolutionary Russia, and try to sort fact from fiction, were John Reed and Louise Bryant, both American journalists with left-wing sympathies. Reed's *Ten Days That Shook the World* became an iconic first-

Investigators [for the Cheka] vary considerably. There are some who are sincere and upright, though demoniacal visionaries, cold as steel, cruel, unpolluted by thirst for filthy lucre, who see the dawn of proletarian liberty only through mists of non-proletarian blood. Such men (or women) are actuated by malignant longing for revenge for every wrong, real or imaginary, suffered in the past.

Paul Dukes, British spy.[8]

Photograph from *Voina i revoliutsiia*, c.1918.

This image was reproduced in early British journals, newspapers and books claiming to show Lenin and Trotsky (the two men in the foreground on the right). It is difficult now to imagine the Russian Revolution without visualising such distinct figures, but clearly this image was of the wrong men entirely. The Russian album *Voina i revoliutsiia (War and Revolution)* identified the two men as Christian Rakovsky (on the right), a Bulgarian communist who unsuccessfully attempted to spark a Bolshevik revolution in the Kingdom of Romania, and Robert Grimm (to his left), a Swiss anti-war socialist.

X.802/4756.

hand account of the Bolshevik revolution. Delegations of trade unionists, socialists and intellectuals from across the world soon followed.

Observers were fascinated, enthralled and repelled by this strange new stage of the revolution. In many cases their responses were intensified by the fact that they were not simply looking at a foreign country. In witnessing the experience of revolutionary Russia, they were contemplating a possible future for their own nations too.

Permanent Revolution and Comintern

It was not just that the outside world was interested in Russia – Russia was itself greatly interested in the outside world. Where Robespierre had said, during the French Revolution, that 'all kings could have led passive lives or die unpunished on their bloodstained thrones, if they had known how to respect the independence of the French people', the Bolsheviks saw the global working class as having a community of interest transcending all national borders. After the Russian Revolution great social upheavals shook the European and global status quo, threatening established social structures everywhere. Foreign states feared that Bolshevik Russia was leading or inspiring these events.

When Lenin and the Bolshevik Party seized power in Russia in October 1917, the concept of world revolution was at the core of both their belief system and their political strategy. First, as Marxists they understood the world to be moving towards ever closer integration as capitalism, in pursuit of greater profits and wider markets, transcended the borders of nation-states to colonise ever more countries and continents. Inaugurating the next stage of history, the proletarian revolution would, in their view, accelerate, extend and transform these globalising

Adolf Strakhov, *Azbuka revoliutsii*
(*ABC of Revolution*), series of posters, 1921.

In this image by Ukrainian Soviet artist
Adolf Strakhov (pseudonym of Braslavskii),
the Russian worker and peasant share
centre-stage as a variety of European and
non-European nationalities approach.

LF.31.b.12070.

dynamics, further dissolving national–territorial distinctions at the same time as it extinguished divisions of class, ethnicity, religion and culture. The revolution would lead to the creation of a unified socialist world-state, and ultimately to worldwide stateless communism.

Secondly, as keen revolutionary strategists the Bolsheviks believed that the survival of the workers' state in Russia, an overwhelmingly peasant country, depended on the proletariat of the industrially more advanced European nations overthrowing their own 'bourgeois' governments and coming to the aid of their Soviet comrades. To this end, Russian revolutionaries strove to incite social upheaval abroad. For many contemporaries, both sympathisers and opponents, the Russian Revolution derived its explosive, momentous power from its expressed ambition to unite anti-imperialist, agrarian, anti-war and socialist movements in one epoch-making world revolution. In March 1918 Lenin declared:

> Regarded from the world-historical point of view, there would doubtlessly be no hope of the ultimate victory of our revolution if it were to remain alone, if there were no revolutionary movements in other countries. When the Bolshevik Party tackled the job alone, it did so in the firm conviction that the revolution was maturing in all countries and that in the end – but not at the very beginning – no matter what difficulties we experienced, no matter what defeats were in store for us, the world socialist revolution would come – because it is coming; would mature – because it is maturing and will reach full maturity. I repeat, our salvation from all these difficulties is an all-Europe revolution …
>
> You wanted the revolution to reckon with you. But history has taught you a lesson. It is a lesson, because it is the absolute truth that without a German revolution we are doomed – perhaps not in Petrograd, not in Moscow, but in Vladivostok, in more remote places to which perhaps we shall have to retreat, and the distance to which is perhaps greater than the distance from Petrograd to Moscow. At all events, under all conceivable circumstances, if the German revolution does not come, we are doomed.[11]

The belief in an imminent German revolution was echoed by Trotsky, speaking in the same month:

> We declare that the moment of social explosion in all states is inevitably approaching, and we, to whom history has given victory sooner than the rest, with all the possibilities that follow from this, must be ready, at the first thunderclap of the world revolution, to bring armed help to our foreign brothers in revolt.

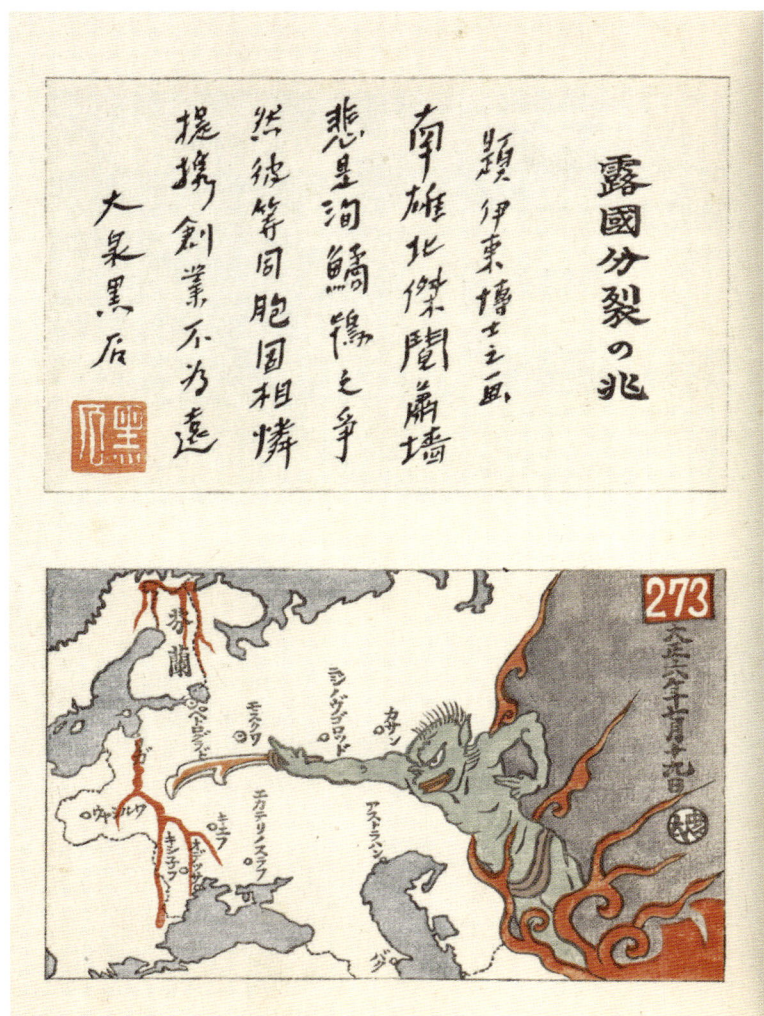

And, in particular, at the moment when the German proletariat, which is nearer to revolution than any other, when this proletariat, enveloped in the flames of militant enthusiasm, comes out into the streets – and it will come, whatever has been said by the croakers of ill-omen in their party, who have struck themselves forever out of the International – we must be prepared, organised in fighting units to go to their aid.[12]

The Brest-Litovsk Treaty may have left swathes of the old Russian Empire outside of Bolshevik control, but it did give them time to organise and arm themselves. They combined their preparations with an intensive propaganda campaign among the German soldiers which soon bore fruit. One German general recalled, 'the troops actually melted away before my eyes'.[13] Many revolutionaries were unhappy with this compromise, and even at this early stage were arguing that the Bolsheviks had betrayed the world revolution for the purposes of retaining their own state power. With this in mind, in July 1918 the Left Socialist Revolutionaries assassinated Count Mirbach, the German Ambassador, hoping to spark a further conflict between Germany and Russia which could develop into a general revolutionary conflagration. Lenin, however, resisted being pulled into this adventure, knowing it would endanger the beleaguered new Soviet state even more greatly.

With the war turning sharply against the Central Powers, social unrest in these countries became revolution. In Germany in November 1918, with armed workers, soldiers and sailors in the streets pushing for an end to the war, the Kaiser abdicated and a Social Democratic cabinet replaced the imperial government before surrendering to the Entente. Many Germans saw this as a national humiliation, and the idea grew of the 'stab in the back' – a belief that the nation could have won the war if it had not been betrayed from within. In *Mein Kampf* Adolf Hitler recalled:

> The dignified old gentleman seemed all a-tremble as he informed us that the House of Hollenzollern should no longer bear the German imperial crown; that the fatherland had become a 'republic'; that we must pray to the Almighty not to refuse His blessing to this change and not to abandon our people in the times to come … I could stand it no longer. It became impossible for me to sit still one minute more. Again everything went black before my eyes; I tottered and

Image from German satirical magazine *Simplicissimus,* vol.22, no.47, 19 February 1918.

The formerly liberal magazine *Simplicissimus* adopted a more conservative and nationalistic tone during the First World War. In this cartoon from early 1918, two Russian peasants bring a red Trojan Horse, packed with armed revolutionaries, into the very centre of Berlin. A wave of strikes in Germany in January 1918 had stoked fears of Bolshevik-supported revolution.

LOU.F459.

groped my way back to the dormitory, threw myself on my bunk, and dug my burning head into my blanket and pillow.[14]

For the Bolsheviks, who had celebrated the first anniversary of their seizure of power just days previously, this German revolution was taken as a vindication of their gamble. German troops began to withdraw from the occupied territories, and in Germany itself Workers' and Soldiers' Councils were formed. In Alsace, then a part of Germany, a Soviet republic was declared (but quickly fell when French troops intervened to restore order). The mass movement of the workers and soldiers in Germany threatened everywhere to escape the control of its leaders. History appeared to be repeating itself.

However, the new government of moderate Social Democrats had themselves learned the lessons of the Russian Revolution. When mass demonstrations and a general strike in January of 1919 turned into an armed uprising, the government responded with harsh repression. The Freikorps, a network

(below right) Erich Wollenberg, *Als Rot-Armist vor München: Reportage aus der Münchener Räterepublik* (*Red Army Soldier in Munich*), Berlin: Internationaler Arbeiter-Verlag, 1929, cover.

Wollenberg had been a lieutenant in the German army in 1918, becoming an active revolutionary soldier in the same year and fighting for the short-lived Munich Soviet Republic. After the failure of the German revolutionary movement he fled to the Soviet Union in 1923 and joined the Red Army.

X.700/10339.

(left) *Was Will Spartakus? (What does Spartacus want?)*, German poster, 1918.

The Spartacist League, on the far left of German socialism, supported the Bolshevik revolution, and was transformed into the German Communist Party (KPD) at the end of 1918. The poster's unknown artist replied to the question posed in the image by illlustrating that Spartacus would not stop after slaying only the monarchist head of the hydra, but would also lop off the heads of the Church, the Junker, the capitalists and the militarists.

Imperial War Museum, PST 7849.

of radical right-wing paramilitary units, mobilised to crush the Spartacist uprising, and the figureheads of the German revolutionary movement, Karl Liebknecht and Rosa Luxemburg, were brutally killed.

Though multiple attempts were made to rekindle the revolution in the following years, and a Bavarian Soviet Republic managed to last for one month in 1919, momentum soon passed to the fiercely anti-Bolshevik far-right.

Austro-Hungary had been, after Russia, the second of the great empires to disintegrate in the closing years of the First World War. In March 1919 the Hungarian communists, in coalition with more moderate socialists, succeeded in forcing the resignation of the government of Mihály Károlyi. Instability, warfare with neighbouring countries and the exercise of state terrorism marred the 133 days of the Hungarian Soviet Republic's existence. Defeated by the Romanian army and shaken by mass peasant resistance, the communist regime was replaced by

Elöre a vörös rém ellen! (Forward Against the Red Monster!), Hungarian anti-revolutionary poster, Szeged, c.1920.

The poster calls on Whites to 'advance against the Red monster!'

Imperial War Museum, PST 5945.

Workers listening to Béla Kun, Hungarian Communist Party leader, in 1919.

Dankó, Ödön. Védd meg a proletárok hatalmát (Defend Proletarian Power), Hungarian revolutionary poster, Budapest, 1919.

The poster calls on the embattled supporters of the Soviets to 'defend proletarian power' against the moneybags.

Imperial War Museum, PST 4986.

VÉDD MEG!

A PROLETÁROK HATALMÁT

Delegates at the Second Congress of the Comintern, 1920.

Maxim Gorky stands immediately behind Lenin. To the right stands Grigori Zinoviev and Indian revolutionary M. N. Roy. Karl Radek and Nikolai Bukharin smoke in the background on the left.

the dictatorship of Admiral Horthy and a ferocious counter-revolutionary White Terror. The agrarian revolution which in 1917 so aided the Russian Bolsheviks had now helped to secure the defeat of the Hungarian communists.

In March 1919 Lenin founded the Third Communist International (Comintern). With this new organisation based in Moscow, the Bolshevik regime hoped to bring centralised leadership and coordination to the spontaneous revolutionary struggles being launched across the globe.

Western governments took the threat posed by the Comintern seriously. America in particular was gripped by a fear of revolution far outweighing the actual level of anarchist violence and labour unrest it experienced in these years. What has been called the 'First Red Scare' lasted from 1919 until the middle of 1920, when a predicted May Day uprising failed to materialise. In that time thousands were arrested and deported. Among these was the Russian-born anarchist Emma Goldman. In her memoirs she wrote:

> I looked at my watch. It was 4:20 A.M. on the day of our Lord, December 21, 1919. On the deck above us I could hear the men tramping up and down in the wintry blast. I felt dizzy, visioning a transport of politicals doomed to Siberia, the étape of former Russian days. Russia of the past rose before me and I saw the revolutionary martyrs being driven into exile. But no, it was New York, it was America, the land of liberty! Through the port-hole I could see the great city

Deiateli Kommunisticheskogo Internatsionala (Delegates of the Second Communist International), Petrograd, 1920.

This souvenir edition was published for the second congress of Comintern in August 1920. Around this time, national communist parties affiliated to the Comintern were forming across the world, attempting to unite all revolutionary socialists into one global revolutionary party. In France, for example, a majority of members of the socialist French section of the Workers' International split to form a Communist Party, while most of its parliamentarians remained with the reformist Second International. The split in the world socialist movement between Social Democrats and Communists was now institutionalised.

LF.31.b.1026.

receding into the distance, its sky-line of buildings traceable by their rearing heads. It was my beloved city, the metropolis of the New World. It was America, indeed, America repeating the terrible scenes of tsarist Russia! I glanced up – the Statue of Liberty! …

The strains of Russian melodies, ringing from a hundred throats, were resounding through the *Buford*. The men were on deck, and their lusty voices rose above the rolling of the waves, reaching us in our cabin. The powerful baritone of the leader intoned the first stanzas, and then the entire crowd joined in the chorus. Revolutionary songs they sang, forbidden old Russian folk-tunes surcharged with the grief and yearning of the peasant, or echoing Nekrassov's women who heroically followed their lovers to prison and exile. All aboard grew silent, even the guards ceasing their march and listening with strained ears to the heart-rending melodies.[15]

Although initially a sympathiser, Goldman was to become a critic of the Bolsheviks after the suppression of the Kronstadt uprising in 1921, branding them betrayers of the world revolution.

2nd EDITION – revised

THE STORY OF THE LIMERICK SOVIET

the 1919 general strike against british militarism

D. R. O'Connor Lysaght, *The Story of the Limerick Soviet, April 1919*, Limerick Branch of Peoples Democracy, 1981.

It is known that Lenin spoke English with an Irish accent, having been taught the language by an Irish tutor. Less well known is the fact that over 100 soviets formed in Ireland in the years of its own revolution and civil war. Left-wing elements in the labour movement and the IRA hoped to build a workers' republic, rather than be satisfied with independence from the British Empire on a Catholic and nationalist basis. However, the Bolsheviks did not confine their support to these more radical sections, but also supported Éamon de Valera's Irish Free State as an anti-British entity, with diplomatic recognition and smuggled tsarist jewels.

X.809/60571.

In the context of the Jim Crow laws institutionalising segregation and white supremacy, a wave of racist lynchings and the resurgence of the Ku Klux Klan, many African-American radicals also took inspiration from the Russian Revolution's internationalist ideals. Published in the July 1919 issue of the *Liberator*, a US socialist monthly magazine, black poet Claude McKay's poem 'The Little Peoples' condemns the government of Woodrow Wilson for supporting self-determination of European nations while neglecting the oppression of blacks by whites at home:

> The little peoples of the troubled earth,
> The little nations that are weak and white;-
> For them the glory of another birth,
> For them the lifting of the veil of night.
> The big men of the world in concert met,
> Have sent forth in their power a new decree:
> Upon the old harsh wrongs the sun must set,
> Henceforth the little peoples must be free!
>
> But we, the blacks, less than the trampled dust,
> Who walk the new ways with the old dim eyes,-
> We to the ancient gods of greed and lust
> Must still be offered up as sacrifice:
> Oh, we who deign to live but will not dare,
> The white world's burden must forever bear!

While the Comintern struggled to assert its leadership over disparate and disunited communist movements in different countries and imperial territories, spontaneous uprisings were being defeated across Europe. In monarchist Spain, there was a strong wave of popular agitation. General strikes in both 1917 and 1919 spurred the growth of anarcho-syndicalism around the revolutionary trade union the CNT. Nationalist movements in Catalonia and the Basque region were expanding rapidly. In reaction, Captain General Primo de Rivera launched a military coup and established a dictatorship in 1923. This banned political parties and suppressed all revolutionary and separatist tendencies.

Meanwhile, Italian workers staged a general strike in July 1919 in support of the Russian Revolution. The years 1919–1920 became known as 'Biennio Rosso', the 'Two Red Years', during which workers across Italy occupied factories, and organised and armed themselves for revolt. In response to this potentially revolutionary situation, the Fascist movement seized its opportunity. Benito Mussolini, the *Duce* (Leader) of Fascism who had been expelled from the Socialist Party for supporting Italian participation in the war, led the paramilitary Blackshirts in the march on Rome in October 1922. Strongly nationalist and anti-

Marxist, the Fascist regime which resulted from this *coup d'état* crushed the workers' movement.

In Britain, a post-war wave of strikes led by the Triple Alliance of miners, railwaymen and transport workers raised anxieties among the governing elite. Politically the workers' movement, despite the moderation of most of its leaders, united around opposition to the Allied military intervention in Soviet Russia and the economic blockade of the new communist state.

Unrest among demobilised soldiers, race riots in various cities and even strikes by the police led the British government to make secret contingency plans in case a revolution did break out, and to draw up measures to avert an uprising, if it seemed imminent (including increasing the availability of alcohol, to drown unrest in inebriation). The closest Britain came to revolution was on 'Red' Clydeside, where the legendary activist John Maclean had been agitating against the war and capitalism for years. On Red Clydeside, mass demonstrations in favour of Soviet socialism were pacified using tanks and the military.

The same year in Britain, 1918, saw the enfranchisement of women aged over 30 with property and of working-class men, aiding the parliamentary advance of the Labour Party. It seemed to be only a matter of time before a Labour government would be voted in, committed to a reformist and non-revolutionary form of socialism which was, nevertheless, almost Bolshevism in the eyes of many. For the Bolsheviks themselves, however, Labour activists were dismissed as the agents of the bourgeoisie in the working-class movement, diverting workers' energies into futile parliamentarism.

The party that was affiliated to the Comintern was the Communist Party of Great Britain (CPGB), formed in August 1920 out of a number of small socialist groups. Although they won two MPs in 1922 and were active in the trade unions, the CPGB never managed to replace the Labour Party as the chief political representatives of the working-class movement, despite experiments with different political approaches. However, many key figures in the socialist and trade union movements passed through the CPGB at one point or another, as did a number of important cultural figures who exerted a left-wing and pro-Soviet pressure on the socialist movement.

Initially frustrated in its efforts to trigger an immediate revolution in the West, the Comintern turned its attention to the East. As expounded by Lenin, one of the particular innovations of Marxism developed by the Bolsheviks was the idea that capitalism had reached a new stage – the era of monopoly capitalism and imperialism. Crises of capitalism in the most developed countries, Lenin argued, could be reduced or annulled by the exploitation and oppression of colonial peoples. In the absence of recurrent and deepening crises, social democratic parties could win concessions

Banner gifted to the Shipley Young Communist League (YCL) by young communists in Moscow. The YCL was linked to the Communist Party of Great Britain (CPGB).

The Peoples' History Museum, Manchester.

Congress of the Peoples of the East, Azerbaijan, 1920.

The Congress symbolised the Bolsheviks' desire to build relations with the anti-colonial and nationalist revolutionary movements of the East.

for privileged strata in the working class. In such conditions, class antagonisms were not resolved, but simply displaced or sublimated. Communists, by weakening the hold of imperialistic nations over their colonial subjects, could shut off this 'safety-valve' and accelerate the advent of revolution in the countries of developed capitalism.

In 1920 the Congress of the Peoples of the East was held in the city of Baku, then the capital of the Soviet Socialist Republic of Azerbaijan. Grigori Zinoviev, in a speech at the first session, declared:

> Yes, we are moving against bourgeois Britain 'to take the British imperialists by the throat and set our knee on their chest'. British capitalism must be dealt a most powerful blow, aimed at its very heart. That is true. But at the same time we must educate the working masses of the East to hate the rich in general – Russian, Jewish, German, French – and to desire to fight them.
>
> The enormous significance of the revolution that is beginning in the East does not consist in requesting the British imperialist gentlemen to take their feet off the table, only to then permit the Turkish rich to stretch out their feet comfortably on the table. No – we want to ask, ever so politely, that *all* the rich take their dirty feet off the table, so that there may reign among us not luxury, not charlatanry, not mockery of the people, and not idleness, but so that the world may be ruled by the toiler with toil-hardened hands.[16]

The Comintern launched a campaign of anti-racist propaganda in order to shake the myths legitimising colonial rule. Across the African continent – colonised intensively during the pre-war 'Scramble for Africa' – there were initially very few converts to communism, but the anti-racist and anti-colonial message inspired many, particularly among African émigré intellectuals.

Before the war, Russia and Britain in particular had long competed for hegemony over the Middle East and Central Asia – a struggle known in Russia as the 'Tournament of Shadows', but better known to Britons as the 'Great Game'. After the war this struggle for hegemony continued, but took on a very different character.

With the end of the First World War, imperial rule across the world faced multiple and growing crises. During the Turkish War of Independence, as the Turks under Mustafa Kemal Pasha (later Atatürk) sought to carve a new state out of the ruins of the fallen Ottoman Empire, the Soviets provided diplomatic recognition and a substantial subsidy of money and arms in order to strengthen the campaign against British imperialism and its proxies. Egypt was also gripped by the desire for 'self-determination', and a revolutionary uprising against British rule in November 1918 was put down by July 1919, leaving many dead. This revolt, however, succeeded in forcing Britain to grant Egyptian independence in 1922.

India, the 'jewel in the crown' of the British Empire, was an important object of Bolshevik sympathy and ambition. For the Comintern, serious unrest in India would weaken Britain by depriving it of revenue at a crucial moment of instability. They also hoped resistance by such an important colonial possession would inspire anti-imperialist movements in other countries.

The Comintern reached out to the dispersed network of Indian émigré revolutionaries and began to establish links with the Indian nationalist movement. One Indian revolutionary, Mahendra Pratap, attempted unsuccessfully to persuade the Bolsheviks in 1918 and 1919 to invade India militarily in an alliance with the new Germany. Independently of the communists, Gandhi launched a campaign of peaceful civil disobedience in 1920. He felt himself forced to end it in 1922, however, as it threatened to become radicalised out of his control, with other Indian anti-imperialists increasingly turning to Marxism for guidance.

China also became a key site of operations for revolutionary socialists working with nationalist and peasant movements. Young intellectuals associated with the May Fourth New Culture Movement of 1919, together with periodicals such as the *New Youth*, were key in introducing the ideas of Marx and Lenin to the country. With the help of the Comintern, the Chinese Communist Party was founded in 1921, and forged an alliance with the revolutionary bourgeois-nationalist Kuomintang Party.

This global revolutionary wave receded before the Comintern managed to assert effective leadership. Nonetheless, it had forged new formations of class and political alliance, created radical new forces on both the left and the right, and profoundly changed the balance of power between nations in the world system. For the Comintern, it had also left behind

Sergei Dalin, *V riadakh kitaiskoi revoliutsii* (*Within the Ranks of the Chinese Revolution*), Moscow, 1926, cover.

The cover image depicts a Chinese revolutionary trampling the White Ensign, a flag of the British Royal Navy. As a 19-year-old communist, Sergei Dalin first visited China in 1922 as a delegate to the First Congress of the Socialist Youth of China. He then taught at the Sun Yat-sen Communist University of the Toilers of China, a Comintern school based in Moscow, from 1925 to 1930. In 1926, when this book was published, he went to China to recruit more students to the communist school. Dalin continued his career as a scholar, specialising in Chinese studies.

YF.2004.a.9118.

With the rising roar of the 'world revolution' and the striking progress of the 'emancipation of mankind' movement, we must change our old concepts of the issues which we have never doubted before, the methods which we have never adopted before, and the words which we have always been afraid to utter. We doubt what we have never before doubted. We adopt what we have never before adopted. We are no longer afraid.

From an early article by Mao Zedong, 14 July 1919.[17]

great contradictions. In the West, as capitalism recovered, social democrats solidified their support among the working class, while in many countries fascism and national socialism gathered strength. The communists found themselves isolated on the left while still hated and feared by the right.

In the East, the Indian revolutionary M. N. Roy, a key strategist of international socialism among colonial peoples, condemned the Bolsheviks' tactic of boosting bourgeois nationalists who were fundamentally hostile to communism, rather than seeking to break nationalists' hold over the peasantry and workers. Roy was soon proved correct when, at great cost to the international revolutionary movement, nationalists in a number of countries, including Turkey and China, turned violently on their erstwhile communist allies.

However, the most obvious contradiction was this – out of the Bolshevik revolution, initiated in order to smash the tsarist state, hasten the end of global capitalism and prevent Russian imperialism from re-asserting itself, a new multinational empire was to grow. To a great many observers, the new Soviet empire seemed to have much in common with that of the tsars.

From Russian Empire to Soviet Union

The Russian Empire, often referred to as a 'prison house of nations', maintained its control of varied ethnicities, cultures and religions across its vast landmass by force, and by the integration of local elites into Russian rule. 'Self-determination of nations' in these conditions was a key slogan for many of the revolutionaries.

In the weakening and overthrow of Russia's central governments throughout 1917, nationalist and socialist currents of revolution found expression in these subjugated nations, who were newly freed to pursue their own paths in the world. In some areas, nationalist and communist aspirations were in harmony, but more often they contradicted and conflicted with one another. Newly emerging states were thrown into chaos involving civil war, class war, agrarian revolt and local uprisings. In the disorder of a suddenly dissolving empire, they were also prey to the ambitions of larger states – and of each other.

Part of the deal reached at Brest-Litovsk in March 1918 involved limiting Bolshevik propaganda in the territories formerly under tsarist rule and now occupied by Germany, including Ukraine, Belarus, Finland, Poland and the Baltic states. In order to get around this, nominally independent revolutionary communist parties were formed in each area. They were organised through Stalin's Commissariat for Nationalities, in an organisation known unofficially as the 'Little International', a precursor of the Comintern.

As these newly independent nations made a bridge between Russia and Germany and therefore between the revolution and

Europe, their role was crucial to the world revolutionary project – and indeed to the counter-efforts of enemies aimed at preventing the revolutionary flames from sweeping into Western Europe. With the German army in retreat at the end of 1918, a pattern of 'revolution from abroad' was set. These pseudo-independent communist parties would incite their followers to overthrow the governments left behind by the Germans, then invite the Red Army to come to their defence and consolidate their victories.

In this manner the Reds quickly swept westwards. They were halted by the organised resistance of nationalist armies before reaching Germany, however, and faced counter-attacks by Latvia, Lithuania and Poland. The line between liberation and military annexation became blurred. In the experience of many of the nations that had gained autonomy or independence after 1917, the new Soviet internationalism with its headquarters in Moscow appeared little different from the old Russian imperialism.

In Ukraine, revolutionary nationalism proved to have stronger appeal among the population than proletarian socialism. Throughout the spring and summer of 1917 the Ukrainian Central Rada had wrangled with the Provisional Government for autonomy and a federal relationship with Russia, but after the Bolshevik coup they declared complete independence. Nationalist forces under Symon Petliura struggled to assert this independence in the midst of broader conflicts – the civil war between Reds and Whites, the German occupation, Polish attempts to annex territory, regional and anarchist uprisings, and the Bolshevik attempts to spread revolution. When the Germans pulled out of the country in early 1919 a Ukrainian Soviet Socialist Republic was declared, but fighting continued until 1921.

Johannes Erwig, *Rødt eller Hvidt? Sandheden om Finland* (*Red or White? The Truth about Finland*), København, 1918.

Finland, which had been a Grand Duchy under the tsars, declared independence in December of 1917. For the first few months of 1918 Finland experienced a bloody civil war, as Reds backed by Soviet Russia and Whites backed by Germany struggled for control. The Finnish White Guards were ultimately successful, and the nation became an independent republic.

8095.ee.23.

Russian Imperial stamps over-printed with the symbol of the Ukrainian Rada, 1918.

The Ukrainian Rada was the parliamentary body that became a central focus of Ukrainian progressive and nationalist vision.

Philatelic collections (BL).

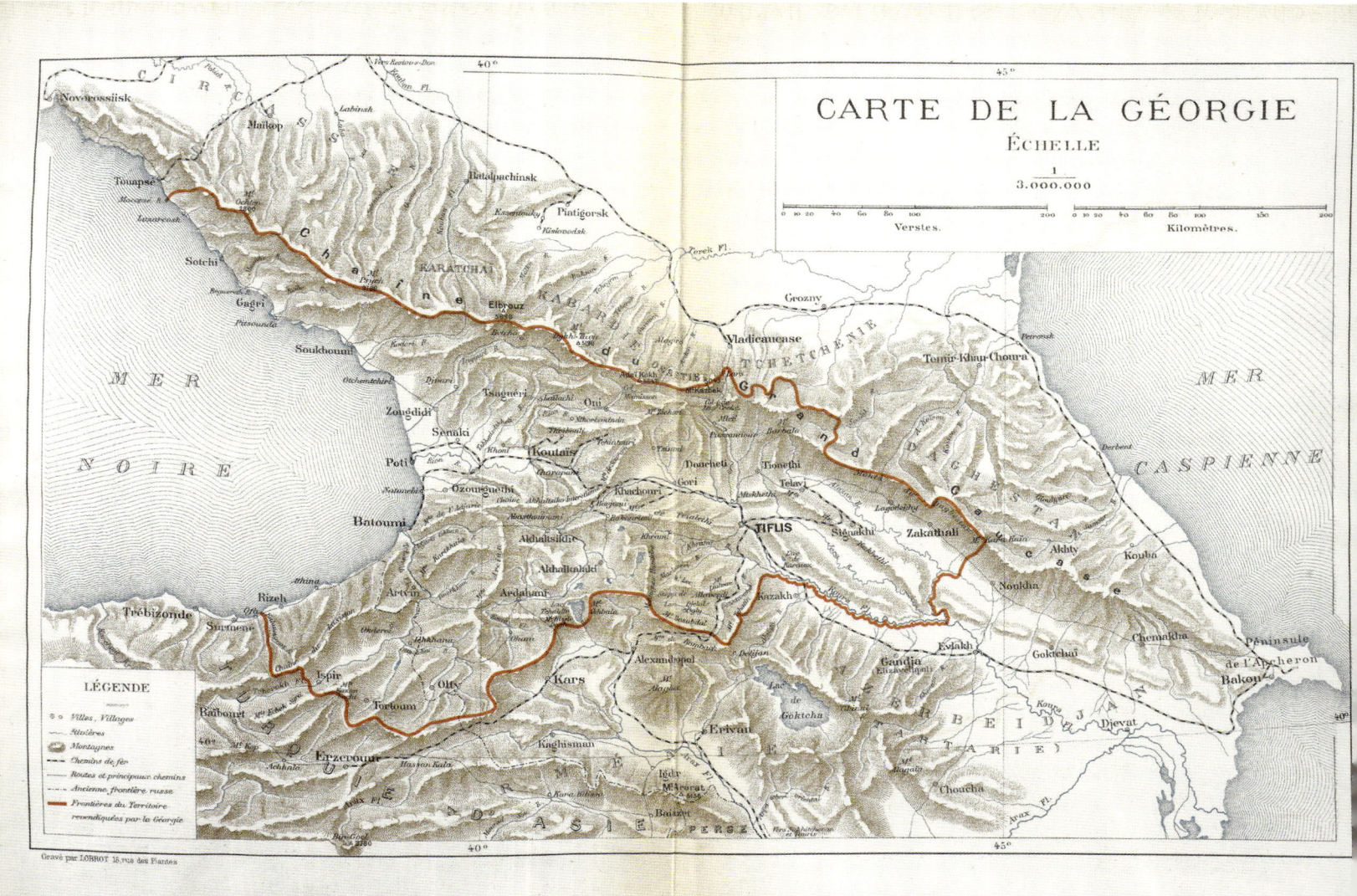

CARTE DE LA GÉORGIE

ÉCHELLE

1
3.000.000

Memorandum presented to the Peace Conference, Political Claims, Frontiers. Followed by the Act of Independence of Georgia and a Map, Paris, 1919.

This map of the borders for independent Georgia was presented to the Paris Peace Conference of 1919.

08028.i.10.

Revolutionaries across the new nations were faced with a dilemma similar to that articulated in the diary of the first Ukrainian Prime Minister, Volodymyr Vynnychenko. The painful compromises they were forced to reach with the different contending forces shaped the future of their nations. In June 1920 Vynnychenko sought an agreement with the Bolsheviks, but struggled to come to terms with what he saw as their Great Russian chauvinism. In his diary he wrote: 'Once again I have the same tragedy that has been tearing me apart for almost two years. To join the Russian Bolsheviks means to oppress my nation and myself with my own hands. To join Petliura and the reactionary forces means to oppress the revolution, myself, and everything that I consider to be good for the whole of mankind.'[18] Disillusioned, he emigrated to Europe three months later.

Similar dynamics drove the revolution in the Transcaucasian colonies of the former Russian Empire. The soviets set up in

Georgia, Armenia and Azerbaijan were hostile to the Bolsheviks from the beginning, and national, ethnic and religious rivalries cut across any politics based on social class. In April 1918 they voted to secede from Russia and form an independent Transcaucasian Democratic Federal Republic. This collapsed after a month, splitting the three nations into independent republics. Azerbaijan and Armenia were brought under communist rule in 1920, by the action of both native Bolshevik revolutionaries and invasion by the Red Army.

Eghishe Charents, an Armenian revolutionary poet who served in the Red Army throughout 1918 and 1919, was disappointed when Soviet treaties in 1921 ceded Armenian land to Turkey, including Kars, his city of birth. Many Armenian revolutionaries felt conflicted, believing that their newly won national independence had been sacrificed to a broader anti-imperialist and world revolutionary strategy, but Charents was among those who retained their loyalty to the Soviets in spite of this. His poem 'Soma' of 1919 had issued a powerful call to join the world revolutionary conflagration:

> Hey, distant brothers and friends,
> do you not hear our invitation
> joyous, festive, even proud
> to come to join our circle-dance?
> Come.
>
> Whoever does not see
> the sky-scraping flame
> is blind.
> Let whoever has a heart
> that can be kindled, come, now.
>
> Whoever comes, must bring with him
> a heart to be sacrificed.
> Come join the dance
> of universal fire.
>
> Let it spread,
> this cleansing fire,
> this incandescent flame
> and let the old life
> which smouldered in vain
> turn to ash and pass.[19]

Independent Georgia was at first declared a German protectorate, governed by the Mensheviks, and was forced to fight to secure its independence against the Bolsheviks, the Whites and the Turks. Between 1918 and 1921 Georgia held out as a Menshevik stronghold. In February 1921 disorder broke out

(left). *Tol'ko Sovetskaia vlast' vedet proletariev Vostoka i Zapada k osvobozhdeniiu (Only the Soviet Power is Leading the Proletariat of East and West to Liberation)*, Kazan', 1920; reprinted in *Plakat sovetskogo Vostoka*, Moscow, 2013.

The text is in Russian and the Tatar in Arabic script.

YF.2014.b.518.

(below). *Khăzir mīndă ăzad! (Now I Too am Free)*, poster in Tatar in Arabic script, 1921.

A Muslim woman turns her back on the mosque; two men invite her to the Youth Organisation. In the absence of a sizeable proletariat in Central Asia, the Soviets hoped that Muslim women, as the most oppressed group in the region's patriarchal structure, could become agents of social change. Muslim women as agents of revolution were tasked to bring Enlightenment and socialist values to traditional pre-capitalist society.

Cup.645.a.6.

(opposite). Dmitrii Moor, *Bud' na strazhe (Be on your Guard!)*, poster, 1920.

From the start, the Bolsheviks' vision of world revolution co-existed with a countervailing strategy aimed at consolidating territorial power – in particular by securing and strengthening the new socialist state's external borders against its hostile neighbours. Here the Red Army soldier personifies the state. His body is the body of Soviet Russia (his right shoulder and raised leg mark out the western state border, and his back rests against and fuses into the Urals, depicted as the bony 'spine' of the country – in Russian the same word means both 'spine' and 'mountain range'). The vitality and resilience of the state is equated with the strength and will of its citizenry-in-arms.

Maps CC.5.a.545.

which, exaggerated by Stalin and his allies in order to convince Lenin to sanction the use of the army, was used as a pretext for an invasion.

Russia's treatment of Georgia at this time became a key point of conflict between Lenin and Stalin. Stalin, though himself Georgian, was accused of 'Great Russian chauvinism' in his dealings with the small nation. As Stalin became increasingly powerful, the old calls for 'self-determination' sounded increasingly hollow in the face of the communists' centralising drive.

Similar ambiguities afflicted the course of revolution in the predominantly Muslim Central Asian parts of the former Russian Empire. Here conflicts between Reds, Whites and other intervening foreign powers forced revolution on to populations from outside. In Turkestan, the Tashkent Soviet succeeded in forcefully pacifying an Islamic nationalist surge, while in

Kto w Boga wierzy – w obronie Ostrobramskiej, pod Sztandar Orła i Pogoni! (*Whoever Believes in God – Defend the Icon of the Mother of God Under the Polish-Lithuanian Banner*), poster, 1920.

A gallant Polish soldier watched over by the Virgin Mary strikes at a bestial Red invader, who is depicted with stereotypical Jewish physical traits. Poland was seen by many counter-revolutionaries across the world as the first line of defence for Christian civilisation against atheistic Bolshevism.

LF.37.b.277.

the Kazakh steppe, as White forces refused to grant autonomy and as the civil war turned against the Whites, the Bolsheviks took control.

In what was then 'Outer' Mongolia, which had gained independence from China in 1911, the Reds, the Whites and the Chinese struggled for supremacy. The Mongolian People's Party, in alliance with the Soviets, fought to expel the Whites in what has become known as the 'People's Revolution of 1921'. In 1924 the Mongolian People's Republic was formed.

In the Middle East, the experience of the Soviet Socialist Republic of Iran, also known as the Gilan Republic, encapsulates the key contradictions of the Comintern's international policies.

The Bolsheviks had long cultivated links with the Jangalis, the revolutionary nationalist movement in Iran led by Kuchek Khan. With the aid of Red Army troops, a coalition of the Jangali movement and the Iranian Communist Party established a Soviet state in 1920. Quickly the two partners came into conflict – the Jangalis opposed British imperialism and the traditional elites of Iranian society, but they also hoped to preserve private property against the country's rising peasant movement.

With the Gilan Republic riven by strife and liable to be overrun at any time, the Soviets forced the issue, bargaining away its existence in the discussions for the Anglo–Russian trade agreement reached in 1921. In order to improve revolutionary Russia's trade relations, the Iranian revolutionary movement was dismantled. Imperial Britain was then allowed to pursue its neo-colonial goals through a government of Iran's traditional elite.

The Iranian poet Abolqāsem Lahūtī was among the revolutionaries who found exile in the USSR after the fall of the Gilan Republic. As the revolutionary wave receded, supporters of the Soviets began to stress the wise statesmanship of the men in the Kremlin more than the liberatory potential of mass movements, as in this extract from Abolqāsem Lahūtī's 'Qasidai Kremel' ('Ode to the Kremlin') of 1923:

> Suddenly the earth trembled and dreaded heaven's
>   vicissitudes
> When the red banner proclaimed the end of tyranny.
> The armies of oppression fled, the chain of terror snapped
> From the downtrodden toiler and the naked worker.
> The house of God settled peacefully in this building;
> The world was illumined by freedom rays.
> The Soviets of the oppressed wrote the government decree
> In letters of red over the summit of the royal tent.
>
> The day, when triumphantly, with the ideology of our time,
> The world becomes one, and the times are balanced,
> Labour will be the sovereign, and conscience the judge,
> Man will find peace, and the world will be prosperous,

Ignorance will fall, and knowledge will come to beautify
   the land,
There will be freedom for everyone, a cure for every pain.[21]

Poland, with the aid of the Entente, achieved independence at the end of 1918 and was immediately engaged in wars and diplomatic struggles with its neighbouring states. For the Bolshevik leaders, Poland was a key target through which the revolution must spread in order to reach the border with Germany and aid the revolution there, while the Poles pressed to expand their territorial control to the east. War broke out between Soviet Russia and Poland in 1919. Early Polish successes were hampered by their inability to come to any agreement with the White Armies, and soon gave way before a strong Bolshevik advance. The world's nations anxiously looked on as events threatened to drag Europe into another general war.

In August 1920, at the height of the Russo–Polish War, this anti-Bolshevik statement by the Polish Socialist Party was received by the British Labour Party. It was addressed: 'To the socialists of all free countries'. Most of the world socialist movement, even the most fiercely anti-Bolshevik, blamed Polish expansionism and Western imperialism for encouraging the war, not the Soviets.

> The Polish proletariat shall and will defend their independence, the independence of Poland is a historic necessity. It is not the result of an accident. Our Polish proletariat will have their free Motherland as every other link of the International. With your help or without it, it will conquer it. Deprived of your help we shall struggle for it through a sea of blood and through sufferings without measure. Forsaken by you, we shall double multiply by tenfold our energy and martyrdom.[20]

The Red Army was halted at the Battle of Warsaw in 1920, and in early 1921 Soviet Russia and Poland finally concluded a peace treaty. Neither side had managed to fulfil its ambition, though Poland did secure its independent status, and the westward sweep of the Bolshevik revolutionary army had been decisively halted.

A number of new states emerging out of the Russian Revolution, such as Poland, Finland, Estonia, Latvia and Lithuania, managed to retain their status as independent, non-socialist republics.

The Union of Soviet Socialist Republics, or Soviet Union, was created at the end of 1922, uniting the Russian, Ukrainian, Belorussian and Transcaucasian republics into one multi-national federal structure. It was an ambitious attempt to create a revolutionary state form intended to harmonise the different nationalities without stifling cultural uniqueness, a precursor to the world state of the future. Predictably, the USSR's relations with the rest of the world were fraught. It faced diplomatic isolation and the constant threat of war with the capitalist world.

As the boundaries of the USSR were gradually settled, conflict developed between the Sovietised nations and the Russian centre. Some Bolshevik leaders in Moscow argued that the ambition for national autonomy in these new countries represented a nationalist deviation away from proletarian internationalism, while many of the national elites protested that Moscow's desire for centralised communist control of their territories was merely a mask for an authoritarian Russian nationalism.

In 1923 the Soviet Union launched an 'indigenisation' programme that strove to promote cultural, social and economic development in its constituent national republics, while ensuring that this did not threaten political integration and centralised communist control. At the same time Moscow permitted poets, writers, educators and artists of all kinds among the national minorities greater scope than ever before to pursue their own linguistic and national cultures under the slogan 'socialist in content, nationalist in form'. However, the tension between the Russian centre and the aspirations of many of the Soviet nationalities would continue, and in response the union became increasingly centralised and chauvinistic.

Revolution Continues

As we have seen, the 'Russian' Revolution was, in reality, only the most visible, explosive and resonant episode in a longer-term, complex and global revolutionary convulsion. In the turbulent years between the fall of the tsar and the proclamation of the USSR, the interaction of different forms of political upheaval and unrest transformed the world in chaotic, unpredictable ways.

The Soviet Union continued to invoke proletarian internationalism as its legitimating ideology and driver of cultural development. However, from the middle of the 1920s political forces emphasising state development gained precedence over the commitment to aiding world revolution. The Soviet regime resolved to pursue international relations with the capitalist world insofar as a limited integration into the world capitalist economy could help the state develop industrially in order to build 'socialism in one country'.

British journalist and author Michael Farbman, in his 1924 book *After Lenin*, wrote:

> Radek, the witty Bolshevik journalist, tells the following story of an English admirer of the Bolsheviks. 'He is disappointed with us,' says Radek, 'because we failed to supply him with the fifth chapter of his book – the story of

Nikolai Punin, *Pamiatnik III Internatsionala / proekt khudozhnika V. E.Tatlina* (*Monument to the Third International by Vladimir Tatlin*), Petrograd, 1920.

Known as 'Tatlin's Tower', this technologically innovative structure was to house radio stations, cloud projectors, congress halls and offices for the future communist world government. Never built, it nevertheless became an icon of the Bolsheviks' global ambitions and modernist visions. Art historian Nikolai Punin wrote: 'We have here an ideal, live and classic manifestation of the international union of the workers of the globe in a pure and creative form'.

Cup.410.g.214.

how the heroes died, fighting gallantly till the last. He has never forgiven us for our impudence in continuing to exist as the ruling party in Russia.' In this story Radek, to my mind, stresses the most remarkable feature of the present situation in Russia, the fact that the very party and the very men who led the Revolution through its destructive phases are now responsible for the policy of reconstruction. To speak in terms of the French Revolution, it is as if the leaders of the Terror were undoing their own work and were inaugurating Thermidor.[22]

After Stalin consolidated his power in the late 1920s, launching the five-year plans of industrial development and agricultural collectivisation, the rhetoric of proletarian internationalism increasingly gave way to a new 'Soviet patriotism'. This stressed the need for internal security and ideological vigilance in defence of the Motherland.

The global revolutionary wave had receded, but it left behind a dramatically altered world structure and shaped the conflicts that would define the twentieth century and beyond. In the maelstrom, long-standing European continental empires had been destroyed and anti-imperialist mass movements had arisen, threatening Western states' hold over their overseas colonies.

Liberal democracy was challenged from all sides by a new mass politics. On the right, populist nationalists arose, fiercely hostile to communism and impelled by ideologies of ethnic or racial uniqueness or supremacy. On the left, the international socialist movement had been invigorated, but also disrupted (and many would argue, perverted) by the Bolsheviks' victory and by the creation in Russia of an entirely new state form that would define the contours of progressive politics for decades – the world's first self-proclaimed workers' republic.

NOTES

1. Arthur Lynch MP, speech delivered at the Royal Albert Hall, 31 March 1917 in *Russia Free: Ten Speeches Delivered At The Royal Albert Hall London on 31st March 1917.* London: 1917.
2. British Library. Koteliansky papers. Add MS 48967. Letters from David Herbert Lawrence. Vol. II (1917–1926).
3. Claude Anet [pseudonym of Jean Schopfer], *Through the Russian Revolution: Notes of an Eye-Witness, from 12th March – 30th May.* London: Hutchinson & Co, 1917.
4. Louis de Robien, *The Diary of a Diplomat in Russia, 1917–1918,* trans. Camilla Sykes. London: 1969.
5. Alice Ziska Snyder and Milton Valentine Snyder, *Paris Days and London Nights.* New York: 1921.
6. Quoted from Nick Baron, *The King of Karelia. Col. P. J. Woods and the British Intervention in North Russia 1918–1919.* London: 2007.
7. Arthur Ransome, *The Truth about Russia.* London: 1919.
8. Paul Dukes, *Red Dusk and the Morrow: Adventures and Investigations in Red Russia.* London: 1922.
9. Frank to Myfanwy Westrope, 21st November 1918. Papers of Frank and Myfanwy Westrope. Hull History Centre. U DX135/3
10. James Ramsay MacDonald, *Parliament and Revolution.* Manchester: 1919.
11. Extraordinary Seventh Congress of the R.C.P.(B.), March 6-8, 1918. Political report of the Central Committee, 7 March in V. I. Lenin. *Collective works,* vol. 27. February–July 1918. Moscow: Progress Publishers, 1967.
12. Leon Trotsky. 'The Internal and External Situation of the Soviet Power in Spring of 1918.' Speech at the Session of the Moscow Soviet of Workers', Soldiers' and Peasants' Deputies, 19 March 1918 (original: Pravda, 21 March 1918), quoted from: L. Trotsky. *The Military Writings of Trotsky. How the Revolution Armed. Vol. 1: 1918,* trans by Brian Pearce, available: https://www.marxists.org/archive/trotsky/military-pdf/Military-Writings-Trotsky-v1.pdf (accessed 11 November 2016).
13. John Wheeler-Bennett, *Brest–Litovsk: The Forgotten Peace, March 1918.* Macmillan: 1967.
14. Adolf Hitler, *Mein Kampf,* trans. Ralph Manheim. London: 1969.
15. Emma Goldman, *Living My Life vol. 2.* New York: 1970.
16. Grigori Zinoviev, speech at the first session of the Congress of the Peoples of the East, 1920. Quoted from John Riddell (ed.), *To See the Dawn: Baku 1920 – First Congress of the Peoples of the East.* New York: 1993.
17. Mao Tse-Tung, 'Inaugural Statement of "Hsiang-Chiang P'ing-Lun"', Hsiang-Chiang P'ing-Lun (July 1919) in *Collected Works of Mao Tse-Tung (1917–1949),* vols 1–2 (1978). Online at: https://www.marxists.org/reference/archive/mao/works/collected-works-pdf.
18. Volodymyr Vynnychenko, diary entry for 3 June 1920. Quoted in Mykola Soroka, *Faces of Displacement: The Writings of Volodymyr Vynnychenko.* London: 2012.
19. Eghishe Charents, *Land of Fire: Selected Poems,* trans Diana Der Hovanessian and Marzbed Margossian. 1986.
20. The Polish Socialist Party letter, August 1920. Labour History Archive and Study Centre, Council of Action, Foreign file (LHASC/CA/FOR).
21. Quoted from Munibur Rahman, 'Abu'l Qasim Lahuti: Iran's Foremost Marxist Poet', *Journal of South Asian Literature* 27, 2, Summer–Fall, 1992.
22. Michael Farbman, *After Lenin: The New phase in Russia.* London: Leonard Parsons, 1924.

Epilogue
Putting History into Words: Russian Novelists Write the Revolution

Ekaterina Rogatchevskaia

'I want to write something called "No one is guilty in this world". A description of all those people, from executioners to revolutionaries ... To describe this revolution, too ... This topic interests me a lot and it deserves to be written on.'

'A work of fiction?'

'Yes, a work of fiction.'

Lev Nikolaevich [Tolstoy] was silent for a while. 'And this topic is suitable for a work of art,' he added.

Valentin Bulgakov, Leo Tolstoy's Secretary, 19 April 1910.[1]

Understanding historical events and their causes is usually associated with a rational analysis of actions and consequences, conflicts and accomplishments, collisions and motives, movements and aims. But only literature and art can convey the elusive ambiance of the time. It is through the feverish atmosphere of *The Possessed*, created by Fyodor Dostoevsky, the passionate search for a new god in Maxim Gorky's novel *The Mother*, set among industrial workers, the stuffy air that Alexei Kuprin's prostitutes and army officers breathe in his novellas *The Pit* and *The Duel*, the strange, overwhelming atmosphere of provocation projected by Andrei Bely's *Petersburg*, the totality of *Black Square* by Kazimir Malevich, Igor Stravinsky's cacophony in *The Rite of Spring*, and the wild revolt of futurists' lyrics that we experience the true feel of the revolution as an approaching thunderstorm.

It is important to note that the anticipation of change in society was not only registered and reflected in artistic forms. Revolution as the most obvious way forward was part of the world order for a society where modernism dominated its intellectual life. Darwin's *On the Origin of Species* (1859), Nietzsche's *Thus Spoke Zarathustra* (1883–1891), Marx's *Capital* (1867), Freud's *The Interpretation of Dreams* (1899), Ernst Mach's *The Science of Mechanics* (1883), and *Time and Free Will* (1889) by

Henri Bergson – all ground-breaking and controversial works – paved the way to the new world with mankind at the centre of it. Based on the recent achievements in social science, modernism recognised 'a fundamental change' that, in Virginia Woolf's words, 'human nature underwent'.

Although Russian modernism was a complex and heterogeneous phenomenon, it would be fair to say that it played a crucial role in creating an intellectual milieu for the revolution. It opened a new era in which human possibilities seemed limitless – not only technically, but socially as well. The purpose of modernism was to find new means of expression for dealing with life in general. Such concepts as time, human nature and art became the framework for discussions about the future. Thus art started not only to reflect life, but also to change it creatively by suggesting radically fresh ways of expressing feelings, emotions and thoughts. Art was considered to be the main power for reforming human nature and society, as the entire world could be not only described but also changed or created. In Russia, aesthetic experiments were taken to the social sphere. Russian futurists presented their art in 'democratic' forms, such as new 'universal' languages by Velimir Khlebnikov and Aleksei Kruchenykh that, they were sure, the masses would embrace. They understood their task as releasing poetry from the 'prison of the book' and bringing art 'to the streets'.

The intellectual experiment had started well before the political one. To a certain extent, the idea of the future became more important than the future itself: longing for the ideal world in turn provoked a desire to overcome the real one. Utopia became a conceptual frame that helped to formulate the demands to the present world, and the spirit of utopia was one of the intellectual constructs that supported the revolution. After the revolution, the reality of Soviet Russia gradually moved further away from the ideal as it had been dreamed, and the foundations of modernism, such as self-consciousness, irony and rejection of realism, could no longer be sustained. For most artists the level of brutality and de-humanisation was such that the failure of hopes in moral progress, on the one hand, and disillusionment in the ultimate results of the revolution, on the other, by the late 1920s and early 1930s made the closure of the revolution as a cultural project inevitable.

At the same time the revolution became a theme that dominated the Russian artistic scene for many years. Attempts to imagine the scale and understand the meaning and the consequences of this event materialised in fiction, film, visual and performing arts and music. Four Russian-born Nobel Prize laureates in literature – Ivan Bunin (1870–1953), Boris Pasternak (1890–1960), Mikhail Sholokhov (1905–1984) and Alexander Solzhenitsyn (1918–2008) – reflected on the revolution in their works, but only Sholokhov's novel *And Quiet Flows the Don* passed

Joseph Brodksy in New York, 1980s.

Soviet censorship and could be read in the Soviet Union. The works of the three other laureates were officially banned. Until Gorbachev's *perestroika* in the late 1980s, they circulated in *samizdat* as clandestine hand- or type-written copies or amateur photographs.

The fifth laureate – the Russian poet and American citizen Joseph Brodsky (1940–1996), who was born in the Stalinist Soviet Union – recalled that the ubiquitous presence of revolutionary symbols visualised in Lenin's portraits taught him to ignore them and concentrate on his inner self. In his essay of 1976 *Less Than One*, Brodsky wrote:

> I think that coming to ignore those pictures [of Lenin] was my first lesson in switching off, my first attempt at estrangement. There were more to follow; in fact the rest of my life can be viewed as nonstop avoidance of its most importunate aspects. I must say, I went quite far in that direction; perhaps too far. Anything that bore a suggestion of repetitiveness became compromised and subject to removal.[2]

Ignoring the revolution was hardly an option for the other four. For Ivan Bunin, who was born in the same year as Lenin and died in the same year as Stalin, the revolution was the major event, which split his life into two halves – in 1920 he left Russia for good. In 1933 he received a Nobel Prize in literature as a person without citizenship, understood by the Russian émigré community as an official recognition of Russian culture in exile.

Bunin's way of coping with the great tragedy of revolution was to write a diary, which he published – apparently in revised form – as a work of literature under the title *Cursed Days*. It was first serialised in a Parisian Russian émigré newspaper in 1925, and in 1936 appeared as a volume of his complete works published in Berlin. Bunin did not touch on this topic in his works thereafter.

The manuscript is not held among the papers of Ivan and Vera Bunin at the Leeds University Russian Archive. Its whereabouts are unknown, and it is therefore impossible to tell how much (if at all) Bunin changed his accounts. The book keeps the structure of a diary, although quite a few entries look more like full-scale essays. *Cursed Days* breaks into two parts. One describes Moscow in the winter–spring of 1918, and the other describes Odessa, controlled by the Reds in the spring–summer of 1919. Bunin thus included in the book only the accounts related to the periods when he lived under Bolshevik rule. 'My Odessa notes break off here. The pages that once followed them I buried so well in a spot in the ground that when we fled Odessa at the end of January 1920 I could not find them', he stated in a postscript to the book.[3] The book is openly anti-

Bolshevik, although Bunin was not excited about the February revolution either. Recalling his visit to Petrograd in April 1917, he wrote:

> In Petersburg I felt the following in a particularly lively way: there had been a great death in our huge, thousand-year-old home. This home had now been thrown open wide and filled with a huge holiday mob, which no longer saw anything sacred or forbidden in its rooms. Amidst this crowd were the heirs of the deceased, individuals dazed by cares and a need to give orders – which no one, though obeyed. The crowd wandered from chamber to chamber, room to room. They never stopped nibbling or chewing on sunflower seeds; they only looked around and held their tongues, waiting for a better time to talk. But the heirs played up to the crowd, talking incessantly and assuring both the people and themselves that it was precisely they, the sovereign crowd, who, in their 'sacred anger', had broken the 'chains' that bound the deceased and the heirs. They kept instilling into the people as well as into themselves the idea that in no way did they consider themselves heirs – only temporary administrators who supposedly represented the crowd.

In the chaos of those days, Bunin first and foremost saw the vulgarity of the mob and resented those, such as the poet Alexander Blok, who advocated 'listening to the music of the revolution'. Bunin is uncompromising in his views, and it is 'shameful and terrifying' for him to discuss with others 'the terrors and shames' of the time in terms of morality or justice. The entire book-diary evolves around the revolution – there is almost no record of the author's everyday personal or family life. All conversations, scenes, thoughts or actions are related to the discussion around the global event. Bunin often describes his actions using the pronoun 'we', but it is not clear from the book who this 'we' refers to, as they never appear as individuals. It is impossible to say now, whether this was the result of later editing or whether the text organically evolved in this way.

The author documents only the historical time. Therefore he talks a lot about the nervous atmosphere of receiving and discussing news, whether published in newspapers or circulated as gossip or rumour. News is the cause of anguish, hope and despair, although Bunin is clear that most of what he reads or hears is a lie:

> There is so much lying going on around that I could scream. All my friends, all my acquaintances, people whom earlier I never would have thought of as liars, are now uttering falsehoods at every turn. They cannot help but lie; they cannot help but add to *their own lies, their own flourishes* to

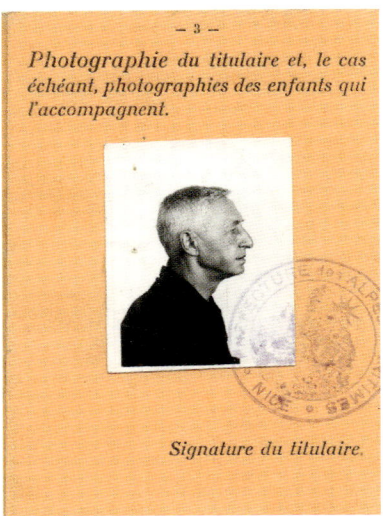

Nansen passport belonging to Ivan Bunin. These temporary travel documents for stateless people were so-named after Fridtjof Nansen, League of Nations High Commissioner for Refugees.

Special Collections, Leeds University Library, LRA Bunin MS 1066/1273.

the well-known falsehoods. And they all do so from an agonising need that everything be just as they so fiercely desire.

One of the leitmotifs of Bunin's book is the physicality of his experience. The author is often physically sick, revolted, numb or in pain while describing the street scenes or his own emotions. And the dominant emotions in Bunin's book are anger, rage and sadness, often conveyed by a sudden change of focus from the atrocities happening among humans to the tranquillity of the nature. These scenes, quite frequently at the beginning, almost disappear as the diary progresses:

> It rained cats and dogs last night. The day was grey, cold. The little tree that has grown green in our yard has burst into flower. But some damned spring this has been! ... I do not *feel* like spring at all. After all, what is spring *now*?

Exploring revolution through epic forms, such as the novel, started when the historical distance between events and their artistic interpretation was still very short. In 1921, Alexey Tolstoy started writing his trilogy *The Ordeal*. The first two novels – *Sisters* and *1918* – appeared between 1921 and 1928. Alexander Fadeev, a future head of the Union of Soviet Writers, published *The Rout*, his debut novel about the civil war, in 1927 and Mark Aldanov, who in the 1920s wrote a tetralogy on the French revolution, ended the decade with *The Key*, the first novel from his trilogy on the revolution in Russia. Similarly, three volumes of Mikhail Sholokhov's epic novel *And Quiet Flows the Don* were completed between 1925 and 1932, and were translated into English in 1934. The final part of the epic, translated into English as *The Don Flows Home to the Sea*, appeared in 1940. The Nobel Prize for Literature was awarded to Sholokhov for this work in 1965, and he remains the only Soviet writer who received the award with the authorities' approval.

The book attracted a lot of controversy, partly because it went through various drastic alterations caused by tightening the rules of socialist realism and total censorship, and partly because of rumours and open accusations of plagiarism. Although a manuscript of the first two volumes was finally found in a private archive in 1999, to be subsequently acquired by the Institute of World Literature in Moscow and published as a facsimile in 2005, the argument has not been fully resolved. Regardless of the question of authorship, the novel remains one of the central works written in Russian in the twentieth century. Many critics view it in the context of the tradition established by Leo Tolstoy's *War and Peace*. According to researchers of Sholokhov's novel, there are at least 883 characters in it, including some 250 historical figures.

However, the story focuses on just one area – the territory of the Don Cossack Host in southern Russia. It is a story of one particular social group – the Cossacks, who before the revolution had lived in self-governing, semi-military and autonomous communities and who were swept away by the revolutionary storm. Stalin's collectivisation in the late 1920s destroyed the last remnants of the Don Cossacks' unique way of life. At the core of the story is the life of one Cossack family, the Melekhovs, which is explored over the period between May 1912 and March 1922. The timeframe in the novel represents the real, historical time, measured by historical events and conduct of historical figures. At the same time, private stories of imaginary characters and their relationships of love and hate are described with a backdrop of nature and the agricultural cycle, such as ploughing, sowing, harvesting, etc., symbolising the complex combination of tradition and modernity in Cossack life.

Although the story takes the characters through the world and civil wars, it is not about choosing sides, but rather about hopelessness; there is no right choice. Any choice that makes people kill or be killed in any conflict is wrong and does not save from total destruction. This tension between human nature and war is constantly stressed by the author. When the main character Grigory Melekhov goes to the First World War he is tormented by a 'dreary inward pain' that makes him thinner and restless. Although unscratched physically, he is psychologically traumatised by necessity to kill. When the earth is 'yearning for human blood', any death becomes ugly, disrespectful and senseless:

As he rode through the district where recent fighting had taken place Grigory noticed a dead Cossack lying at the side of the highway. He lay with his fair head resting on the hoof-pitted road. Grigory dismounted and, holding his nose (the dead man already reeked of decay), searched the body. In his trouser pocket he found his notebook, a stub of indelible pencil and a purse. He removed the cartridge belt and glanced at the pale, damp face that was already beginning to decompose. The temples and the bridge of the nose were turning a moist black; on the forehead a slantwise furrow fixed in mortal concentration was grimed with dust. Grigory covered the face with a cambric handkerchief that he had found in the dead man's pocket and rode on to headquarters, glancing back occasionally. He handed in the notebook to the headquarters clerks, who gathered round to read it and laugh over this other man's brief life and its earthly passions.[4]

The notebook that Grigory took from the corpse was the diary of a young man. In it the writer describes his first love and

Mikhail Sholokhov reading from his novel *Quiet Flows the Don*, Red Hero Club, 1929.

his first encounter with a dead body – someone who had been killed before him. Describing the civil war, Sholokhov introduces many more episodes in which he talks about killings and executions of those who had killed and executed others.

In his private life, Grigory Melekhov is torn between the calm devotion of his wife Natalia and the sinful wild lust of his lover Aksinya. He loses both of them. Much loved and happy in her childhood, Natalia dies as the result of an abortion, undertaken when she learns that Grigory has again left her for his mistress. Aksinya, having been raped in her youth by her father and witnessed his brutal murder by her vengeful mother and brother, is constantly fighting for her love; she is killed by a random bullet when there is no obvious barrier to her happiness. The enclosed world of the Cossack village at the beginning of the novel is no paradise. Violence is part of life, but families managed to remain as functional units and thus resist destruction. Grigory's grandfather takes revenge on his wife's killers, but later re-builds his family life; Aksinya's early trauma does not obliterate her strong desire for happiness. The revolution makes rage and revenge spread out at astonishing speed. We know that the Cossack world is broken beyond repair when Grigory's sister marries the killer of their brother and Grigory's former best friend. Sholokhov shows how 'a plough cuts' through families, relationships and friendships. At the end of the story, we learn that 'black as the fire-scorched steppe was Grigory's life now'. He had lost 'everything he held dear'. Yet the novel leaves readers with a tiny hope that life is stronger than death: 'He was standing at the gate of his own home and holding his son in his arms. This was all he had left, all that still made him kin with the earth and with the whole huge world around him, glittering under the cold sun.'[6]

If Sholokhov's war and peace evolves around a peasant–warrior, Boris Pasternak looks at the fate of Russia through the eyes of Yuri Zhivago – a doctor and a poet. Maybe this dual nature of the main characters of *Quiet Flows the Don* and *Doctor Zhivago* is not a total coincidence; it may reflect the authors' attempts to enhance a three-dimensional picture of the revolution by supplying their characters with mirrors in which they can see their other selves.

It is also important that in *Quiet Flows the Don* the author does not refer to the present time when he was writing the novel. He lives through the past with his characters, not giving away that he knows what happened to the country after the novel's final scene. Sholokhov tries to remember and recreate what he and other people felt and thought at that time. The author of *Doctor Zhivago*, by contrast, is fully aware of the consequences of the tragedy and his own present time. On one of the dead White Army soldiers Yuri finds a small amulet with the text of Psalm 90 that the young man used to wear under his shirt:

The text was believed to be miraculous and a protection against bullets. It was worn as a talisman by soldiers in the last imperialist war. Decades later prisoners were to sew it into their clothes and mutter its words in jail when they were summoned at night for interrogation.[5]

In the novel, Yuri died in 1929; he could not of course know about Stalin's purges of the 1930s to which the passage refers. But at the same time Zhivago's friends, who are reading his poems after the Second World War and probably even after Stalin's death in 1953 (here the author is intentionally ambiguous about the date), feel as if he knew the future and could foresee their state of mind and emotions after all these years:

> Although the enlightenment and liberation which had been expected to come after the war had not come with victory, a presage of freedom was in the air throughout these post-war years, and it was their only historical meaning. To the two ageing friends sitting by the window it seemed that this freedom of the spirit was there, that on that very evening the future had become almost tangible in the streets below, and that they had themselves entered that future and would, from now on, be part of it. They felt a peaceful joy for this holy city and for the whole land and for the survivors among those who had played a part in this story and for their children, and the silent music of happiness filled them and enveloped them and spread far and wide. And it seemed that the book in their hands knew what they were feeling and gave them its support and confirmation.

The time period covered by the novel is about 50 years. It begins in 1903, before the first revolutionary uprising, which Pasternak discussed in his earlier poems. Critics and researchers noticed that before autumn 1917 the time in the novel flows in strict correlation with history: all dates and facts are checked by various sources, calculations of characters' ages are precise and the time is measured in two systems, the civil and the Orthodox Church calendars, as the author keeps referring to Christmases, Easters, saints days, etc. The author shows how enthusiastic Zhivago was at the beginning of the 1917 revolution, how busy he became trying to work for the good cause. Even in October he remained excited, talking about the change as a doctor and poet:

> What splendid surgery! You take a knife and you cut out all the old stinking sores. Quite simply, without any nonsense, you take the old monster of injustice which has been accustomed for centuries to being bowed and scraped and curtseyed to, and you sentence it to death. This fearlessness, this way of seeing the thing through to

Boris Pasternak, *c.*1930s.

the end, has a familiar national look about it. It has something of Pushkin's blazing directness and of Tolstoy's bold attachment to the facts.

Zhivago believes at first that the revolution can change the course of life as a miracle. Yet the revolution does not fix injustice; it rather makes moral categories redundant. Revolution cannot protect Lara Guishar, the most vulnerable and lively type in Pasternak's Russia and, as many critics agree, a symbol of Russia itself. Poor and exploited before the revolution, Lara does not find peace and protection in it. Her relationship with Zhivago develops during the most turbulent years, but just at the end of the civil war she leaves him to go away with the lawyer Komarovsky, who abused her as a girl. All three women in Yuri's life – his first wife Tonya, his lover Lara and his second wife Marina – symbolically represent different aspects in Russia's way of life. Tonya's immigration is the path for the 'old' Russia, while Marina's meekness is the survival tactic for the 'new' state. Lara loves two different decent men – Yuri Zhivago and her husband Pavel Antipov – yet returns to her abuser, symbolising the impossibility of a decent way for Russia under the present circumstances.

The narrative related to the events that occurred after the October revolution starts to reveal anachronisms and inaccuracies, as if time has suddenly become difficult to follow. This creates a special feature in Pasternak's novel, where history and its symbolic interpretation are interwoven in the main characters' lives. In Russian tradition the periods of reaction and stagnation are usually called 'timeless' and 'airless'. It is interesting that the Bolshevik revolution brings the timeless period into Zhivago's world. Twelve years later he will die, having suddenly felt stifled in a crowded tram.

Another poetic feature of the novel is the role of miracles, with some episodes, situations or problems being resolved by the 'deus ex machina' method (for example, the appearance of Yuri's half-brother Yevgraf, who saves him and his family at critical moments). In similar vein are the constant and improbable coincidental meetings and links that create a complex net of connections between all the characters in the book. Leo Tolstoy also used such an approach in *War and Peace*, but his work gives an impression of randomness. In Pasternak's novel, by contrast, these sudden encounters are impossible to miss. They are also part of the world that was arranged at a divine level. By making history people just try to interpret it, and Yuri's interpretation is very different from the one that determined Russia's history since 1917:

There you are. You are a Bolshevik, and yet even you admit that what's going on isn't life – it's lunacy, it's an absurd nightmare'. – 'Of course I do. But don't you see that it's a matter of historical inevitability? It has to be gone through.' – 'Where is the inevitability?' – 'Are you a child, or are you just pretending? Have you dropped from the moon? Gluttons and parasites sat on the backs of the staving workers and drove them to death, and you imagine things could stay like that? And what about all the other forms of outrage and tyranny? Don't you understand the rightness of the people's anger, of their desire to live in justice, of their search for truth? Or do you think a radical change was possible through the Duma, by parliamentary measures, and that we can do without a dictatorship?' – 'We are talking at cross purposes and even if we argued for a hundred years we'd never see eye to eye. I used to be very revolutionary-minded, but now I think that nothing can be gained by violence. People must be drawn to good by goodness.'

An independent philosophical analysis of the revolution and its consequences proved to be too radical even for the post-Stalin period of political 'thaw' (ottepel'). Pasternak was given to understand that his novel could not be published in the Soviet Union, so he took the decision to allow the novel instead to be smuggled beyond the Iron Curtain that during the cold war divided the world into the 'Soviet bloc' and 'the West'. Doctor Zhivago was first published, in Italian translation, in 1957. In short succession it was followed by other translations into major world languages, with the Russian language edition appearing in the Netherlands in 1958. The Nobel Prize for Literature was awarded to Pasternak in the same year, but – under enormous pressure from the Soviet authorities – the laureate had to decline the honour. In 1960, Boris Pasternak died of lung cancer that rapidly developed, probably as a result of a massive propaganda campaign against the writer.

Alexander Solzhenitsyn, born in 1918, belongs to the generation who, according to the official communist ideology, were to become the 'new Soviet men'. His critical mind and experience of the Gulag system were to make him one of the fiercest critics of the communist state. Solzhenitsyn received the Nobel Prize in literature in 1970. In that year he tried to publish the first novel from the epic cycle The Red Wheel, August 1914, in the Soviet Union, but without success; it appeared abroad instead. Solzhenitsyn considered this cycle to be the most important of his writings. He claimed that even as an 18-year-old he aspired to write a big novel about the revolution. Although the author planned to finish the narrative in 1922, as his notebooks suggest, he completed only four novels or 'knots' – 'Narratives in Discrete Periods of Time', as he himself called them – August 1914, October 1916 (in two volumes; it is called November 1916 in the English translation), March 1917 (in four volumes) and April 1917

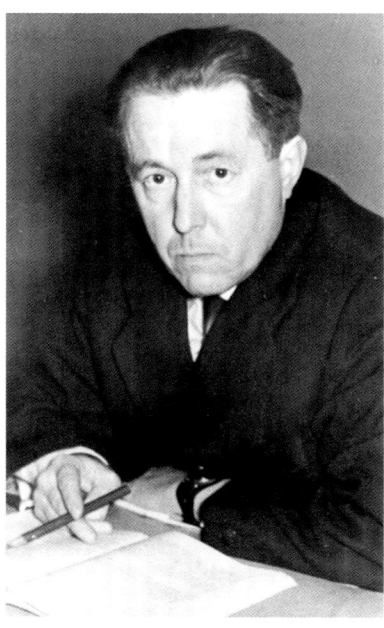

Alexander Solzhenitsyn, 5 November 1962.

(in two volumes which have not yet been published in English). The cycle was published in Russia in 1991.

As an author of a historical epic, Solzhenitsyn, like most Russian writers working in the genre, operates in the orbit established by Leo Tolstoy. But if others use and overcome this tradition, Solzhenitsyn starts with direct polemics against the great authority. A fictional character called Sanya Lazhenitsyn (based on the author's father) visits Tolstoy in his estate in Yasnaia Poliana, some 120 miles from Moscow. Their conversation leaves the young man deeply unsatisfied with Tolstoy's beliefs that Christian love and universal benevolence are all that is needed to reach worldwide peace and brotherhood. For Solzhenitsyn, Tolstoy's ethic was powerless in the face of the evil that Russia encountered at the start of the world catastrophe.

Polemics with Tolstoy continued at the level of literary genre. Solzhenitsyn's novels give an impression of an amalgam of multiple personal stories and lengthy historical essays, without fictional characters and philosophical discussions. Such a structure was unfamiliar to readers of historical fiction. It is unusual because the author, unlike Tolstoy, does not choose main characters to take them on a historical journey. All the characters, fictional or historical, have their turn in the spotlight – the main focus of episodes dedicated to them – they may then disappear from the novel's pages, not to resurface until the next 'knot', if at all. The chaotic and 'mosaic' structure of the novel, noted by critics, has its own internal logic – the logic of historical development as Solzhenitsyn understood it. For example, fictional characters from different episodes do not normally meet one another, nor do they develop relationships and interconnections. Even when their paths cross, they may not interact, as one would expect in a conventional novel. Rather, as in real life, his characters do not pay attention to passers-by and forget those whom they met as a result of an occasional communication. This is not only a skilful method of creating a polyphony of social representation and political views. Every individual story is a unique and important part of the 'big' history; each suggests its own explanation of this greater mosaic and deserves to be recorded.

This technique allows the author to convey a full diversity of opinions and beliefs, with, of course, some personalities and their choices in life being closer to the author than others. Colonel Georgi Vorotyntsev is the fictional protagonist of the novels, as many critics suggest. He is a man of action and has a deep and in many ways intuitive comprehension of history:

> He had refused to take the Warsaw train because he needed to 'feel' every bit of ground the corps had passed over if he was to understand anything at all ... Vorotyntsev needed to 'feel' it for himself because the scalding pain of the war with

Japan had not diminished in the ten years since. Russia's mindless 'educated public' might rejoice in that defeat, as an unthinking child rejoices in the illness which is his excuse for not doing something or not eating something that day, without realizing that it threatens him with disablement for life. The educated public might rejoice and put all the blame on the Tsar and Tsarism, but patriots could only grieve. Two or three such defeats in succession and the spine would be crooked forever. A thousand-year-old nation would perish. There had been two such defeats – the Crimean War and the war with Japan – with the not very great or glorious Turkish campaign as a slightly brighter interlude between them. The war which had now come upon her might therefore prove to be the beginning of a great florescence, but it might just as easily be the end of Russia altogether. That was why any true soldier must smart under the mistakes made in the Japanese war, dread their repetition and strive to prevent it.[6]

Having carried out thorough research based on various primary and secondary sources, Solzhenitsyn uses the background detail as an artistic technique. For example, he includes a collage of newspaper headlines to relate fictional characters to the historical context.

At the same time, quite a few pages of *The Red Wheel* are devoted to vivid and detailed individual portraits of key political and public figures, such as Nicholas II and Lenin. Some retrospective analysis is included, for instance in the case of Petr Stolypin, the prime minister assassinated in 1911. It is important for Solzhenitsyn to examine whether his historical 'knots' could have unravelled differently, and what kind of effort would have been required to achieve this:

But for the stiffness to which his lack of self-assurance condemned him, that man [Nicholas II] might even then have changed the history of Russian: a frank gaze, a big smile, a man-to-man handshake with the deputies, then perhaps he could have mounted the rostrum, stood under that frigid portrait of himself, and opened his heart to his Russian subjects, tell them of his own anxiety, his sadness, but say at the same time that together with the people's representatives (never mind for the moment whether they really were that) he hoped to get the better of Wilhelm, that there would never be a separate peace, that in truth he had never entertained such a thought, had never made a move in that direction, because to do so you would have to be a traitor to Russia and he, her Tsar, who owed her most, strove to serve her to the best of his abilities. And this is not just in words but in a voice that was loud and steady. He should have gone on to replace the Master of Ceremonies with some competent person as Prime Minister – almost any change would have been for the better. But the energy of the dynasty, and its ability to speak out boldly and frankly, had died with Aleksandr III.[7]

In a lengthy chapter on Stolypin, the author examines possibilities of 'defeating revolution with reform'. For Solzhenitsyn, Stolypin was Russia's only chance to divert from sleepwalking into the First World War. Solzhenitsyn placed a strong emphasis on the link between the war and the revolution, showing that once the conflict began the downfall that set the red wheel in motion was unavoidable.

At the beginning of his work, Solzhenitsyn planned to focus on the October revolution. However, he changed his mind in the process, as it became clear to him that the tsar's overthrow had been part of an unmitigated disaster. It is important to understand that this belief is based not purely on the analysis of the historical and political situation of that period, but also informed by the entire complex of Solzhenitsyn's multi-dimensional ethical, political, religious and philosophical views. Thus, in Solzhenitsyn's system of views, the war was a disaster for the entire world because Christian civilisation had lost its spiritual power to restrain evil – of which Lenin was a bearer, as Russia was for him only a means towards personal accomplishment.

The literary masterpieces surveyed in this essay form the core of the Russian cultural interpretation of the revolution. All are works that, I believe, deserve to be seriously and widely read and engaged with. For all the authors, reflection on the revolution played an important part in framing their philosophical, artistic and moral paradigms. Their perception and interpretation of the revolution was dependent on, but not fully determined by, their social and cultural background. Bunin came from a family of impoverished provincial landlords, Sholokhov was a non-Cossack in a Cossack milieu, and Solzhenitsyn's roots were in Russian and Ukrainian peasantry. Pasternak was born in Moscow to intellectual Jewish parents (an established artist and a talented pianist). For his entire life he struggled to overcome his sense of guilt at his relatively privileged upbringing, as well as his marginality as a Jew in an openly anti-semitic country. Another Jewish family, that of Joseph Brodsky, belonged to the so-called 'Soviet intelligentsia'. Brodsky's estrangement, Bunin's straightforward statement and the polyphony of voices created by Sholokhov, Pasternak and Solzhenitsyn allowed readers to appreciate the complexity of the Russian Revolution before multiple opinions recorded in diaries, accounts and documents could make their way from the archives into history textbooks through the hard work of many historians.

I would like to summarise our modest attempt to tell the story of the Russian Revolution by relaying, in parallel to the events and personal experiences so vividly evoked, the words of the Russian poet and literary critic Zinaida Gippius (1869–1945), who embraced the revolution in February 1917 and turned her house into a political club that many guests called a 'branch of the Duma'. The Bolshevik rule, however, was for her a manifestation of 'the kingdom of antichrist'. Having left Russia for good in 1920, Gippius published *The Blue Book: The Petersburg Diary* in 1929 in Belgrade:

> As an author of belle-lettres, I was primarily interested not only in historical events, but also in people. I was interested in every individual, in their image, their personality, their role in that enormous tragedy, their strength and their faults, their path and their lives. Yes, history is not made by people. However, it is made by people as well, to some extent. If we don't see and don't look for separate dots in the spontaneous flow of the revolution, it might stop making sense at all. And the fewer dots – these individual personalities – are left, the more pointless, scary and boring the historical development becomes.[8]

NOTES

1.   V. F. Bulgakov, *L. N. Tolstoi v poslednii god ego zhizni. Dnevnik sekretaria L. N. Tolstogo*, Moscow, 1957.

2.   Joseph Brodsky, *Less Than One. Selected Essays*, New York: Viking, 1986.

3.   Ivan Bunin, *Cursed Days: A Diary of Revolution*, translated form the Russian, with an introduction and notes, by Thomas Gaiton Marullo, London: Phoenix, 2000.

4.   Mikhail Sholokhov, *Quiet Flows the Don*, translated by Robert Daglish; edited by A. B. Murphy, London: Dent, 1996.

5.   Boris Pasternak, *Doctor Zhivago*, translated by Max Hayward and Manya Harari, London: Collins & Harvill Press, 1958.

6.   Alexander Solzhenitsyn, *The Red Wheel: A Narrative in Discrete Period of Time. August 1914*, translated by H. T. Willetts, London: Bodley Head, 1989.

7.   Alexander Solzhenitsyn, *November 1916. The Red Wheel; knot 2*, translated by H. T. Willetts, London: Jonathan Cape, 1999.

8.   Zinaida Gippius, *Siniaia kniga: Peterburgskii dnevnik, 1914-1918*, Belgrade, 1929.

Further Reading

Primary sources

Bonch-Bruevich, M. D. *From Tsarist General to Red Army Commander*. Moscow: Progress Publishers, 1966.

Bunyan, James, ed. *Intervention, Civil War and Communism in Russia: Documents and Materials*. Baltimore: John Hopkins Press, 1936.

Chary, Pauline de, trans. *The Diary of Nelly Ptashkina*. London: Jonathan Cape, 1923.

Denikin, Anton. *The White Army*, trans. C. Zvegintzov. Cambridge: Ian Faulkner, 1992.

Emmons, Terence, ed., trans. *Time of Troubles: The Diary of Iurii Vladimirovich Got'e. Moscow, July 8, 1917 to July 23, 1922*. New Jersey: Princeton University Press, c.1988.

Hickey, Michael C., ed. *Competing Voices from the Russian Revolution: Fighting Words*. Santa Barbara: Greenwood, 2011.

Ilyin-Zhenevsky, A. F. *The Bolsheviks in Power: Reminiscences of the Year 1918*. London: New Park Publications, 1984.

Maylunas, Andrei, and Sergei Mironenko, ed. *A Lifelong Passion: Nicholas and Alexandra: Their Own Story*. London: Phoenix Giants, 1997.

Teffi, Nadezhda. *Memories: From Moscow to the Black Sea*, trans. Robert Chandler. London: Pushkin Press, 2016.

Trotsky, Leon. *My Life: The Rise and Fall of a Dictator*. London: Thornton Butterworth, 1930.

Trotsky, Leon. *The History of the Russian Revolution*, trans. Max Eastman. London: Wellred, 2007.

Wrangel, P. N. *The Memoirs of General Wrangel, the Last Commander-in-Chief of the Russian National Army*, trans Sophie Goulston. London: Williams & Norgate, 1929.

Secondary sources

Acton, Edward, et al, ed., *Critical Companion to the Russian Revolution, 1914–1921*. Bloomington: Indiana University Press, 1997.

Badcock, Sarah. *A Prison Without Walls?: Eastern Siberian Exile in the Last Years of Tsarism*. Oxford: Oxford University Press, 2016.

Badcock, Sarah. *Politics and the people in revolutionary Russia: a provincial history*. Cambridge : Cambridge University Press, 2007.

Baron, Nick. *The King of Karelia: Col. P. J. Woods and the British Intervention in North Russia, 1918–1922: A History and Memoir*. London: Francis Boutle Publishers, 2007.

Baron, Nick, ed. *Displaced Children in Russia and Eastern Europe, 1915–1953: Ideologies, Identities, Experiences*. Leiden: Brill, 2016.

Bullock, David. *The Russian Civil War, 1918–22*. Oxford: Osprey, 2008.

Engel, Barbara, and Clifford Rosenthal. *Five Sisters: Women Against the Tsar*. Routledge, 1992.

Figes, Orlando. *A People's Tragedy: The Russian Revolution, 1891–1924*. London, 1996.

Figes, Orlando, and Boris Kolonitskii. *Interpreting the Russian Revolution: The Language and Symbols of 1917*. New Haven, London: Yale University Press, 1999.

Fitzpatrick, Sheila. *The Russian Revolution*. Oxford: Oxford University Press, 2008.

Hosking, Geoffrey. *Russia and the Russians: A History*. Cambridge, Mass.; London: Belknap, 2001.

Kinvig, Clifford, *Churchill's Crusade: The British Invasion of Russia, 1918–1920*. London: Hambledon Continuum, 2006.

Lieven, Dominic. *Towards the Flame: Empire, War and the End of Tsarist Russia*. London: Allen Lane, 2015.

Lincoln, W. Bruce. *Red Victory: A History of the Russian Civil War*. New York: Simon & Schuster, 1989.

Mawdsley, Evan. *The Russian Civil War*. Edinburgh: Birlinn Ltd, 2008.

Merridale, Catherine. *Lenin on the Train*. London: Allen Lane, 2016.

Miéville, China. *October: The Story of the Russian Revolution*. Verso, 2017.

Montefiore, Simon Sebag. *The Romanovs: 1613–1918*. London: Weidenfeld & Nicolson, 2016.

Pipes, Richard. *The Russian Revolution, 1899–1919*. London: Harvill Press, 1997.

Rappaport, Helen. *Caught in the Revolution*. London: Hutchinson, 2016.

Retish, Aaron B. *Russia's Peasants in Revolution and Civil War: Citizenship, Identity, and the Creation of the Soviet State, 1914–1922*. Cambridge University Press, 2011.

Ruthchild, Rochelle. *Equality and Revolution: Women's Rights in the Russian Empire, 1905–1917*. University of Pittsburgh Press, 2010.

Service, Robert. *Lenin: A Biography*. London: Macmillan, 2000 (1st edition); reprint: London: Pan, 2010.

Service, Robert. *Trotsky: A Biography*. London: Macmillan, 2009 (1st edition); reprint: London: Pan, 2010.

Shukman, Harold, ed. *The Blackwell Encyclopedia of the Russian Revolution*. Oxford: Blackwell, 1988.

Smele, Jonathan D. *The "Russian" Civil Wars, 1916–1926: Ten Years that Shook the World*. London and New York: Hurst; Oxford: Oxford University Press, 2016.

Smele, Jonathan D. *Historical Dictionary of the Russian Civil Wars, 1916–1926*, 2 vols, Lanham, MD: Rowman & Littlefield, 2015.

Smith, Douglas. *Rasputin: the Biography*. London: Macmillan, 2016.

Smith, Douglas. *Former People: The Destruction of the Russian Aristocracy*. London: Pan Books, 2013.

Smith, S. A. *The Russian Revolution: A Very Short Introduction*. Oxford: OUP, 1998.

Stites, Richard. *Revolutionary Dreams: Utopian Vision and Experimental Life in the Russian Revolution*. New York and Oxford: Oxford University Press, 1989.

Swain, Geoffrey. *The Origins of the Russian Civil War*. London: Longman, 1995.

Wade, Rex A. *The Russian Revolution, 1917*. Cambridge University Press, 2000.

Zamoyski, Adam. *Warsaw, 1920: Lenin's Failed Conquest of Europe*. London: Harper Press, 2008.

Fiction

Alexander, Robert. *The Kitchen Boy: A Novel of the Last Tsar*. Penguin Books, 2004.

Dralyuk, Boris, trans. *1917: Stories and Poems from the Russian Revolution*. London: Pushkin Press, 2016.

Gerenstein, Grigori, trans. *The Terrible News: Russian Stories from the Years Following the Revolution*. London: Black Spring, 1990.

Hessian, Dirk. *Constantinople: Escaping the Russian Revolution*. BarbarianSpy, 2014.

Karetnyk, Bryan, ed. *Russian Émigré Short Stories from Bunin to Yanovsky*. Penguin Classics, 2017.

Montefiore, Simon Sebag. *Sashenka*. Corgi, 2009.

Roberts, Wiliam Owen. *Petrograd*, trans. Elisabeth Roberts. Cardigan: Parthian, 2015.

Robinov, Kyra Kaptzan. *Red Winter: One Woman's Struggle to Survive the Russian Revolution*. CreateSpace Independent Publishing Platform, 2016.

Rose, Laura. *The Passion of Marie Romanov*. Memoir House: 2014.

Online Resources

This list is not intended to be comprehensive, but rather to highlight key available online resources which can be used to supplement set texts and other teaching materials covering the Russian revolution.

Marxists Internet Archive
https://www.marxists.org/

An enormous digital archive of Marxist and other leftist textual sources. Includes wide range of sources relating to, and composed by, participants in the Russian Revolution. This is an explicitly ideological project and commentaries provided by archivists reflect their Leninist outlook.

Plakaty.ru
http://www.plakaty.ru/ (in Russian)

Excellent collection of Russian and Soviet posters, beginning before 1917 and spanning the whole of the USSR's existence.

Seventeen Moments in Soviet History: An On-Line Archive of Primary Sources
http://soviethistory.msu.edu/

An initiative by Michigan State University taking an in-depth look at seventeen years in Soviet history – including 1917, 1921, and 1924. The website presents a large amount of key primary sources, with translations and contextualising essays.

Russia's Great War and Revolution
http://russiasgreatwar.org/index.php

Aimed at non-scholarly audiences, the website of this academic project contains popular articles on such topics as Military Affairs, Arc of Revolution, International Affairs, The Home Front, and Culture.

The Russian Revolution in the Internet Modern History Sourcebook
http://sourcebooks.fordham.edu/halsall/mod/modsbook39.asp#The%20Russian%20Revolution

Part of Fordham University's project collecting public domain primary sources, the Russian Revolution section hosts the texts of a number of key sources.

The Russian Revolution and Britain, 1917–28
https://www2.warwick.ac.uk/services/library/mrc/explorefurther/digital/russia/

A strong digital collection of primary sources held by the Modern Records Centre at the University of Warwick which touches chiefly on the response of the British Labour movement to the Russian Revolution.

Illustration Credits

Index